The RAJ *Revisited*

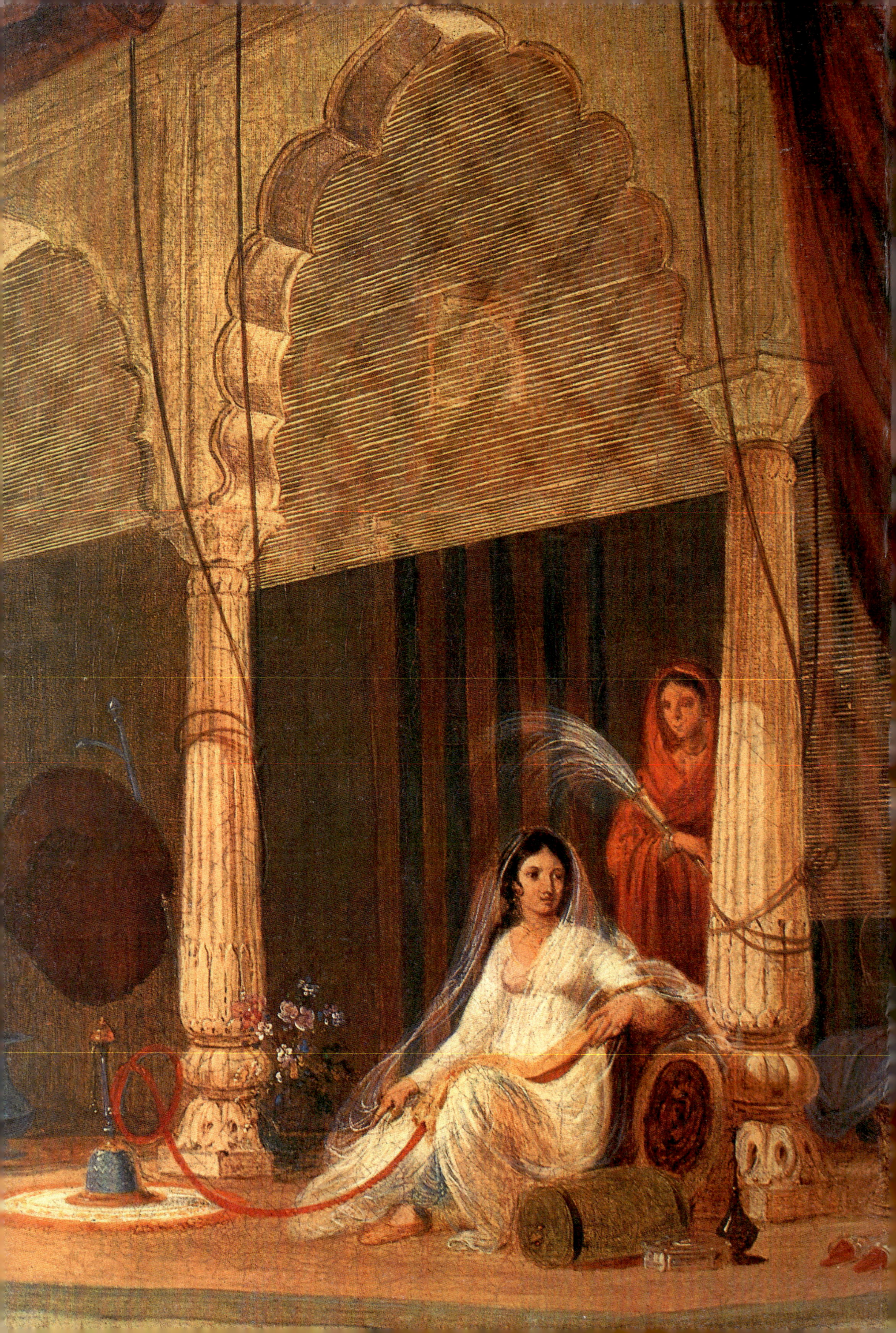

The RAJ *Revisited*

Pran Nevile

NIYOGI
BOOKS

Published by

NIYOGI BOOKS

D-78, Okhla Industrial Area, Phase-I
New Delhi-110 020, INDIA
Tel: 91-11-26816301, 49327000
Fax: 91-11-26810483, 26813830
email: niyogibooks@gmail.com
website: www.niyogibooks.com

Editing and Design: Malini Saigal

ISBN: 978-93-81523-28-5
Publication: 2012

Printed at: Niyogi Offset Pvt. Ltd., New Delhi, India

Contents

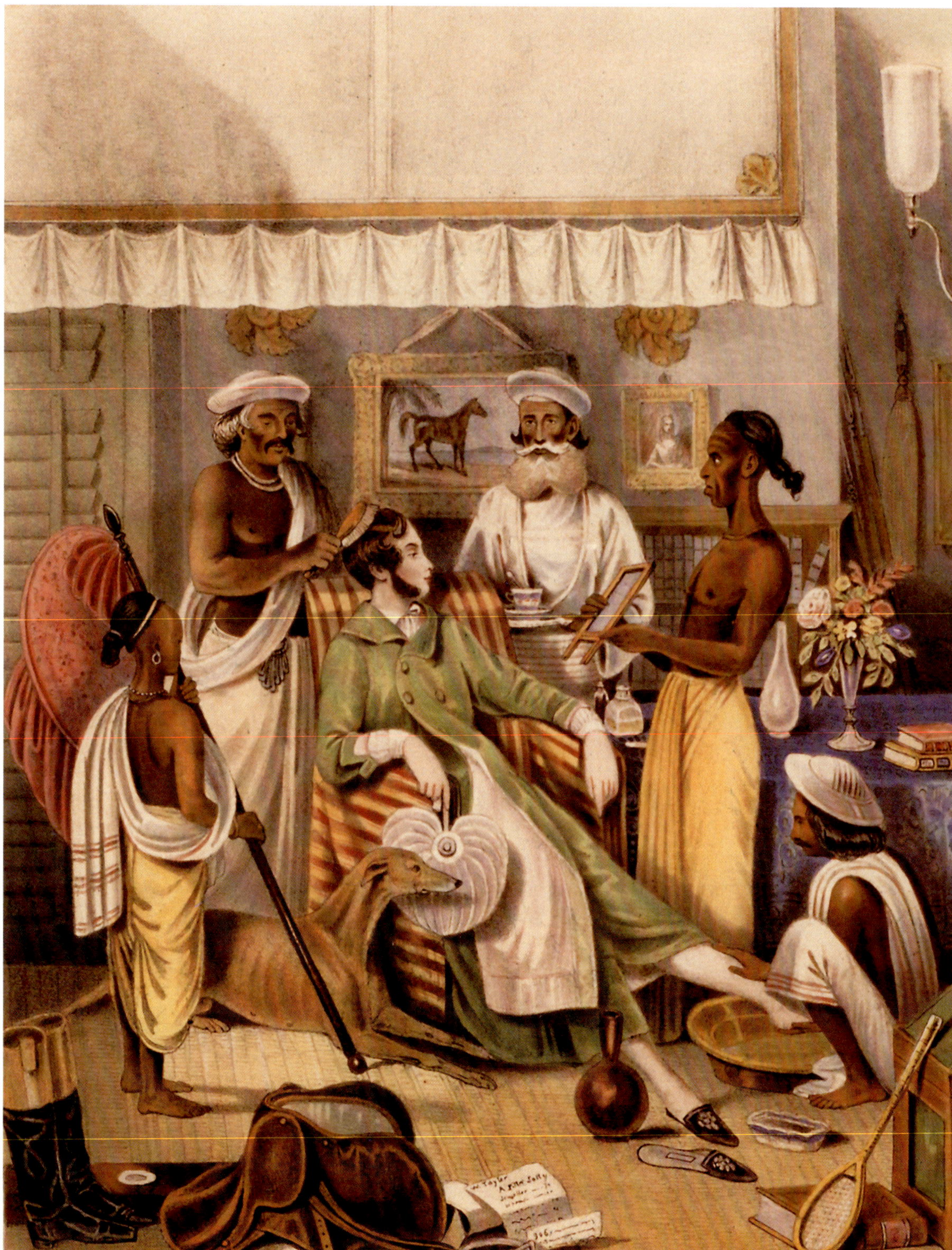

Introduction

RALPH FITCH visited India in the 1580s, and was the first Englishman to record the glorious splendours of Mughal India. On December 31, 1600 the East India Company was established by a royal charter granted by Queen Elizabeth I of England. Other European traders such as the Portuguese had already made inroads into India. William Hawkins, a merchant sea-captain, was the first British crown representative to visit India in 1608 and seek trading concessions from the court of the Mughal Emperor Jahangir, though without success. Sir Thomas Roe came as the crown ambassador in 1615 and got permission to establish factories. Throughout the seventeenth century the East India Company set up a cluster of factories on the Indian coasts, such as those at Surat, Bombay, Madras and Calcutta.

The following century saw not only the decline and disintegration of the Mughal Empire with all its political turmoil and chaos, but also the assumption of a wide administrative and political role by the East India Company. The British military and political exploits in the post-Plassey period of the eighteenth century proved extremely rewarding, so much so that the 'Company Bahadur' emerged as the dominant political power in India.

It was during this period that the Company officials, both civil and military, amassed fortunes not only due to the enormous profits through private trade, but also through the huge sums they extracted in gifts and presents from Indian Nawabs and princes who came seeking their protection. These wealthy gentlemen were known as `Nabobs'. They lived in luxury and splendour emulating the style of native ruling chiefs with their zenana of bibis, or the unofficial Indian wives, and an army of servants. They built magnificent mansions in Calcutta making it famous as the 'City of Palaces.' When some of these wealthy nabobs returned to England, they were viewed as social upstarts. Still they managed to acquire palatial country houses and even buy positions of influence either as Justices of Peace or as Members of Parliament.

Rich in historical and human interest, Raj literature comprises journals, diaries and memoirs by officials, scholars and travellers. It provides a rare insight into British social life in India during this period. The late eighteenth century also saw a flowering of British interest in India's history, literature and the culture of its people.

Governor-General Warren Hastings was surrounded by eminent Indologists of the time like Charles Wilkins, Colebrook Davis and Sir William Jones, the renowned scholar and founder of the Asiatic Society of Bengal in 1784. There was a lively interest in collecting illustrated

Title page: *'A Zenana Scene,' the Bibi of an unknown protector.*
Oil on canvas by Thomas Daniell, c. 1804, courtesy Dr. Mildred Archer and Margaret Paish, London.

Left: *The Young Civilian's Toilet.*
Coloured lithograph after a drawing by William Tayler, 1842.

manuscripts and miniature paintings. This also encouraged a number of British professional artists to visit India in search of fame and fortune, especially when their financial prospects in Britain were rather bleak at that time. For landscape artists there was the additional attraction of seeing exotic oriental scenery in their pursuit of the cult of 'Picturesque.' They brought with them the art of illusionist oil painting and naturalistic watercolours as well as the techniques of engraving and lithography. Until then, there was no true to life visual record of the Indian scene and its people. There were some published accounts by travellers with illustrations but these were largely imaginative. India was then described as a land of palm trees infested with cobras, with people of strange faiths and customs and with bejewelled kings in marble palaces adorned with harems of dusky beauties in gauzy veils. It was only in the early part of the nineteenth century that a visual image of India based on direct observation reached England, and it was seen as a country of infinite variety, picturesque landscape, marvellous monuments, and diverse communities with their rich civilization and culture. It has to be admitted that no other colonial power in history has left such an enormous volume of visual material recording the country's panorama, its people and their way of life with such fidelity and telling detail.

The varied landscape of India ranging from flat plains, great rivers and the snow-capped Himalayas provided superb subjects to suit the contemporary vogue for the 'Picturesque and the Sublime.' The monuments that attracted foremost attention were Hindu temples, then called 'pagodas,' as imposing, free-standing structures or cut

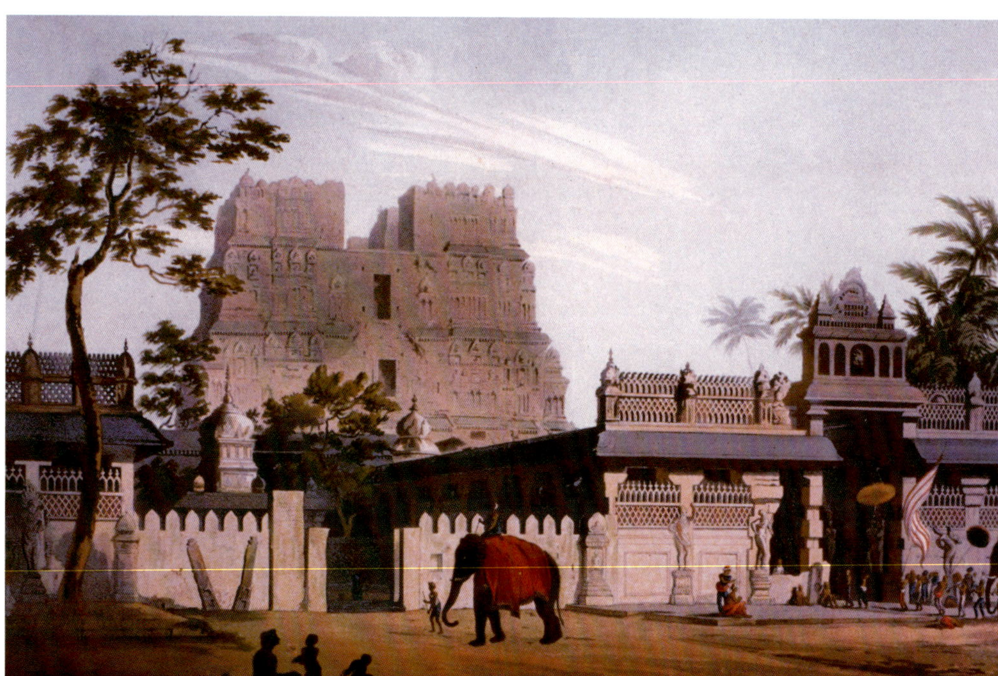

Pagoda at Ramiseram, Madras. Hand-coloured aquatint after a drawing by Henry Salt, 1809.

out in the rocks. This was because of their origin in the B.C. era and also on account of the marvellous sculptured figures embellished in a unique way. Among the most notable artists who captured the Indian panorama in their paintings were William Hodges, who travelled to India between 1780–83, producing his *Select Views of India* in 1787, and the uncle and nephew team of Thomas and William Daniell who toured the country extensively. They made numerous sketches and watercolours which they took back to England and produced their famous six-volume series of aquatints, *Oriental Scenery*. Their pictures offer the most resonant examples of the British vision of 'Picturesque and Sublime' and India. Their work was greatly appreciated and this inspired several landscape artists to visit India such as William Simpson and Edward Lear, who brought out many scenic views of India including its ancient monuments and other historic edifices.

Other artists like A.E. Davis and Emily Eden applied their talents to the portrayal of the diverse people of India with their colourful costumes and strange customs and manners. There were also a number of British portrait painters who worked in India during 1780–90 and amassed fortunes, thanks to the patronage of the Indian nawabs and rajahs, and also the British merchant princes who were keen to have portraits of their glamorous lifestyle with Indian bibis. Due to purdah, Indian women of aristocracy would not sit for portraits by the male artists. But the bibis of English sahibs were free from purdah and gladly agreed to sit for their portraits. The leading portrait painters included Tilly Kettle, Johann Zoffany, Thomas Hickey, Robert Home, Francesco Renaldi and George Chinnery. They were also at times commissioned by the John Company to make pictures of historical events of imperial interest.

Portraits were regarded as records of one's wealth and social status to be handed over to their succeeding generations. It was a costly affair as seen from the following advertisement that appeared in a local newspaper in April 1798:

> *Mr. Morris having taken a house in Wheeler Place directly behind the Governor's house, begs leave to inform such ladies and gentlemen who may be inclined to favour him with their sittings, that he is ready to paint them at the following prices:*
>
> *A head size: 15 gold mohurs*
> *Three quarters: 20 gold mohurs*
> *Kit cat: 20 gold mohurs*
> *Half length: 40 gold mohurs*
> *Whole length: 80 gold mohurs*

The portrait price varied depending upon the reputation of the artist and the status of the patron. Mr. Morris, not so famous, charged

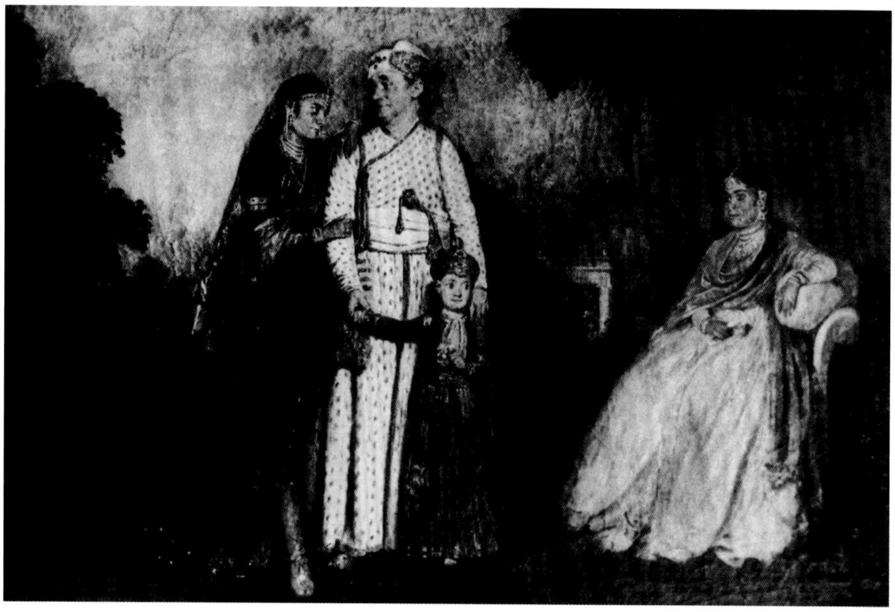

A European in Nawabi dress with his family.
Oil on canvas by
Francesco Renaldi, c.1795.

80 gold mohurs or Rs.1500 for a full-length portrait while Zoffany charged Rs. 2500 for Mrs. Hastings's portrait. The portraits of high dignitaries were also commissioned to be hung in public buildings like the town hall and Government offices.

It was the lure of wealth that brought Englishmen to India, "the land of the boiling sun and scorching wind." The picture of Englishmen in eighteenth century India that emerged from the Raj literature was that they lived in luxury and enjoyed a standard of living befitting the upper classes in England. The social interaction between the British and the Indians changed with the passage of time. The early adventurers who had come to make a fortune cultivated the ruling classes to win commercial contracts. Once established in their various trades they developed contacts with the native gentry. This period saw much social intermingling between the two. With the East India Company graduating from a trading venture to a political force, there was a change in attitudes. Social relations gave place to power equations. The situation deteriorated further during the first half of the nineteenth century when the British, who were now the rulers, kept Indians at a greater distance. The relationship had changed into one of master and servant. The Mutiny of 1857 swept away what little social intercourse had existed between the two races.

Two of the Indian entertainments became particularly popular with the Sahibs. One was smoking the hookah, described as a most curious device for smoking tobacco through water; the smoke being conveyed by a long tube called a snake which was washed with rose water. The other was the nautch or Indian dance; the English became almost addicted to the nautch. It was similar to attending the ballet in Europe. Professional nautch girls and their performances have been described in detail by European visitors, missionaries, and John Company's civil and military officials. Nautch represented a form of cultural interaction between the native and the early English settlers in India. Many British artists have depicted the captivating performances in their glamorous and glittering costumes. It was such a popular and common form of entertainment until the middle of the nineteenth century that even the Governor-General and the high-ranking British ruling elite attended the nautch parties organized by Indian nobility.

The English were greatly impressed by the folklore and hectic gaiety of the people singing and dancing at the celebration of their fairs and festivals which had a religious and also regional flavour. They were also amazed by the feats of the Indian jugglers, magicians and other street performers. Some of these performances have been recorded by both professionals and amateur artists. The snake charmers usually find ample mention both visually and also in writings. Indian mendicants, sadhus, astrologers, ascetics also attracted the attention of the Sahibs, some of whom were not only impressed by their knowledge but also by their predictions when these came true.

Among other unusual amusements were the animal fights involving tigers, buffaloes, elephants and rams. Then there were also bird fights, especially cock fights, a popular pastime of the nobility and commoners alike. We come across graphic accounts by Capt. T. Williamson of the Bengal army in his famous classic *Oriental Field Sports,* (1819). The native princes and nawabs organized special shows of animal fights to entertain English guests. The English were introduced to the big game hunting of lions and tigers by the Indian ruling princes for whom it had been a traditional outdoor sport from time immemorial. There are fascinating accounts of the hunting trips by some English sportsmen. The most popular game with English civilians and soldiers alike was pig-sticking or hog-hunting according to Bombay phraseology. Practically all these sports have been covered in drawings and paintings by some British artists.

The British recorded their impressions of India in their letters home or in their memoirs. Many English families made it a tradition to send one or two members to India for a promising lucrative career. Apart from letters, another good way to keep in touch with relatives home was through portraits or drawings. Before the advent of camera these served the purpose of snapshots.

The contribution of amateur artists in depicting India is equally noteworthy. From the mid-eighteenth century onwards, upper and middle classes in Britain regarded the learning and practice of drawing as a desirable accomplishment. It was one of the most popular and commendable occupations for their leisure. Then it became a part of liberal education and youngsters received instructions in drawing by art teachers in their schools or at home. Many British men and

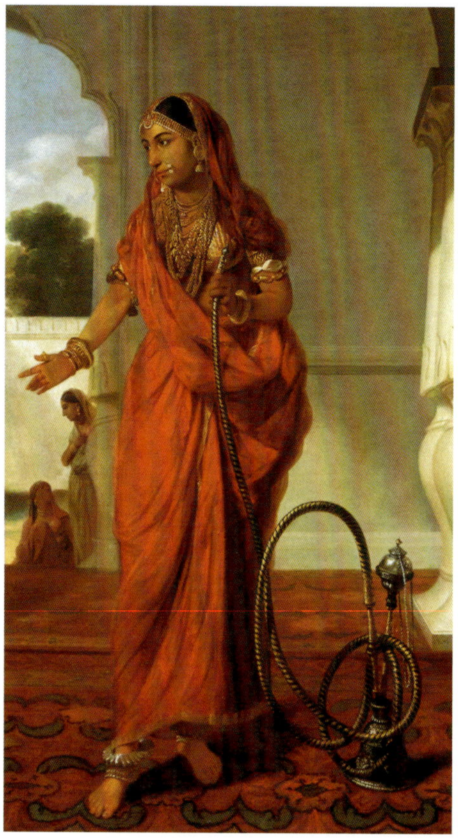

Dancing-girl Faizabad
Oil on canvas by Tilly Kettle,1772.

women who came to India had acquired such training. No wonder, there were a number of talented amateur artists among the East India Company's civil and military officials whose works frequently reached a high standard comparable in certain cases to those of the professional artists. The British women amateur artists did not lag behind the men as they were also as competent with pencil, pen and brush. Moreover, though very much a part of the Raj, women artists were not burdened by a sense of imperial mission. They had an open mind and took genuine interest in depicting the country and its people. Also as their sketches and drawings were mostly meant for their own selves and not for any competitive market, they were executed quite freely and are thus more intimate observations of the Indian scene.

The amateur artists depicted not only the delightful landscape but illustrated the mode of life, the varied means of transport, native costumes, customs and manners, festivities and amusements. Certain drawings even show their mansions, military camps and their large retinue of servants.

Among these amateur artists the most accomplished was Sir Charles Doyly (1781–1845) followed by J.B. Fraser. Both of them had received training from George Chinnery, a famous professional artist, who spent over twenty years in Calcutta. Other notable artists were Captain Charles Gold (1842), James Forbes (1749–1819), R.M. Grindlay (1786–1877), Emily Eden (1797–1869), S.C. Belnos, Fanny Parks and Marianne Postans. They have all bequeathed to us a very valuable collection of drawings, watercolours and sketches which provide an interesting visual record of the English life during the Raj and their perception of the Indian scene.

By the late eighteenth century, the new employees of the Company coming in from England were from the educated, cultured middle classes, who took an interest in intellectual pursuits. Many of them shared the fashionable interest in the 'Picturesque' and the 'Exotic'. They were fascinated by the variegated landscape of the country, its magnificent monuments and the diversity of its people. They wanted to acquire pictures of their new environment, but not all of them could afford to buy the works of British artists. They had also no access to the works of amateur artists as these were generally not sold. As a result, many British Company Officials began commissioning Indian artists to produce paintings of their chosen subjects. They were keen to collect these as mementos and souvenirs for their friends and relatives in England. For the British, almost every aspect of life in India was worth sketching. Their favourite subjects, however, were historic monuments with their novel architecture, people of different classes in colourful costumes, festivals and rituals, crafts and occupations, different modes of transport, and dancing girls. For many of them, paintings and drawings were the best record and became one of their most valued possessions.

Indian artists, on their part, welcomed the opportunity to work for their new British patrons, especially because the traditional patronage of Indian rulers and their courts was rapidly declining. While adopting some features of western art they took care to preserve traditional elements. Since their own skills were more than adequate, they did not need formal training from the British. However, they gave up using gouache in favour of European paper and changed colour patterns to replace the brilliant hues of miniature painting with mute tones and sepia washes which appealed to the British.

The first European professional artist to devote himself to the neglected field of drawing true-to-life pictures of Indian people of different classes and professions was Balthazar Solvyns at Calcutta. He made a comprehensive study of the Indian communities and their occupations and produced 250 colour etchings (1799). His work was not only of great historic value but it had also a tremendous influence on the fortunes of Indian painters who were then seeking patronage of the emerging English masters. They looked for subjects that would appeal to their British clients and they found Solvyn's sketches as the best guide.

A Gentleman Delivering a letter to a Soonta-Burdar or silver Baton-Bearer. Hand-coloured aquatint engraving after a drawing by Sir Charles Doyly.

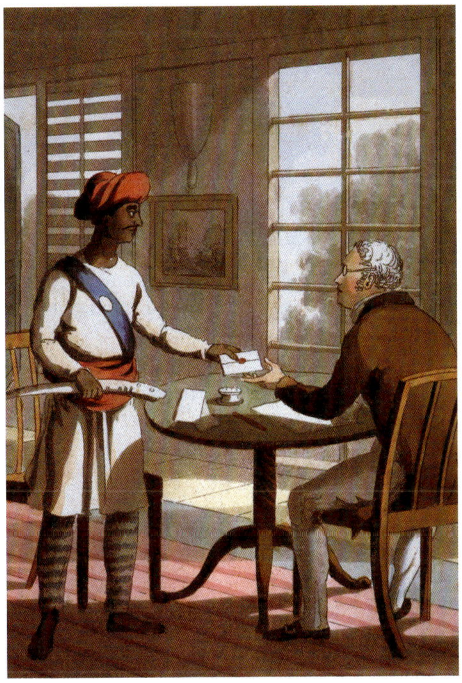

One of the most remarkable manuscripts covering trades, occupations and social classes is *Tasrih-al-Aqvam* by Col. James Skinner. It is an outstanding work in Persian dealing with the castes, sects and tribes of Punjab. Skinner was one of the most glamorous personalities of the Raj. Famous for his 'Skinner's Horse,' he was the son of a Scottish father and Rajput mother, and had opted for an Indian lifestyle with an estate at Hansi near Delhi. A Persian scholar and a great patron of Indian arts, he commissioned several native artists to work for him. The *Tasrih-al-Aqvam* is profusely illustrated with paintings in the Delhi 'Company' style combining European naturalism in the human figures with certain Indian elements. The medium of painting is watercolour on paper which is pasted on card and bound in leather.

Another remarkable collection of paintings by Indian artists as commissioned by British patrons is the Fraser Album discovered in 1979 in Scotland. These marvellous paintings of great aesthetic merit were commissioned by James Fraser (1783–1856), a gifted amateur artist himself, and his brother William Fraser (1784–1835) then stationed in Delhi as an assistant to the British Resident. With over a hundred water colours this album portrays a wide range of Indian characters and the pattern of everyday life in Delhi. These fine portraits are noteworthy for their striking likeness and graphic detail that captured every last detail of hair and wrinkle and also the subject's mood and expression — a rare combination of humanity and realism transcending the common depiction of human figures.

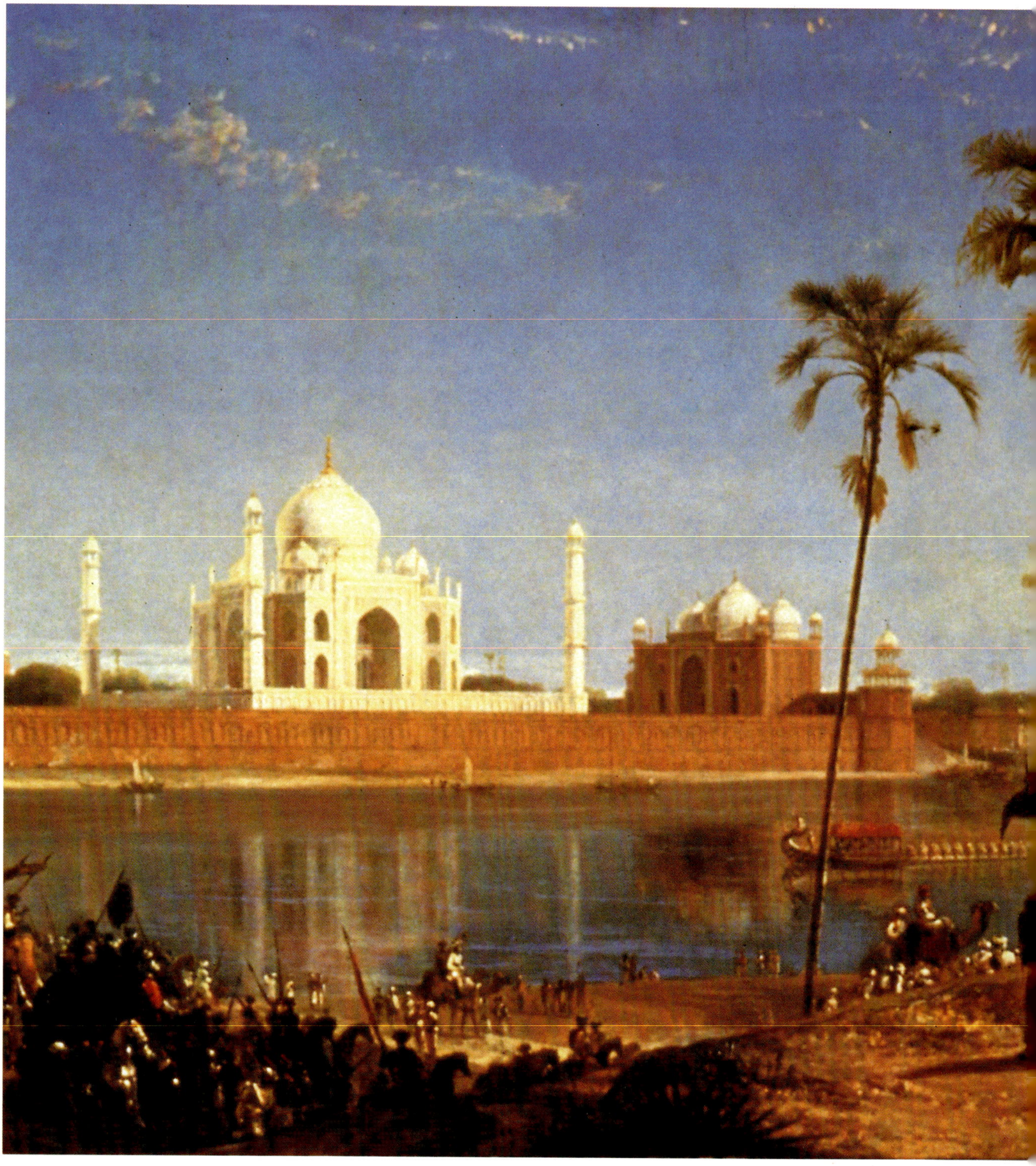

FIRST VIEWS OF INDIA

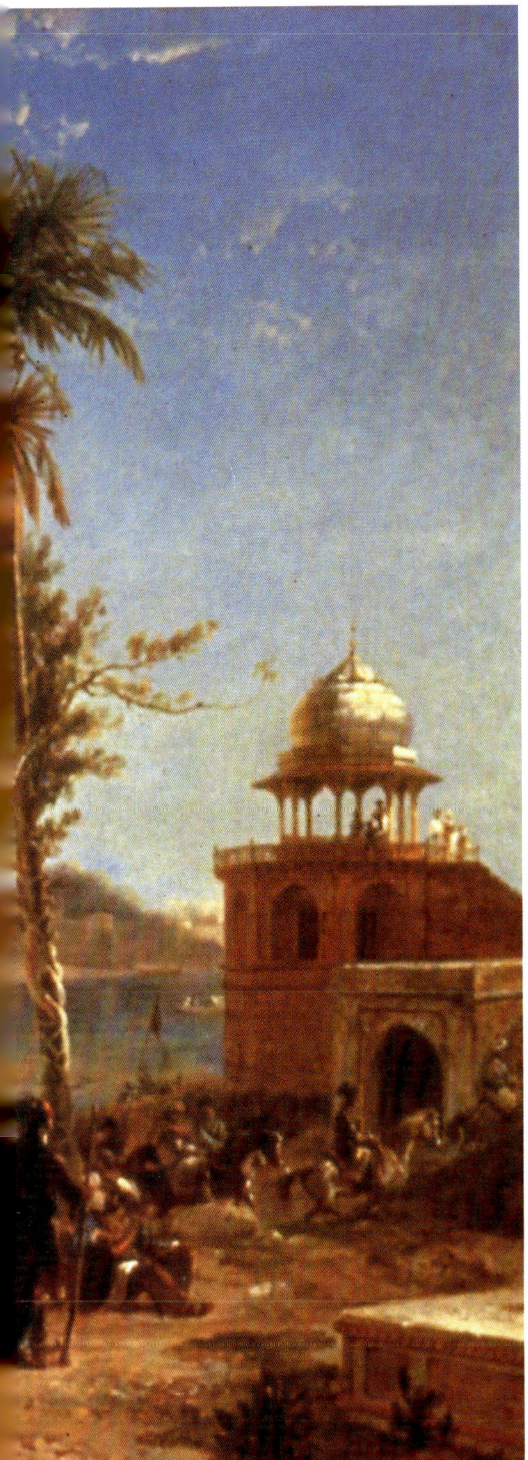

The Taje Mah'l at Agra viewed from the opposite side of the River Jumna. Oil on canvas by William Daniell, 1829.

BRITISH PROFESSIONAL artists began to visit India in the late eighteenth century. Until then there was no visual record of India, based on first-hand observation. A number of published travelogues had carried illustrations by engravers who had never visited India except in their fantasy and imagination. These accounts carried imaginary tales of India as a land of palm trees, bejewelled kings, majestic Mughal monuments like the Jama Masjid, Taj Mahal and the Qutab Minar, as well as imposing Hindu temples adorned with gold idols However, those who had not seen them had no idea what they looked like! In earlier centuries Indian artists left marvellous miniature paintings of emperors, their court life and also of religious and mythological themes, but they had no tradition of applying their talent to landscape painting.

The first professional landscape artist to visit India was William Hodges (1744–97). A prolific painter, he came to India in 1780 and soon became a protégé of the Governor-General Warren Hastings who extended immense help to him in his ambitious plans. Hodges spent three years in India and travelled extensively in the interior both by land and boat. He was dazzled by the grandeur of Indian monuments. On his return to England he published a series of aquatints titled *Select Views of India.* They depicted for the first time many places and buildings in India that became famous later.

Hodges was followed by the legendary uncle-nephew duo of Thomas (1749–1840) and William Daniell (1769–1837) who spent over eight years in India (1785–1794). After an initial year in Calcutta they travelled extensively in North India visiting Agra, Delhi, Lucknow, Benaras and even Garhwal in the lower Himalayas. They then made a tour of South India visiting Madras, Bangalore, Madura, Rameswaram, Tanjore and Mahabalipuram, recording the famous Hindu temples and antiquities in those little known parts of the country. From here they journeyed by sea to Bombay and visited the massive rock-cut temples of Western India. Both the Daniells were well acquainted with the British taste for the 'Picturesque and the Sublime.' Throughout their travels they made exquisite drawings of every spot or building they thought noteworthy and interesting. Most of these places were being depicted for the first time in an exquisite classical style that earned

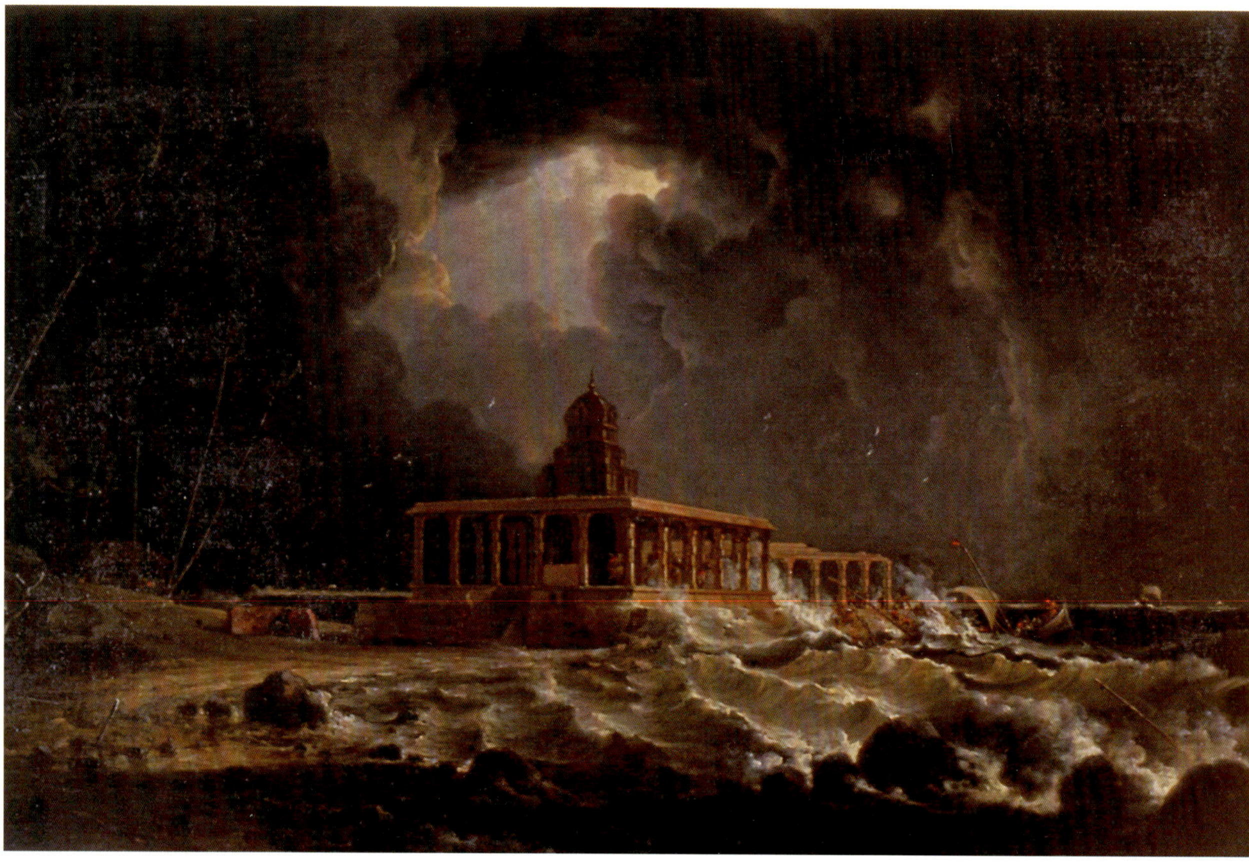

An Hindoo Temple on the Island of Ramiseram near Cape Comorin; with the approach of the north-east Monsoon. Oil on canvas by William Daniell, 1802.

them universal acclaim. India had never before been explored to identify such a rich treasure of pictorial subjects nor had they been recorded in this evocative manner. On their return to England the Daniells produced a colossal publication in six parts between 1795 and 1805, entitled *Oriental Scenery* with 144 aquatints. This phenomenal work offered a comprehensive visual record of India's scenery and it is no wonder that it became an important source of the image that the outside world had of India.

Another contemporary of the Daniells was James Wales who made a large number of sketches of the rock-cut temples of Western India and the city of Bombay. Another artist who also depicted scenes of Bombay was William Westall. Some of his drawings were published as aquatints in Captain R.M. Grindlay's *Scenery, Costumes and Architecture Chiefly on the Western Side of India* (1830).

Indian views by Hodges and Daniells were supplemented by Henry Salt (1780–1827), a professional landscape artist who accompanied Lord Valentia on the latter's grand tour of India. He visited Southern and Western India sketching all the picturesque places he passed through such as the ghats of Benares, the Rajmahal Hills and also the Lucknow scenery. A number of his drawings in 1809, skilfully engraved, were published as illustrations in Valentia's travelogue.

The artist James Moffat (1775–1815) spent over 25 years in India recording the Indian countryside and its monuments. He produced views of Calcutta and a number of other Indian towns that he visited between 1798 and 1810. His most well-known work is *South East View of New Government House,* Calcutta, which was engraved and published in England in 1805.

George Chinnery was another professional artist who spent over twenty years (1802–25) in India. Though he earned his living through giving lessons in painting and doing portraits, he had a passion for landscape painting especially the countryside, with its wayside villages, mud huts and roaming cattle. His only published drawings date to the time he was in Madras (1802–07) entitled *Views in Madras.*

Hardly any professional artist came to India after the advent of the camera, until William Simpson who was commissioned to make drawings of India by the London publishers Day & Son. From 1859 to 1862 Simpson travelled widely in India and made 250 drawings. Unfortunately only about 50 have survived as illustrations in the book titled *India Ancient and Modern,* published in 1867 with a descriptive text by the historian J.W. Kaye. The last major professional artist to visit India was Edward Lear in 1873. He made around 3000 drawings in two years and most of these were acquired in the first half of the 20th century by American collectors. They are now in the collection of the Houghton Library of Harvard University.

The body of work on India was significantly augmented by amateur artists most of whom were East India Company civilian and military officials. Their work was of a quality comparable to professional artists. During the period 1770–1810, many of their drawings were engraved and published in London. One of the earliest and finest of these amateur artists was James Forbes, a Company official in the Bombay presidency from 1765 to 1784. He produced many drawings covering the Indian scene which served as illustrations in his monumental work *Oriental Memoirs* published in 1813. Among others of merit were Samuel Davis, Colonel Francis Swain Ward, Lieutenant R.H. Colebrooke, Major John Luard and Commander Robert Eliot. No list of amateur artists would be complete without the mention of J.B. Fraser who was not a Company official, but his sketches of Calcutta and the Himalayas rank amongst the finest images of India. However, the most famous and prolific of all amateur artists was Sir Charles Doyly, a senior Company official who had taken lessons from George Chinnery. Though his forte was landscape painting, he was the most versatile of artists. His delightful drawings of Calcutta, *The City of Palaces*, were highly acclaimed on their posthumous publication in 1848.

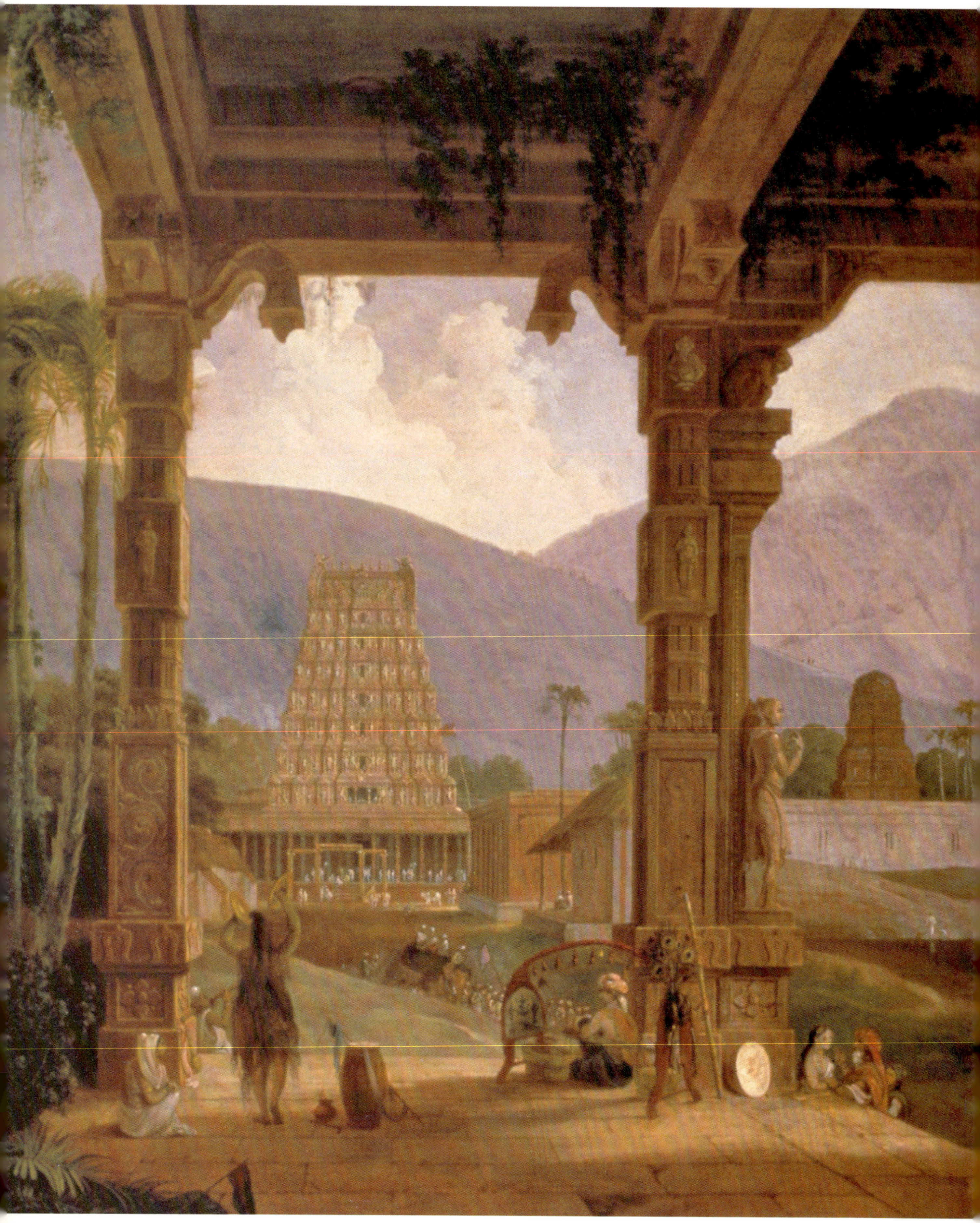

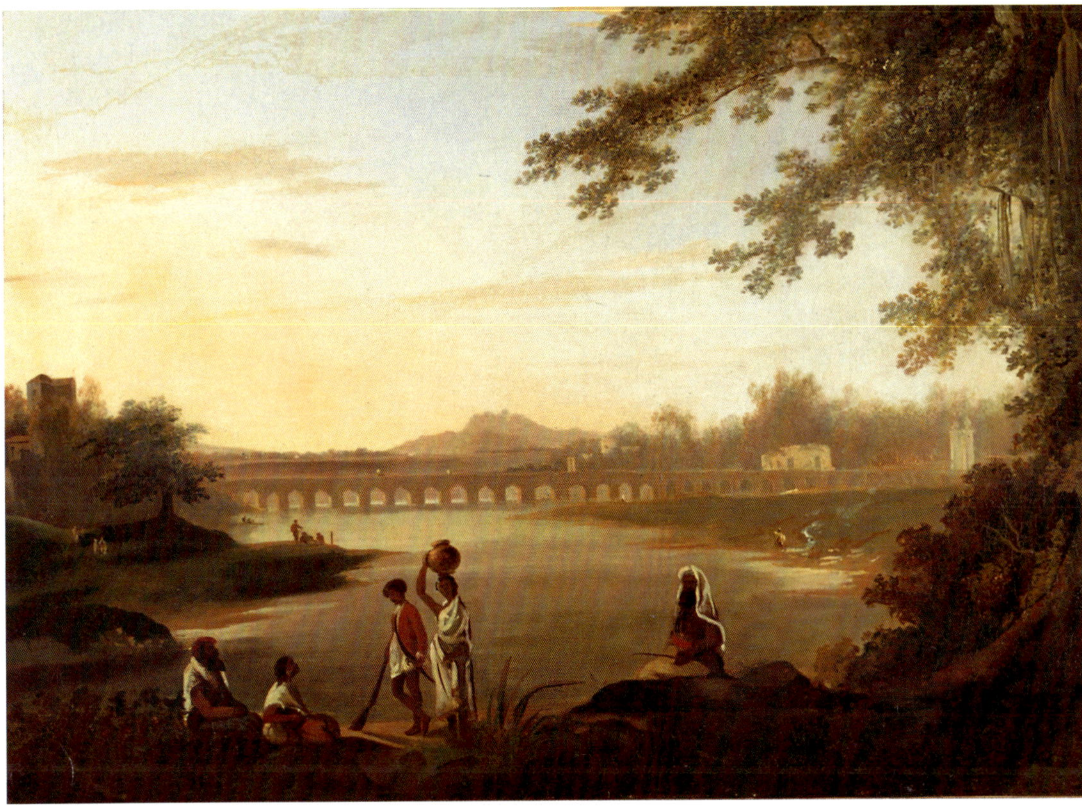

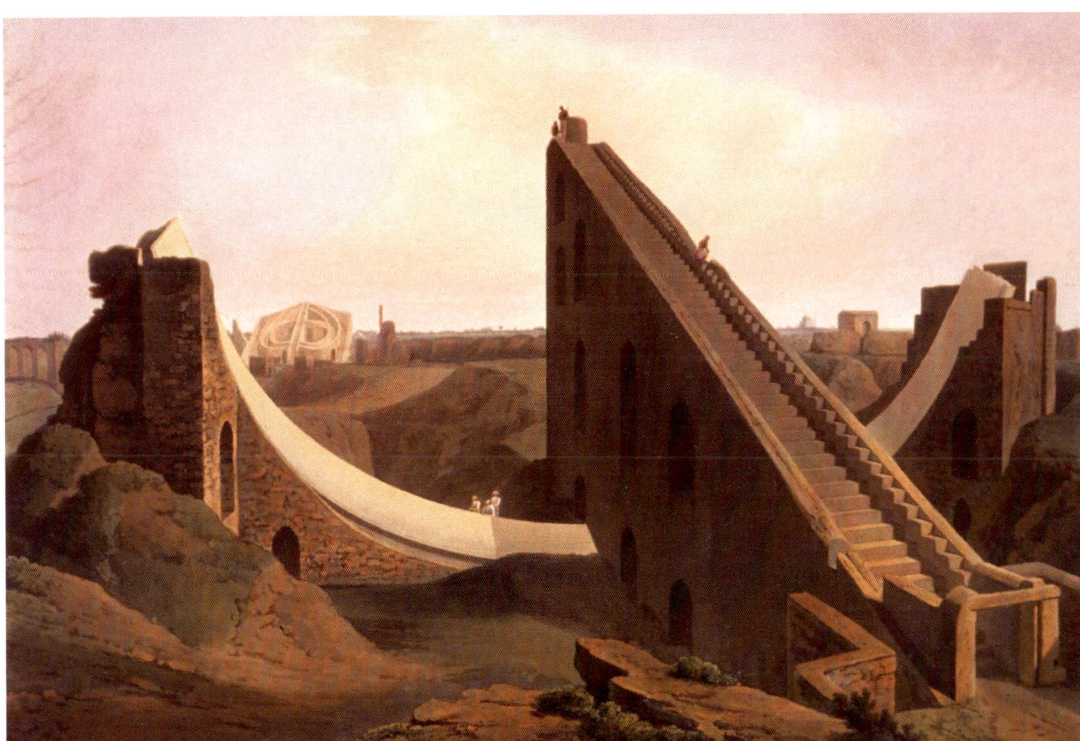

Facing page: *Gateway to the Lower Temple, Trichangodu.*
Oil on canvas by Thomas Daniell,1822.

Top: *A view of the Armenean Bridge Madras.*
Oil on canvas by William Hodges, c.1780.

Above: *The Observatory at Delhi.*
Aquatint by Thomas and William Daniell (1808) after a drawing by Thomas Daniell (1789).

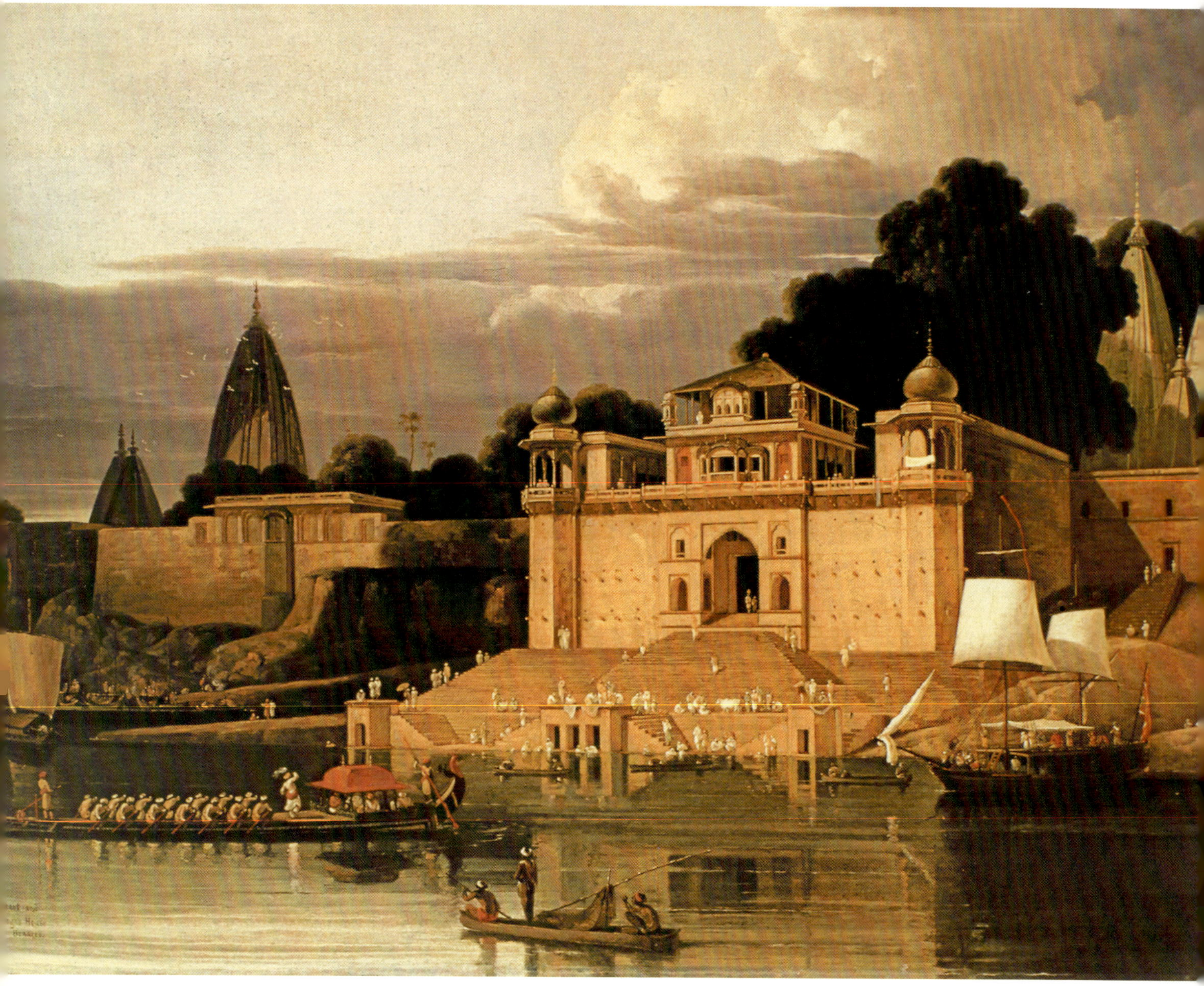

Shuwollah Gaut, Benares on the River Ganges.
Oil on canvas by William Daniell
exhibited at the Royal Academy, 1802.
(Private collection)

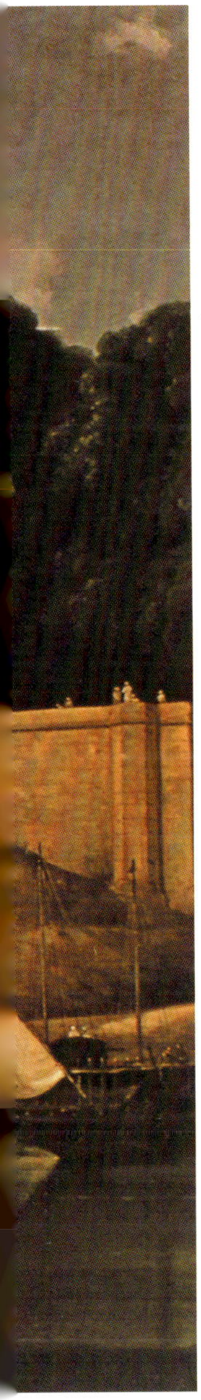

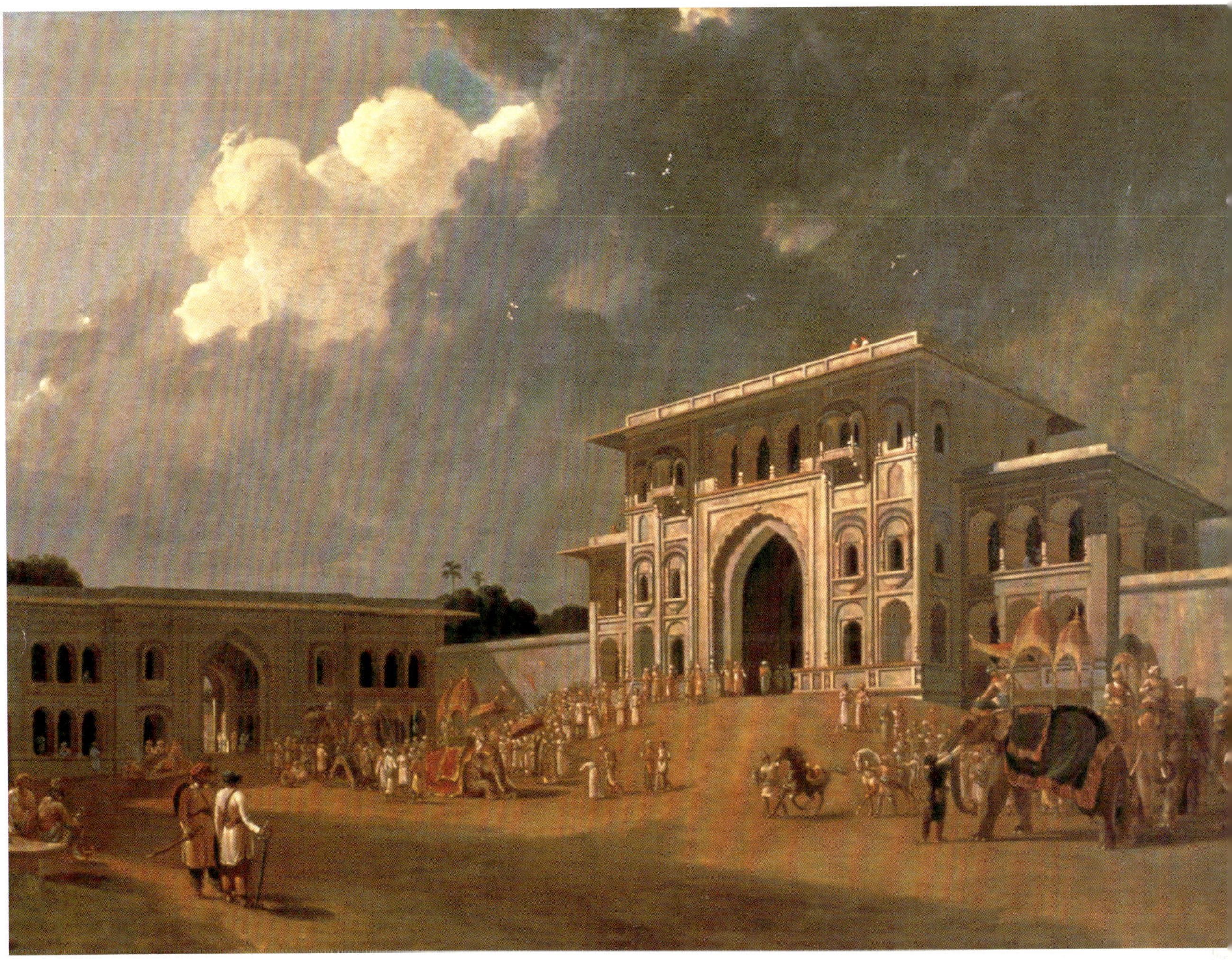

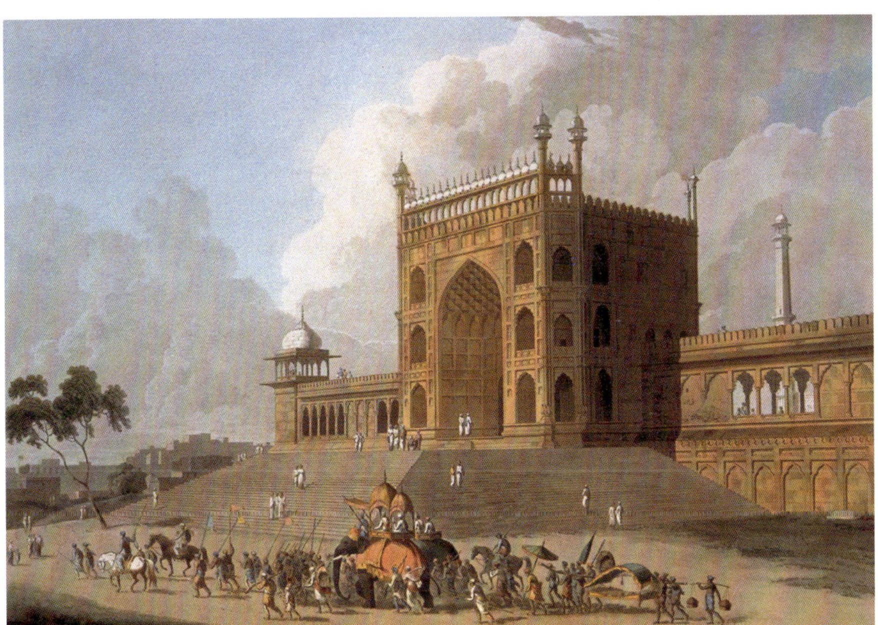

Above: *The Entrance to the Palace at Lucknow.* Oil on canvas by William Daniell, exhibited at the Royal Academy, 1801.

Left: *Eastern Gate of the Jummah Musjid at Delhi.* Aquatint by Thomas Daniell after a drawing by himself, 1795.

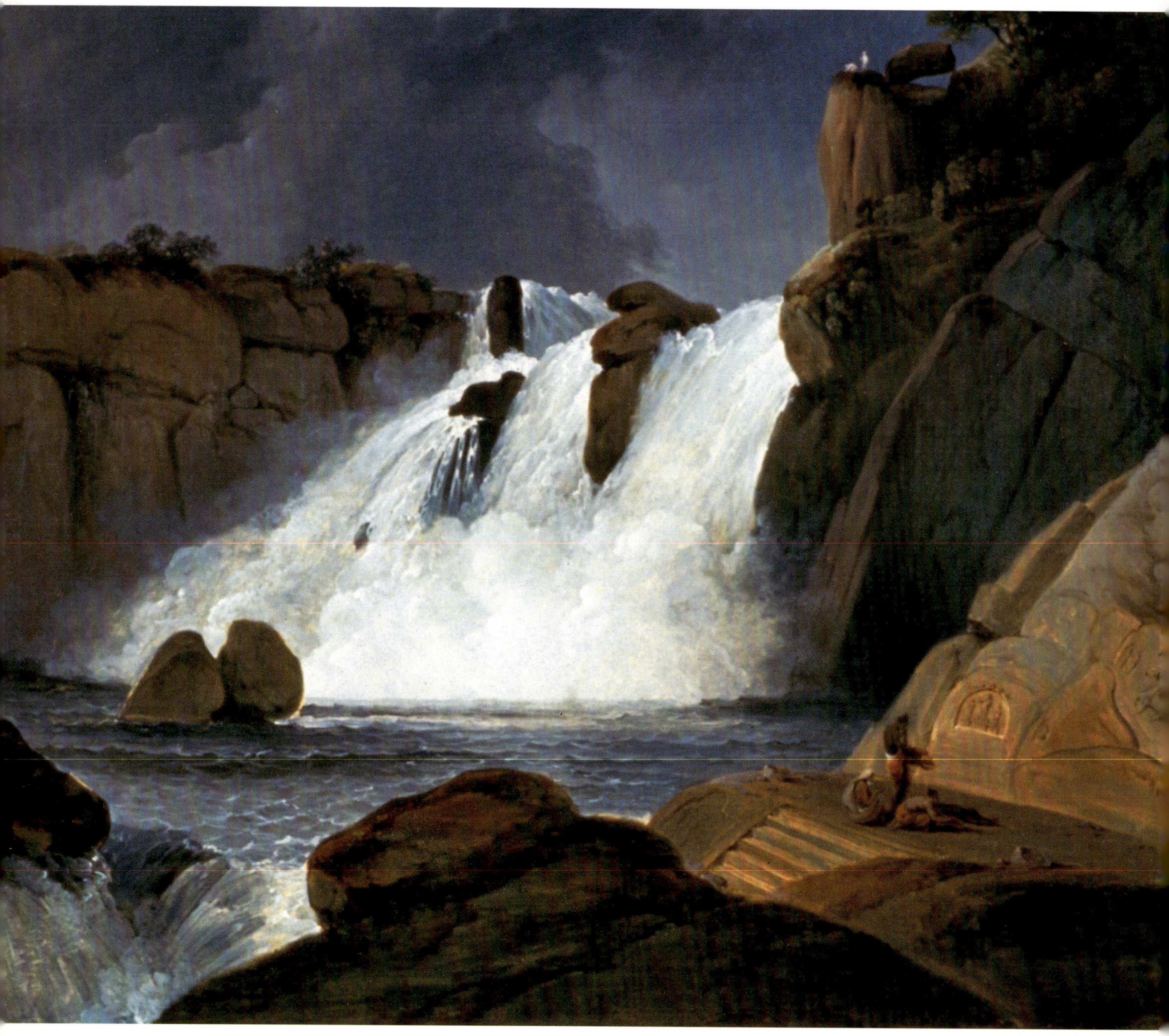

Above: *The waterfall at Puppanassum in the Tinnevelly District.* Aquatint after a drawing by Thomas Daniell, 1792.

Facing page above: *The Rope Bridge at Sirinagur (Garhwal).* Aquatint by Thomas and William Daniell, 1805.

Facing page below: *Hindoo Temples at Agouree on the River Soane, Bahar.* Aquatint by Thomas Daniell after a drawing by himself, 1790.

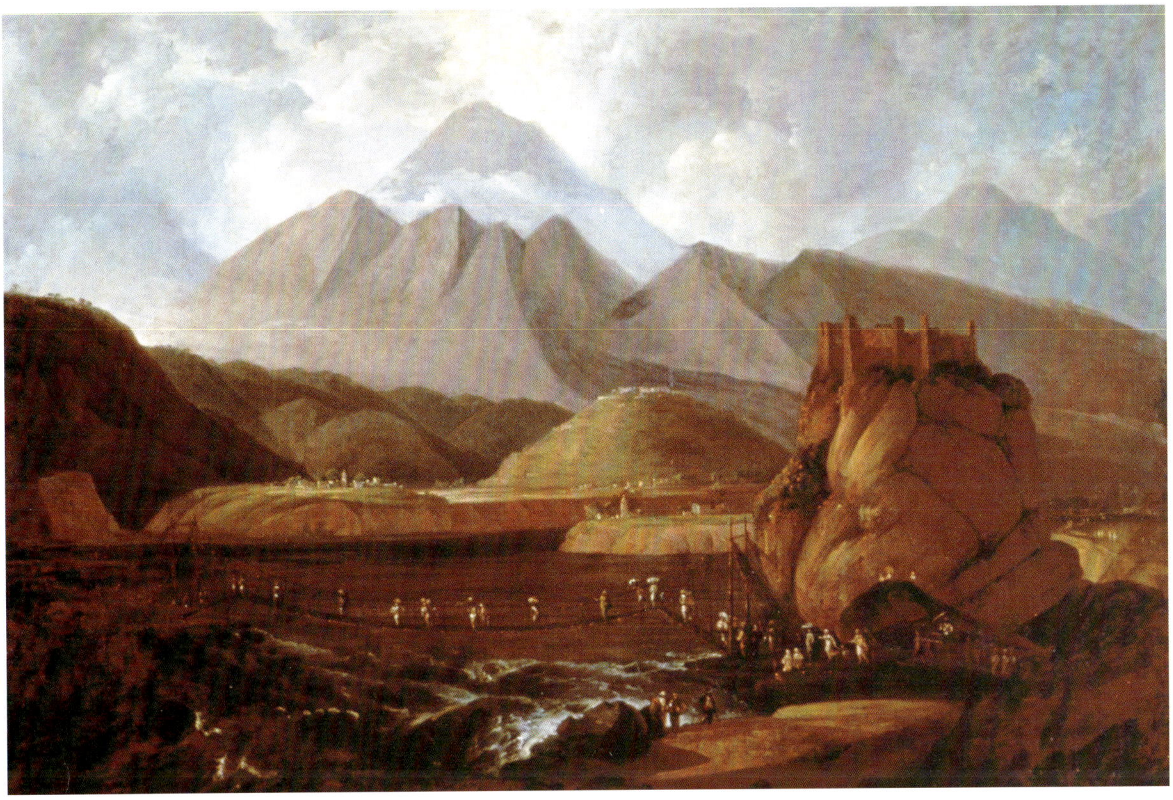

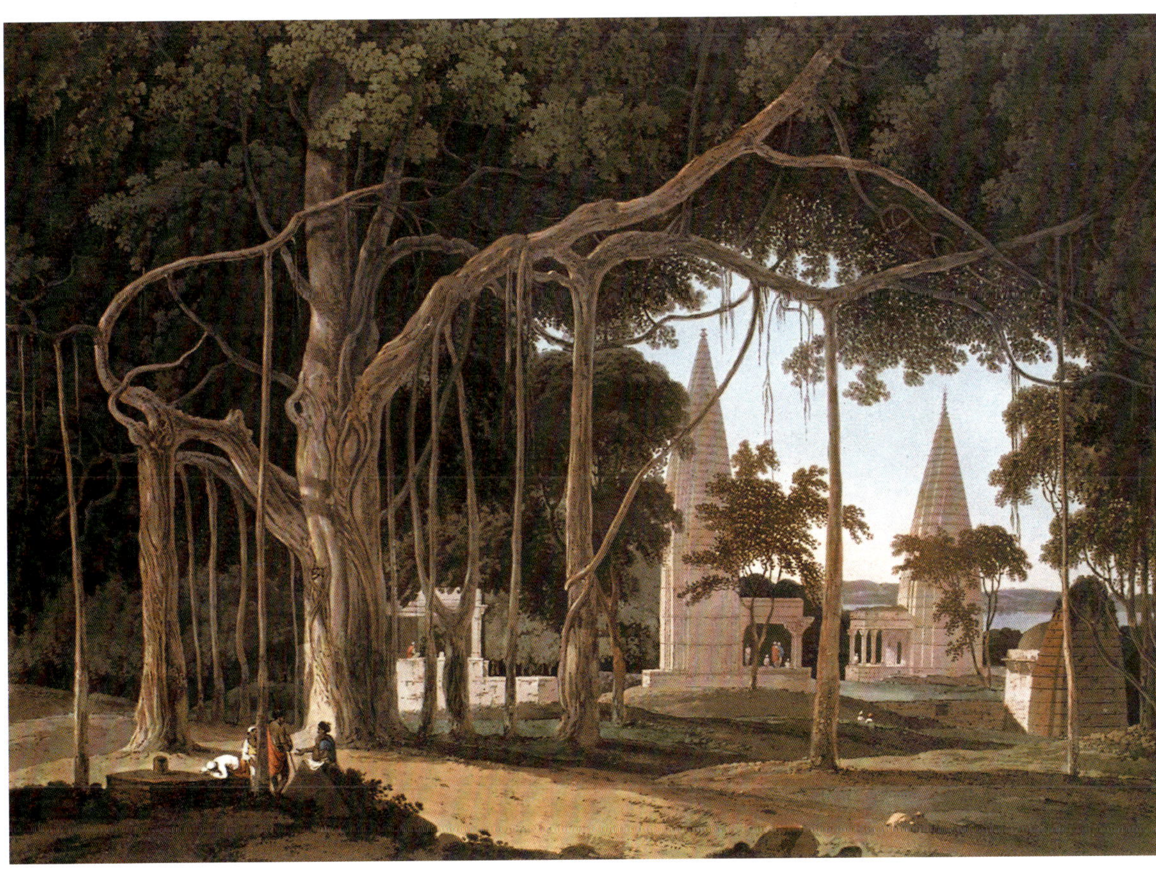

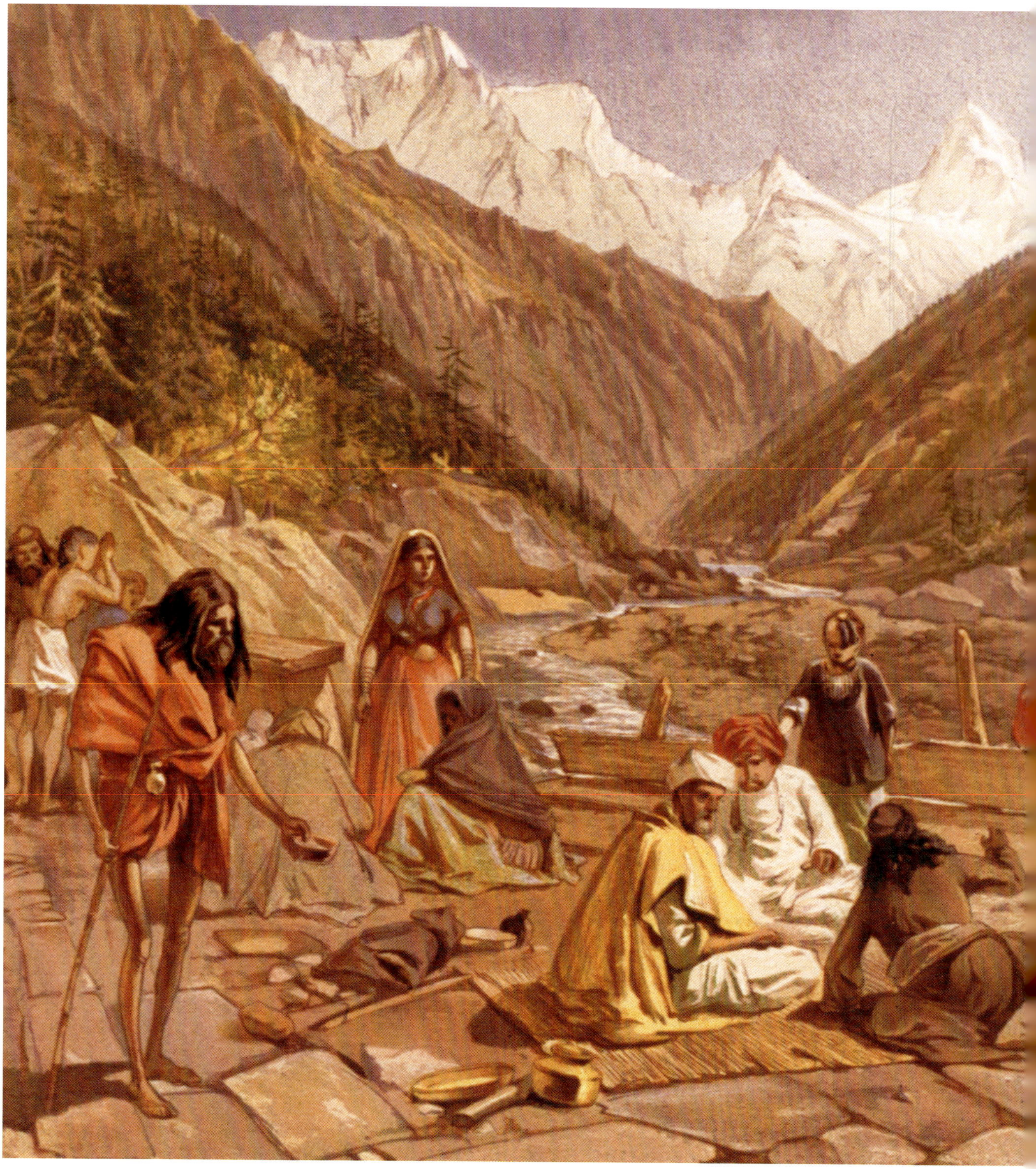

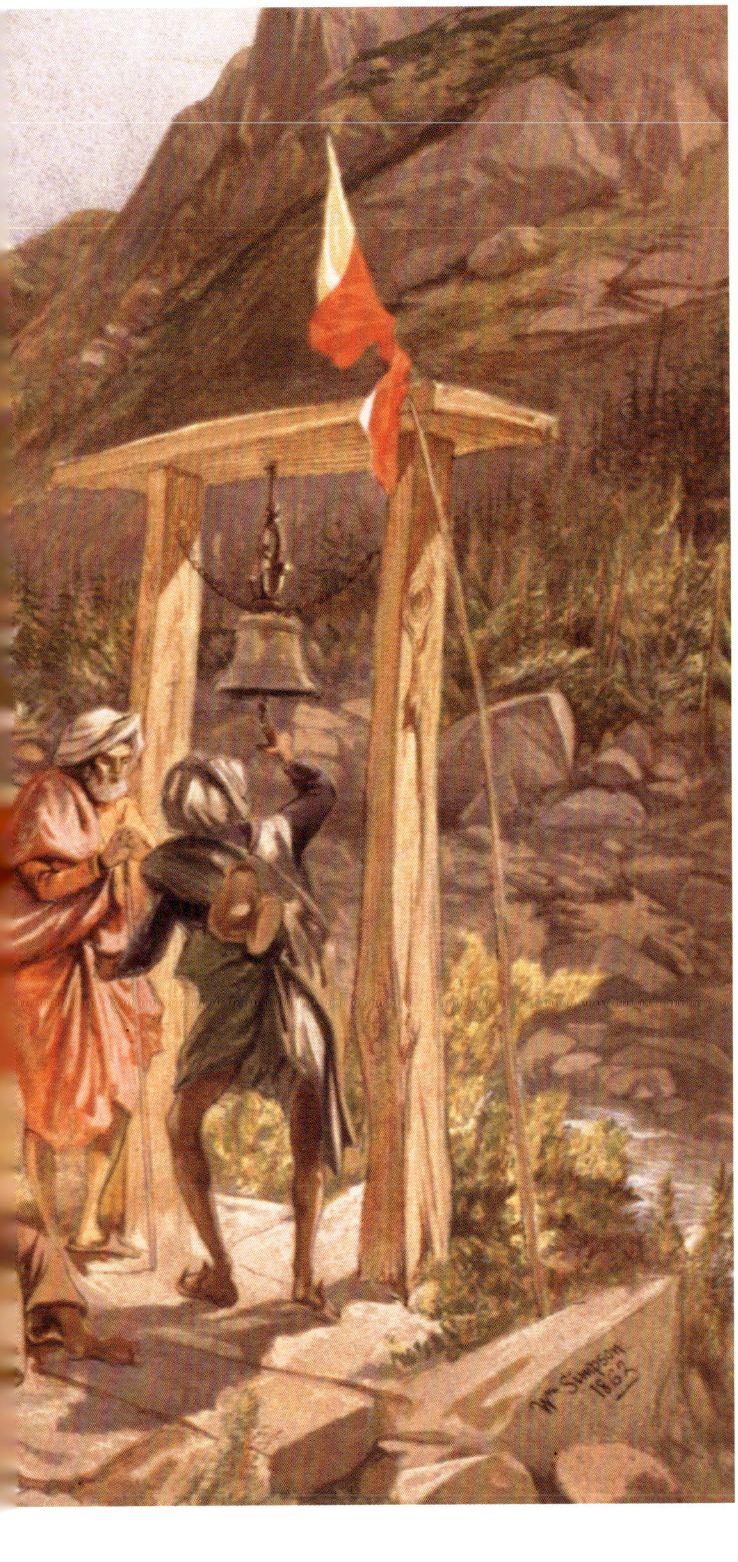

A sketch of Pilgrims to Gangotri.
Chromo-lithograph after a drawing
by William Simpson, c.1860.

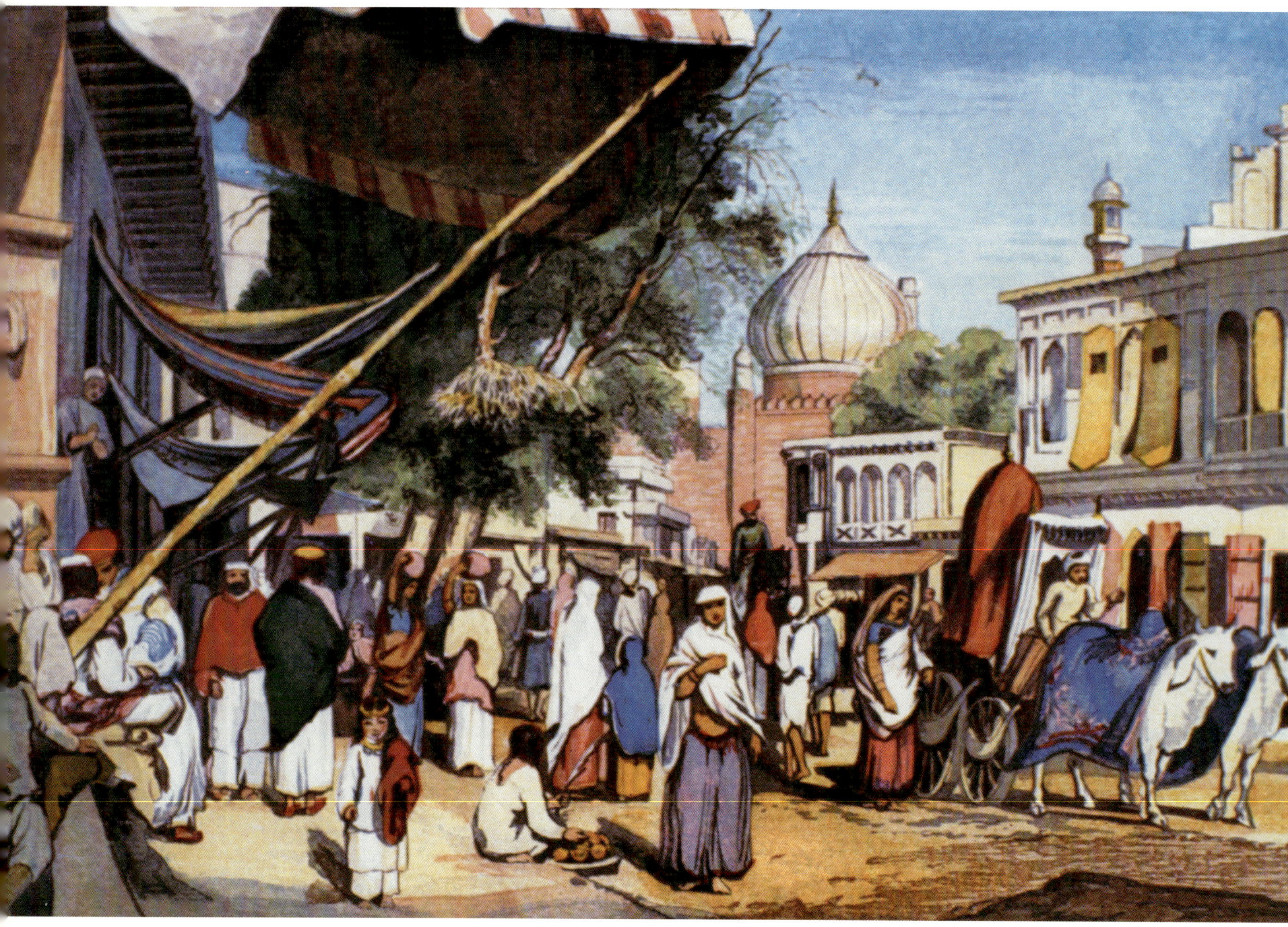

Delhi, a street at Back of Juma Musjid. Coloured lithograph after a drawing by William Carpenter, c.1855, 'Illustrated London News.'

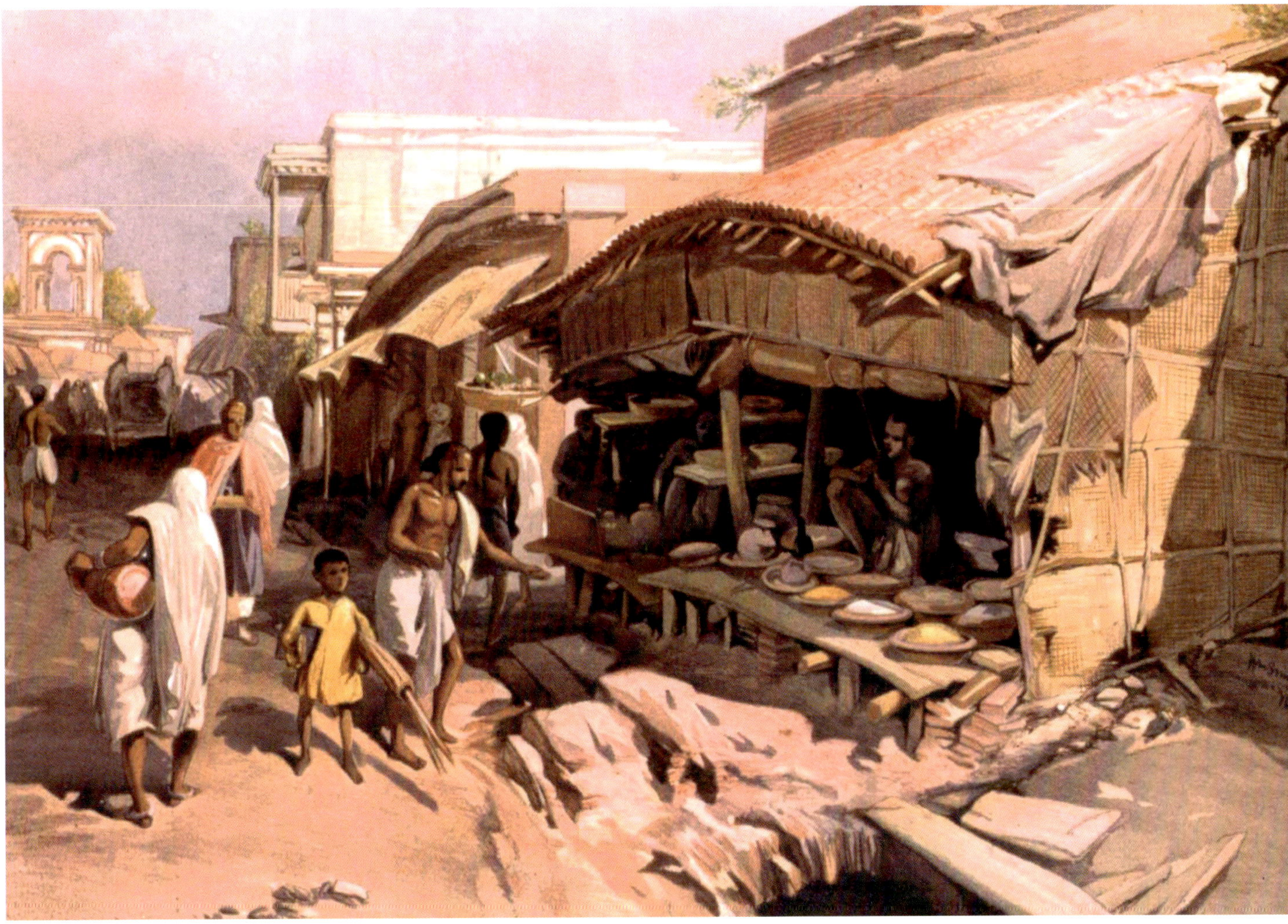

Native shop in a Calcutta Bazaar.
Chromo-lithograph after a drawing
by William Simpson, c.1860.

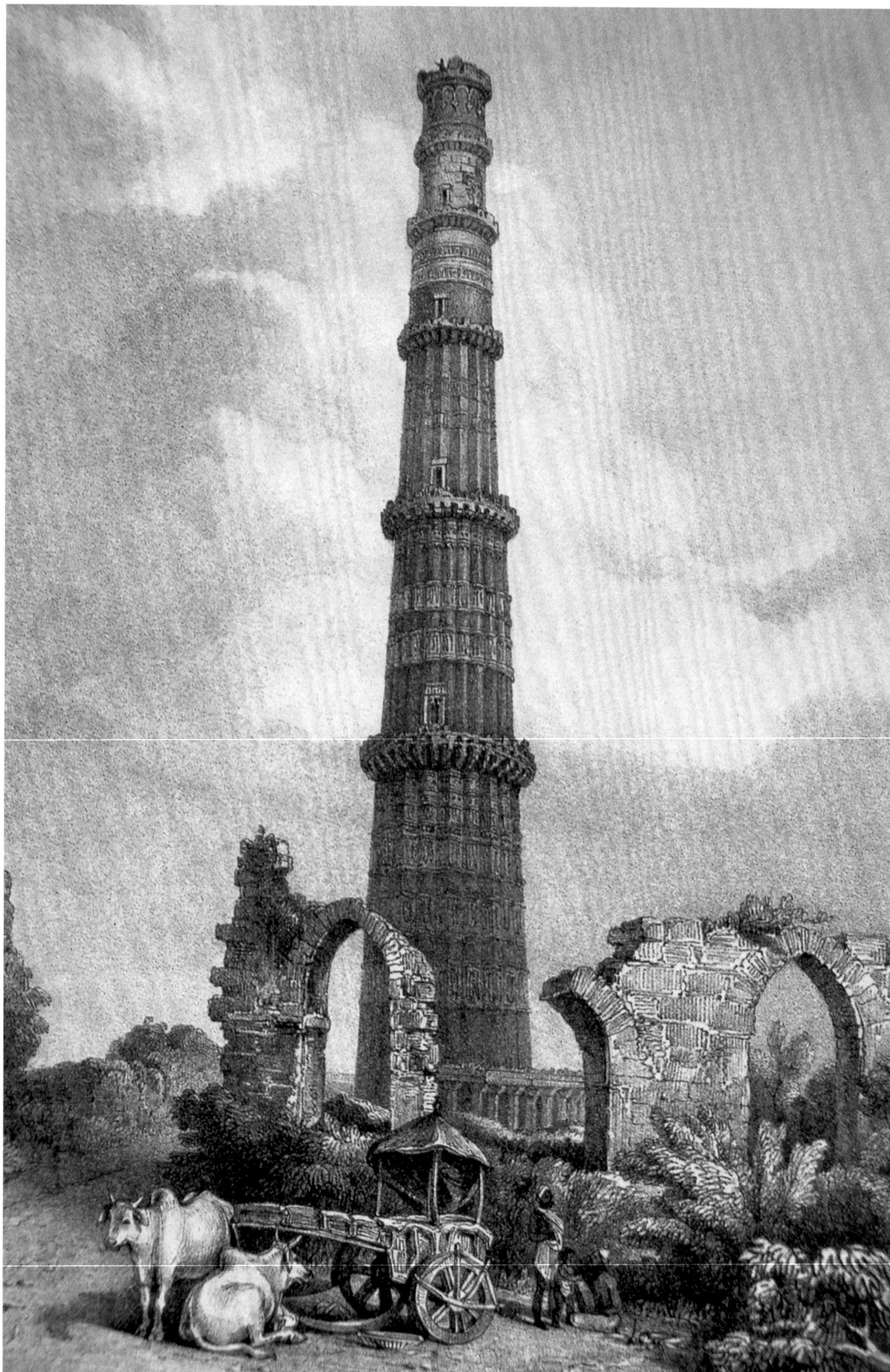

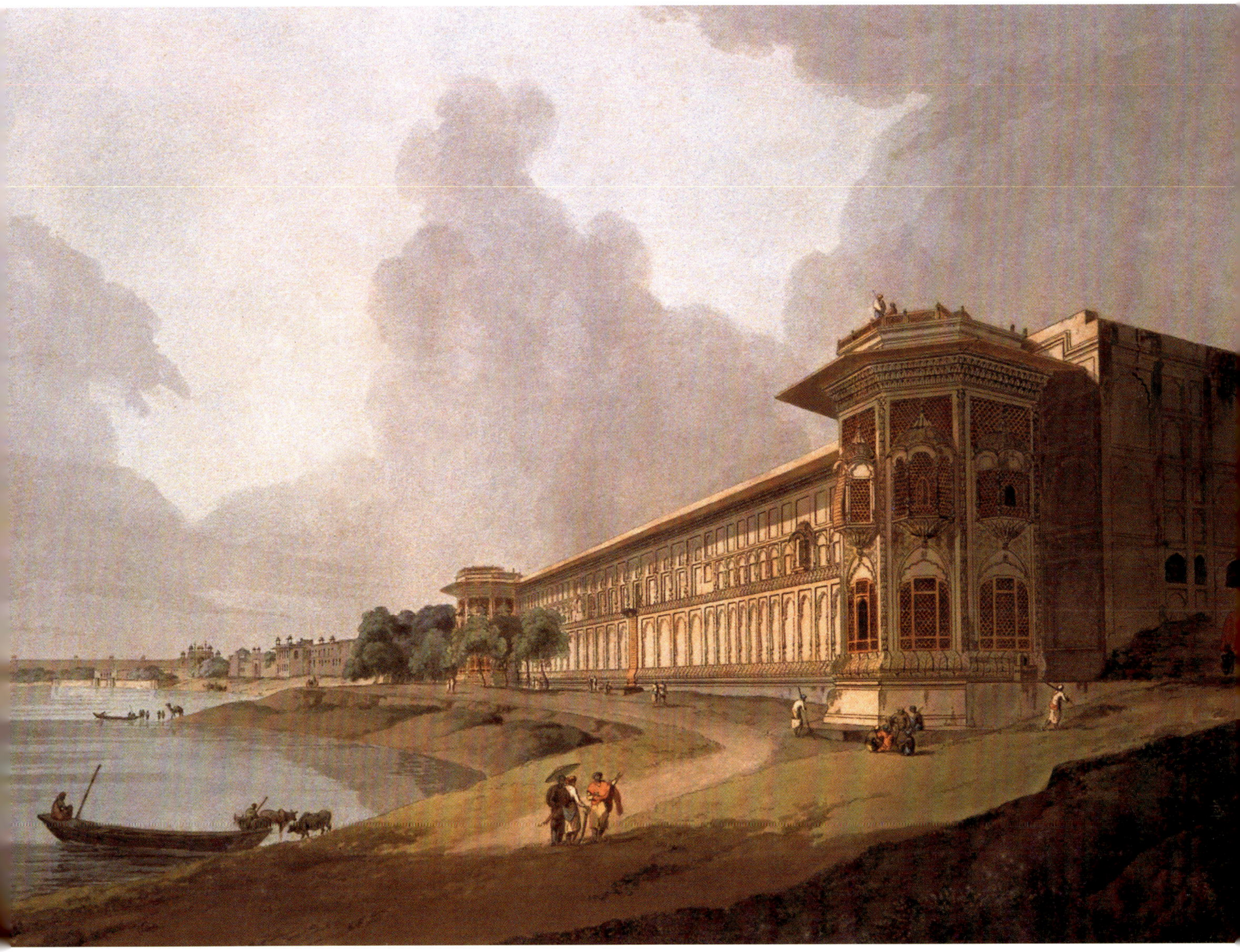

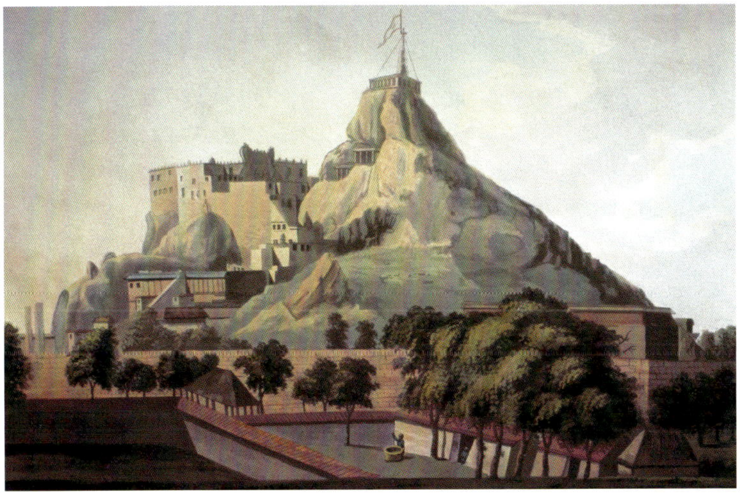

Facing page: *Qutab Minar.* Engraving after a drawing by Lt. Col. C.R. Forrest, 1824.

Above: *North East View of the Cotsea Bhaug, on the River Jumna, Delhi.* Aquatint by Thomas Daniell after a drawing by himself, 1789.

Left: *South East View of the Rock of Trichinopoly.* Engraving after a drawing by Col. F.S. Ward, 1804.

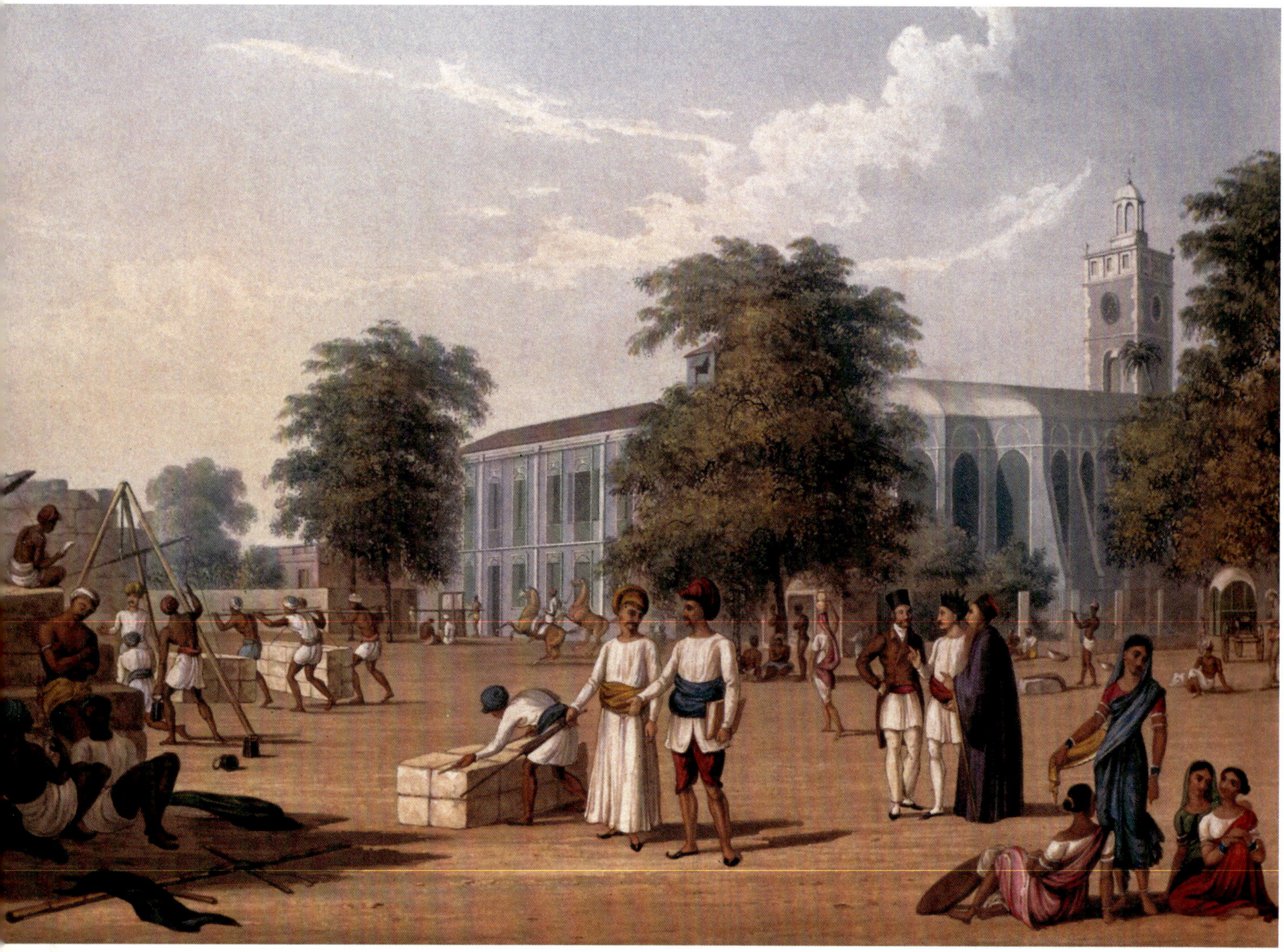

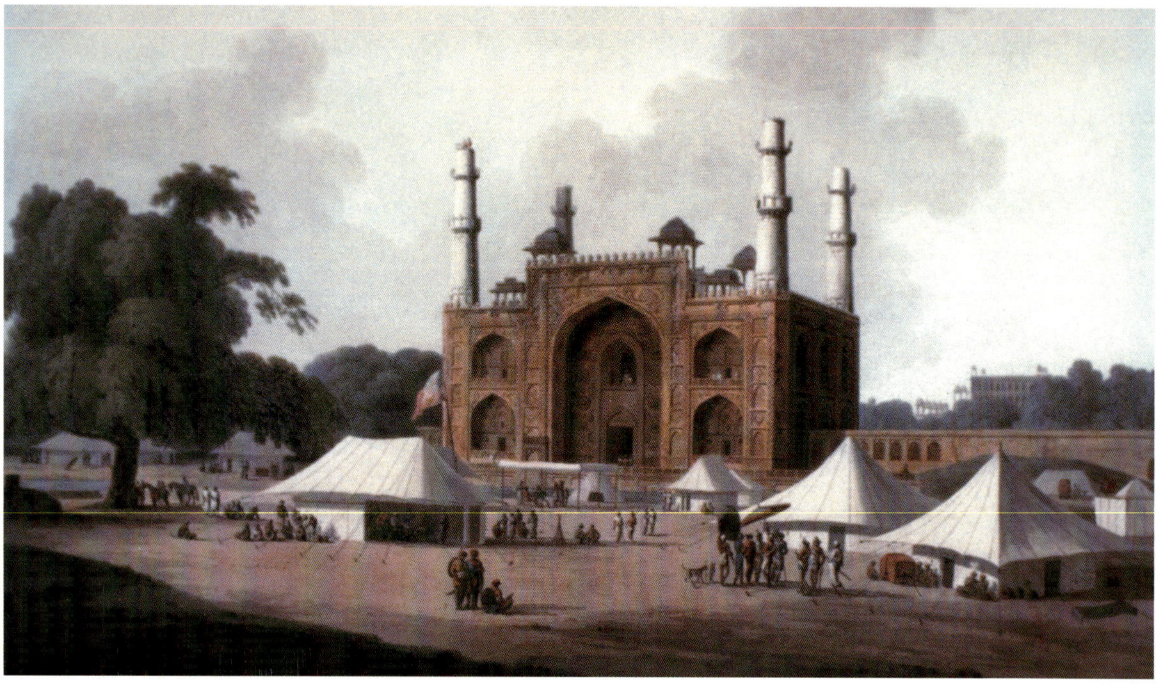

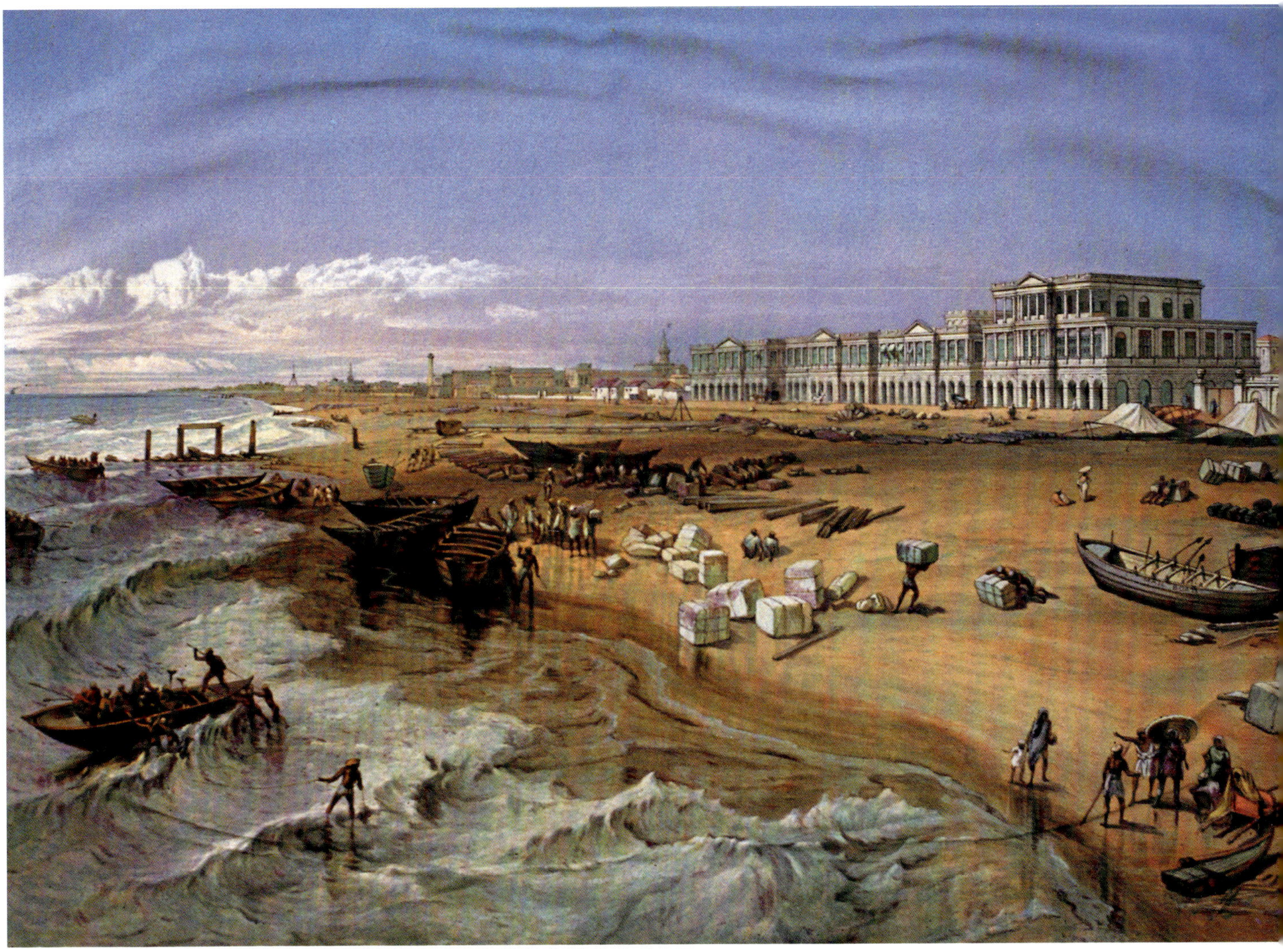

Above: *Madras.*
Chromolithograph after a drawing by William Simpson, c.1860.

Facing page above: *Scene in Bombay.*
Engraving after a drawing by Captain R. M. Grindlay, 1811.

Facing page below: *Gate of the Tomb of the Emperor Akbar at Secundra, near Agra.*
Aquatint by Thomas and William Daniell, 1795.

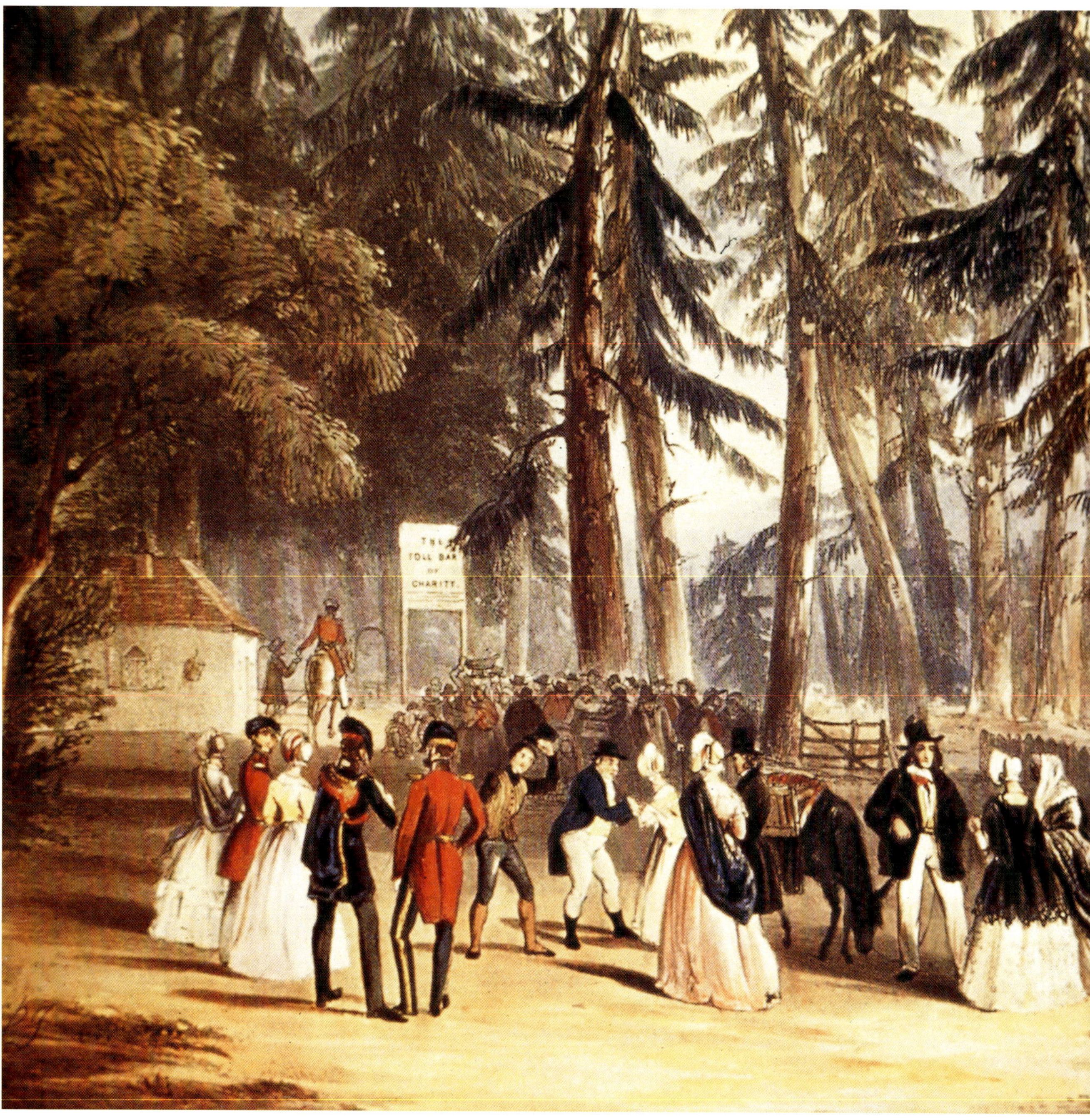

Fancy Fair at Annandale, in Simla in 1839.
Lithograph after a drawing by
Captain G.P. Thomas, 1846.

THE SAHIB'S LIFESTYLE

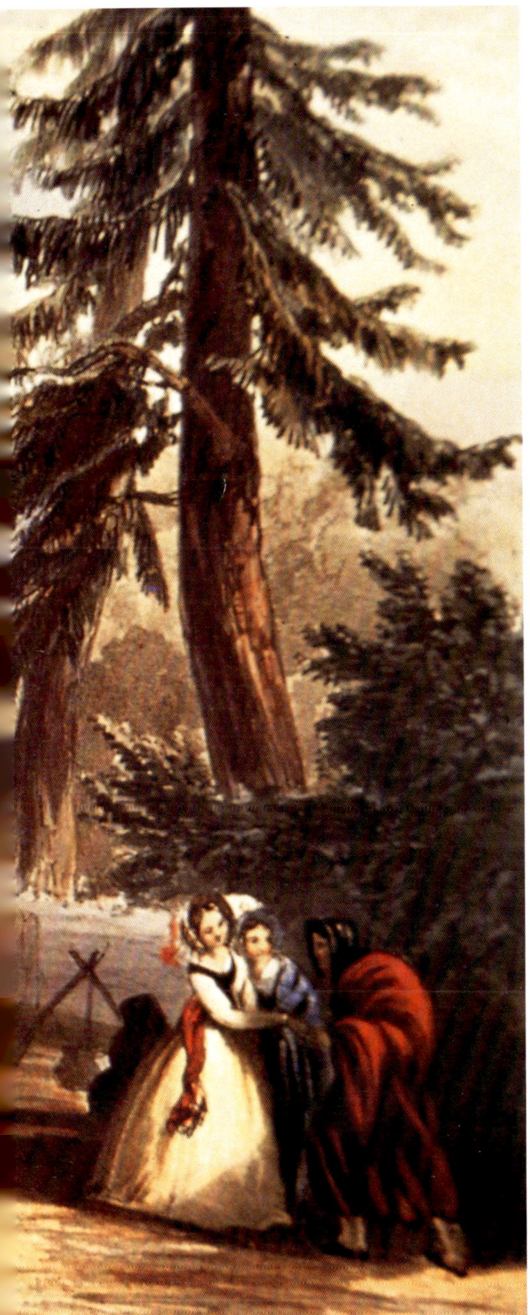

THE SECOND half of the eighteenth century witnessed the transformation of the British from traders to rulers. This phenomenon ushered in the 'Age of Nabobs,' during which the East India Company's civilians and soldiers made their personal fortunes through private trade and other means fair or foul. This brought a notable change in the pattern of their everyday life. They lived in a grand manner and Indian influence could be seen occasionally in their mansions, in their elaborate meals, and in their opulent dress. It was also visible in their entertainments especially the 'nautch.' In the manner of Indian aristocracy, these English Nabobs employed an army of servants to serve their every possible need and to lend an aura of grandeur and prestige to their status in society.

The picture of the life of the English in eighteenth-century India that emerges from travel books is that they lived in bungalows the size of small palaces, surrounded by the luxuries of oriental splendour. Attended by troops of dusky, white-clad servants, they would relax on a pile of cushions and enjoy smoking perfumed tobacco from their bejewelled hookahs while sipping cool sherbet or Shiraz wine. In the evening, they would go out in their gilded palanquins or riding on their Arabian horses. Contemporary accounts mention their overindulgence in food and excessive drinking. According to Raikes (1867), "It was nothing uncommon for them to sit over their cups until death came to claim one of the revellers." Many of them were so fond of gambling that card parties began on Saturday and continued till Monday and vast sums of money changed hands.

Most of the Sahibs found a solution to their sexual isolation by keeping Indian bibis or setting up zenanas. The bibis dominated the scene until the middle of the nineteenth century. For the British Nabob a large zenana became a status symbol. It was said to be more economical to keep a dozen Indian mistresses or bibis than maintaining a European wife. There was no shame attached to these liaisons. Contemporary paintings depict the intimacy between the Sahib and his bibi.

There is a fascinating account of 'A day in the life of an English sahib in Calcutta,' in *Macintosh Travels,* 1771–82. "About the hour of seven in the morning, his durwan opens the gate and the Veranda is free to his circars, peons...The head bearer and jemmadar enter the hall and his bedroom at eight o' clock. A lady quits his side and is conducted by a private staircase either to her own apartment or out of the yard." There is detailed description of his daily chores including supper at 10 and the company of guests till between 12 and 1 in the

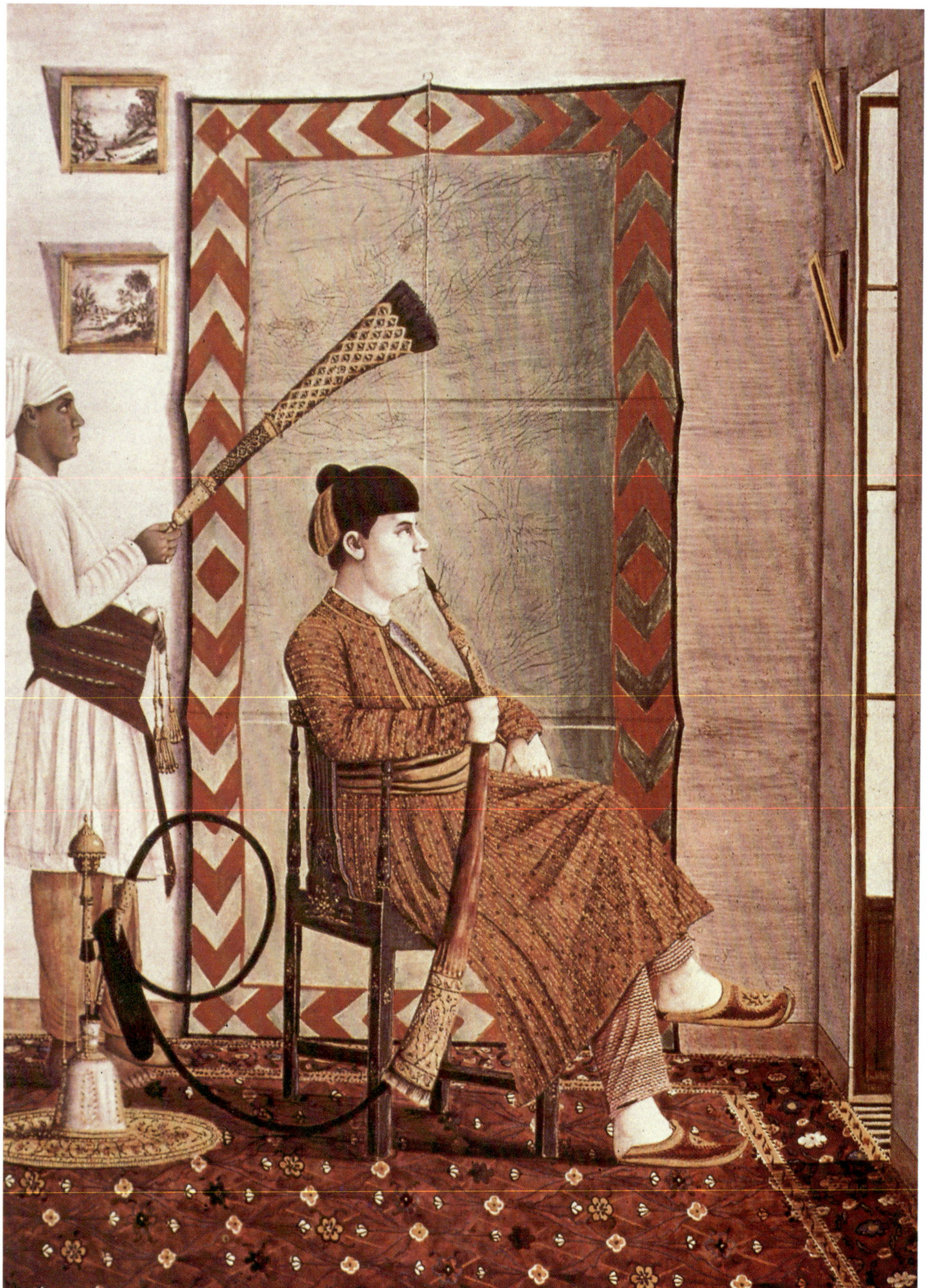

morning after which our hero is conducted to his bedroom, where he finds a 'female companion to amuse him.' The author concludes that with no greater exertion than these do the Company's servants amass the most splendid fortunes.

The following poem presents a vivid picture of a Sahib and his personal attendants:

Here they rise very late and beginning to dress
Are surrounded by slaves for they can't do with less.
For the heat is so great that unfortunate selves
They've scarcely the pow'r to accountre themselves!
So languid and weak, they are frequently known
To rise as fatigued as at night they laid down
Then the natives of India to cast do so cling
ou scarcely get two to perform the same thing
One puts on stocking, one holds a serie
Another with chilumchee stands ready bye
A third has a mirror, he brings to your view
A fourth fellow is tying, the string of your shoe
Or perhaps undressing a bearer's undoing
Your shoes or cravat there is another champoeing
Your arms or your legs which'er he may lighten
Like famed Dean Mohmed champoes at Brighton
(The Life and Adventures of Shigram-Po, Calcutta, 1821.)

An English lady's life was equally leisure-oriented and her every comfort was taken care of by her female servants who were constantly in attendance. During their stay in India memsahibs learnt well the art of never moving from their perch if they could avoid it. A contemporary account gives an interesting description about the memsahibs:

They lie on a sofa, and if they drop their handkerchief, they just lower their voices and say, 'Boy!' in a very gently tone, and then creeps in perhaps, some old wizen, skinny brownie, looking like a superannuated thread-paper, who twiddles after them for a little while, and then creeps out again as softly as a black cat, and sits down cross-legged in a verandah till `Mistress please to call again.'

John Wombwell, the Paymaster and Auditor-General to the Oudh Nawab's troops under British Command. Watercolour by Dip Chand, c.1780.

As the nineteenth century rolled on and the steamships increased their sailings to India, British women came out to India in increasing numbers in search of husbands with wealth and position. By the middle of the century they had driven out the bibis and after the Mutiny of 1857, the zenana virtually vanished from the scene. Many young English girls married men twice their age, who showered them with jewels,

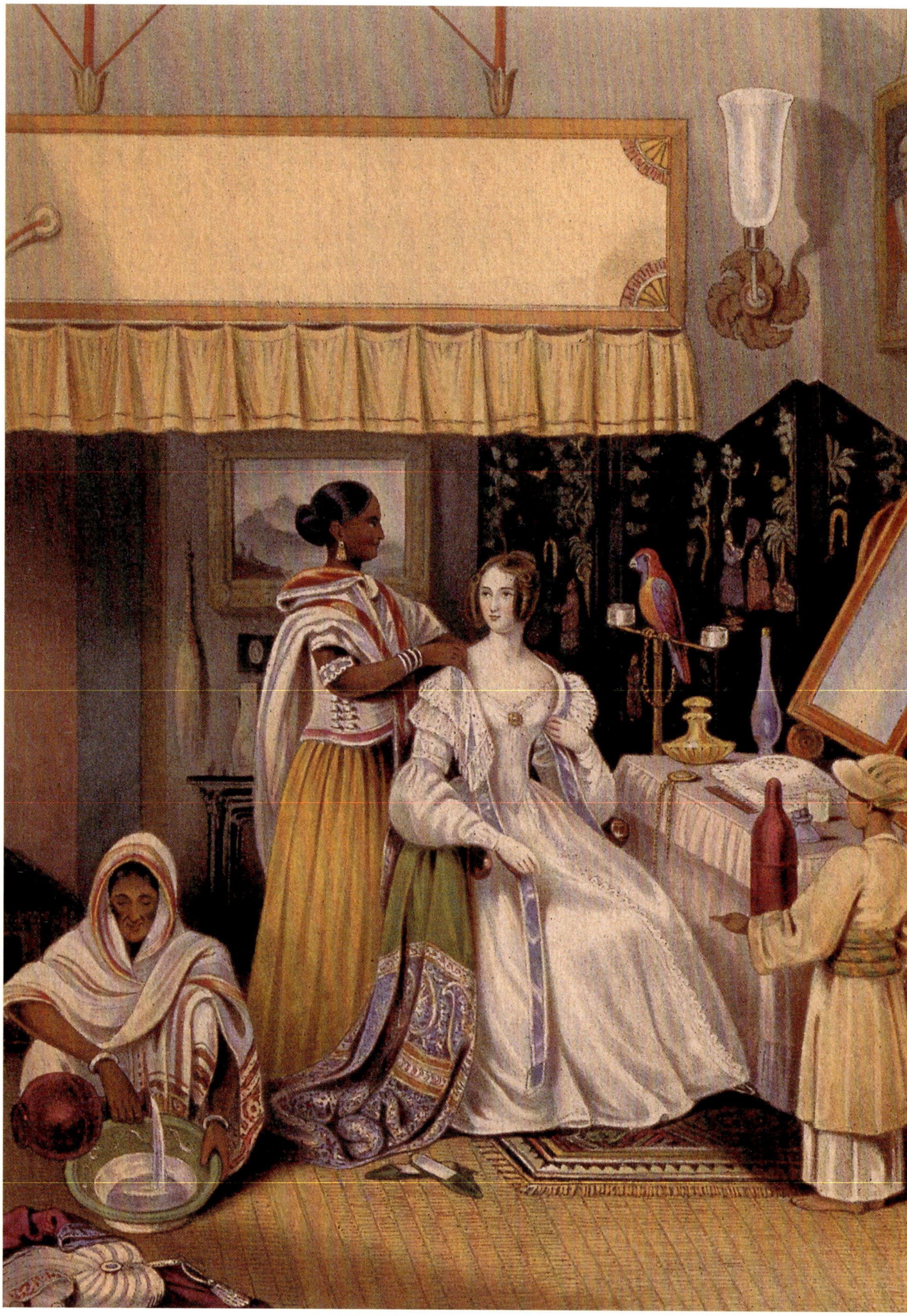

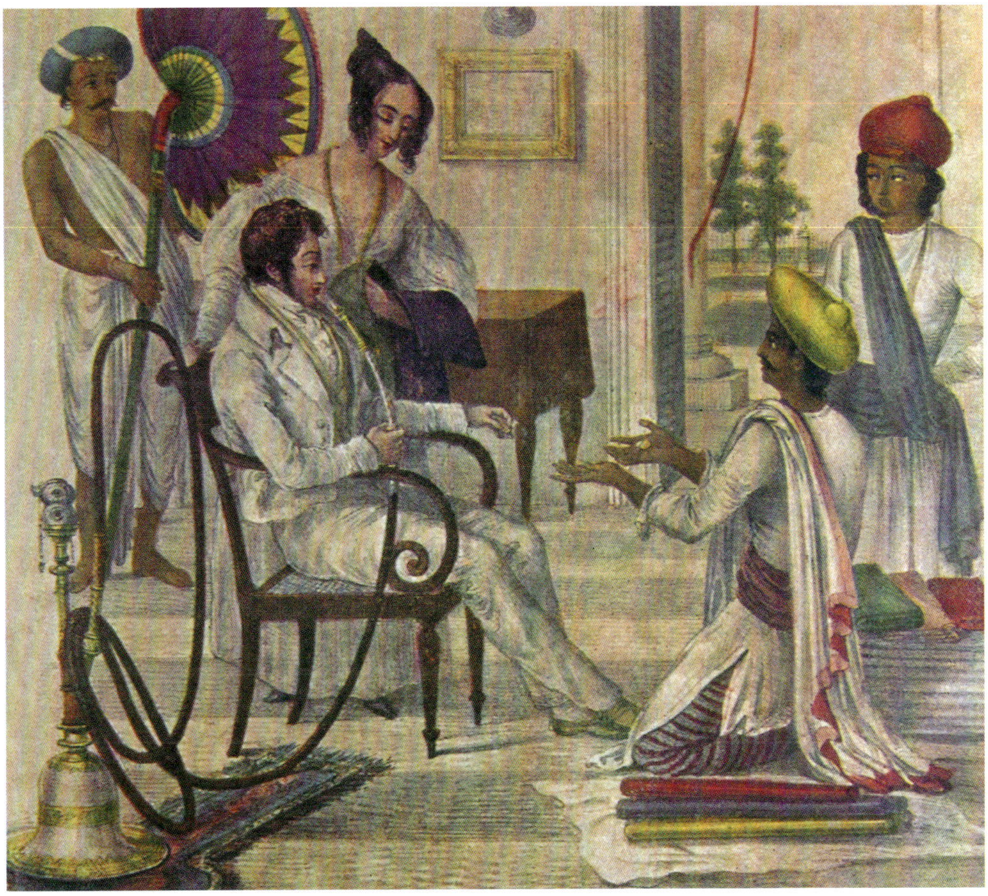

Above: *Cloth and Silk Marchant.* He is supposed to have sold some pieces of silk to the Lady for which the gentleman pays him in gold mohurs. Coloured lithograph after a drawing by S.C Belnos, c. 1820.

Facing page: *The Young Lady's Toilet.* Coloured lithograph after a drawing by William Tayler, 1842.

costly clothes and carriages to win their love. Many alliances were also concluded in utter haste without knowledge of the family background of the prospective bridegrooms. Devoid of attachments many such ill-matched unions led to illicit affairs and scandals. Young civil and military officials with no financial means to afford a European wife were ever willing to offer their services and pay their homage to the fashionable married women who looked for amours outside wedlock.

This brings us to the 'Age of Memsahibs'. They brought a sea change in the sahibs' lifestyle with the spread of racial gulf between the rulers and the ruled. Small `Englands' were created in a chain of civil and military stations where social life came to revolve within the community. There were exclusive clubs for entertainment of the English gentry. Hill-stations came up, led by the summer capital of Simla, the pride of the Raj. It became well-known for its round of lively parties, fancy dress balls, romantic escapades, riding and sports. Kipling's image of Simla as a resort for philandering and frivolity, and his damaging remarks about memsahibs as 'frivolous', vain adultresses irritated the government circles and he was dismissed as a `subversive pamphleteer'. Despite Simla's butterfly reputation, the British managed to rule one-fifth of mankind from that remote resort in the Himalayas.

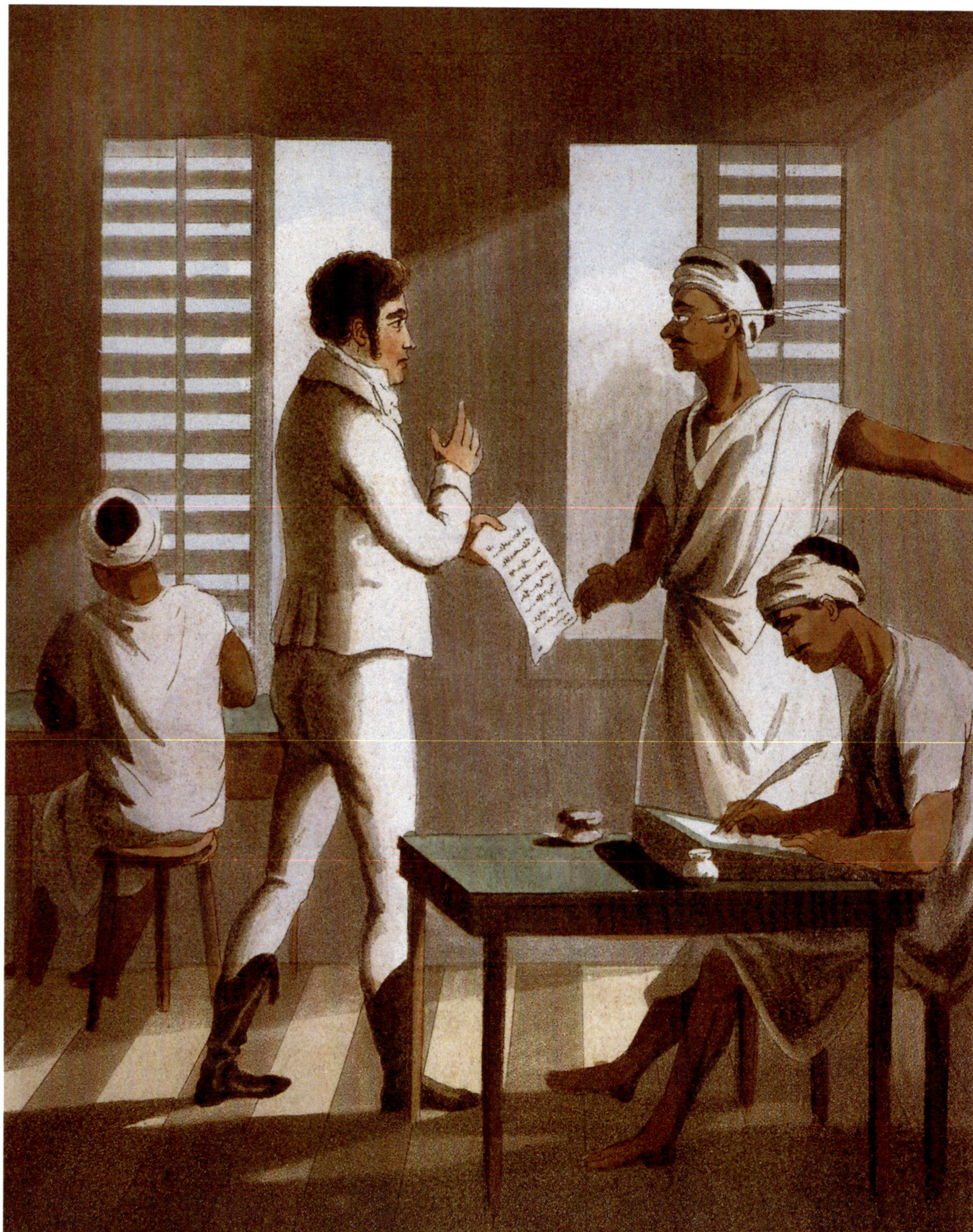

A Gentleman in a Public Office attended by the Crannies or Native Clerks. Hand-coloured aquatint engraving after a drawing by Sir Charles Doyly, 1813.

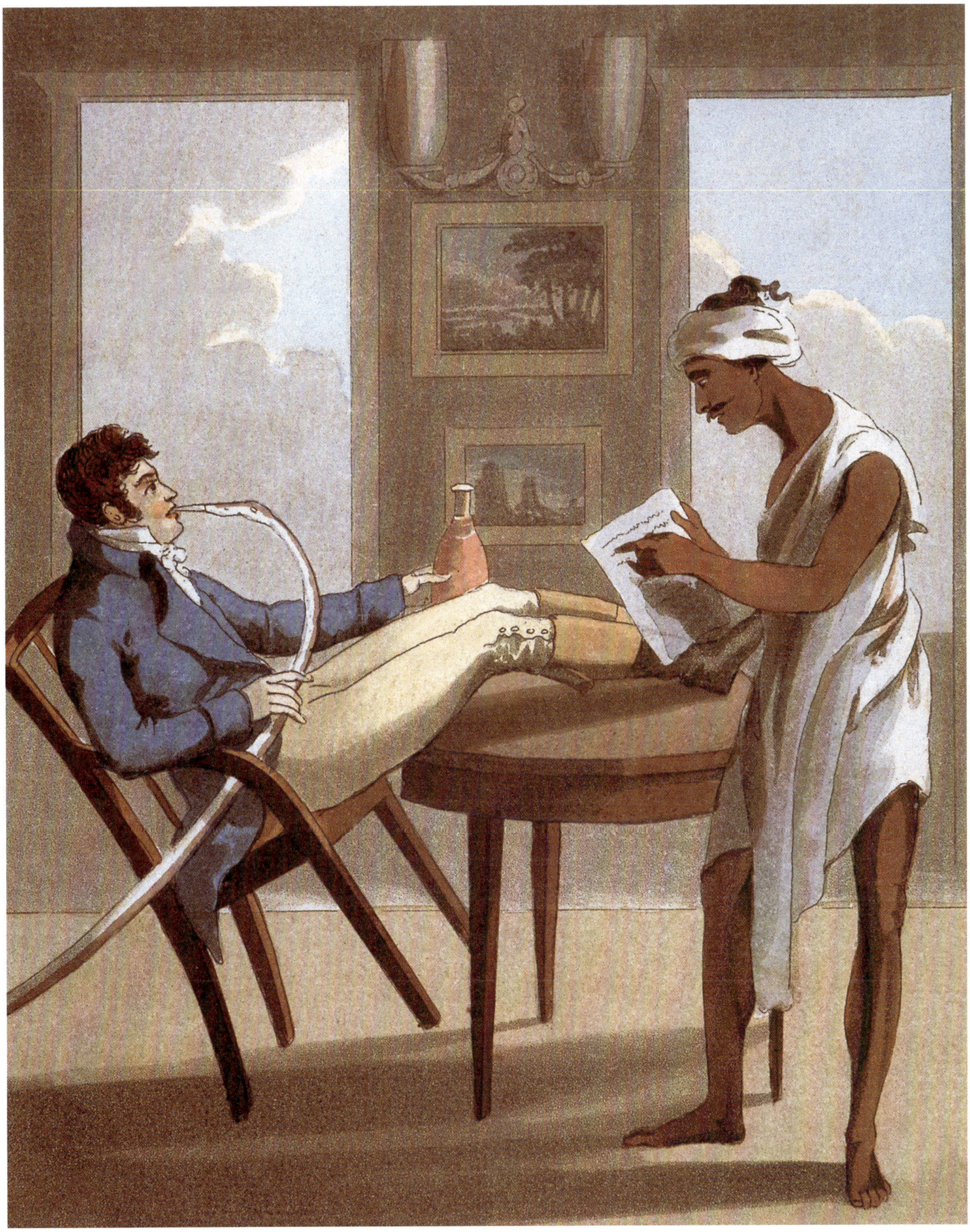

A Gentleman with his Sircar or Money-Servant.
Hand-coloured aquatint engraving after a drawing by Sir Charles Doyly, 1813.

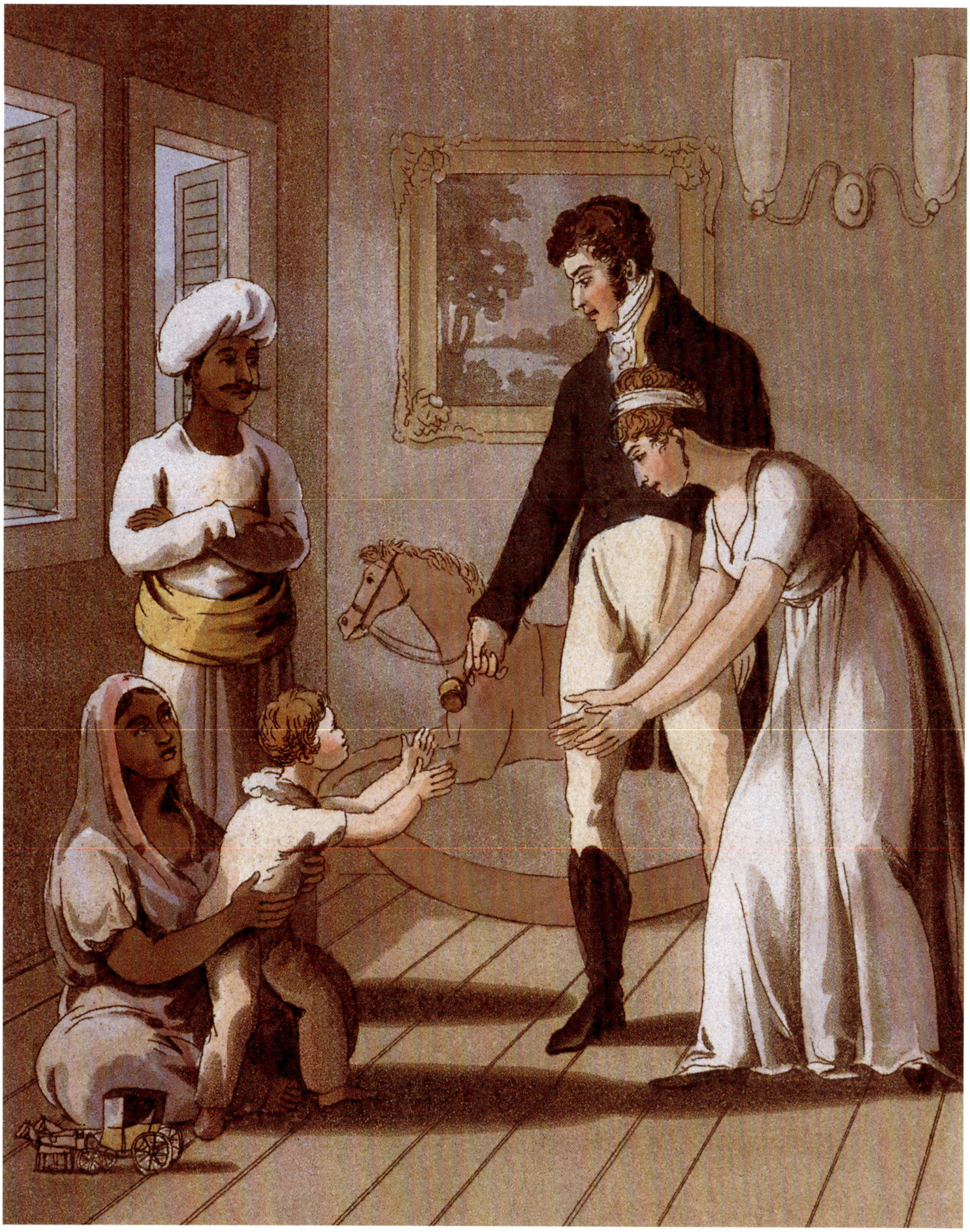

A European Lady and her Family, attended by an Ayah, or Nurse.
Hand-coloured aquatint engraving after a drawing by Sir Charles Doyly, 1813.

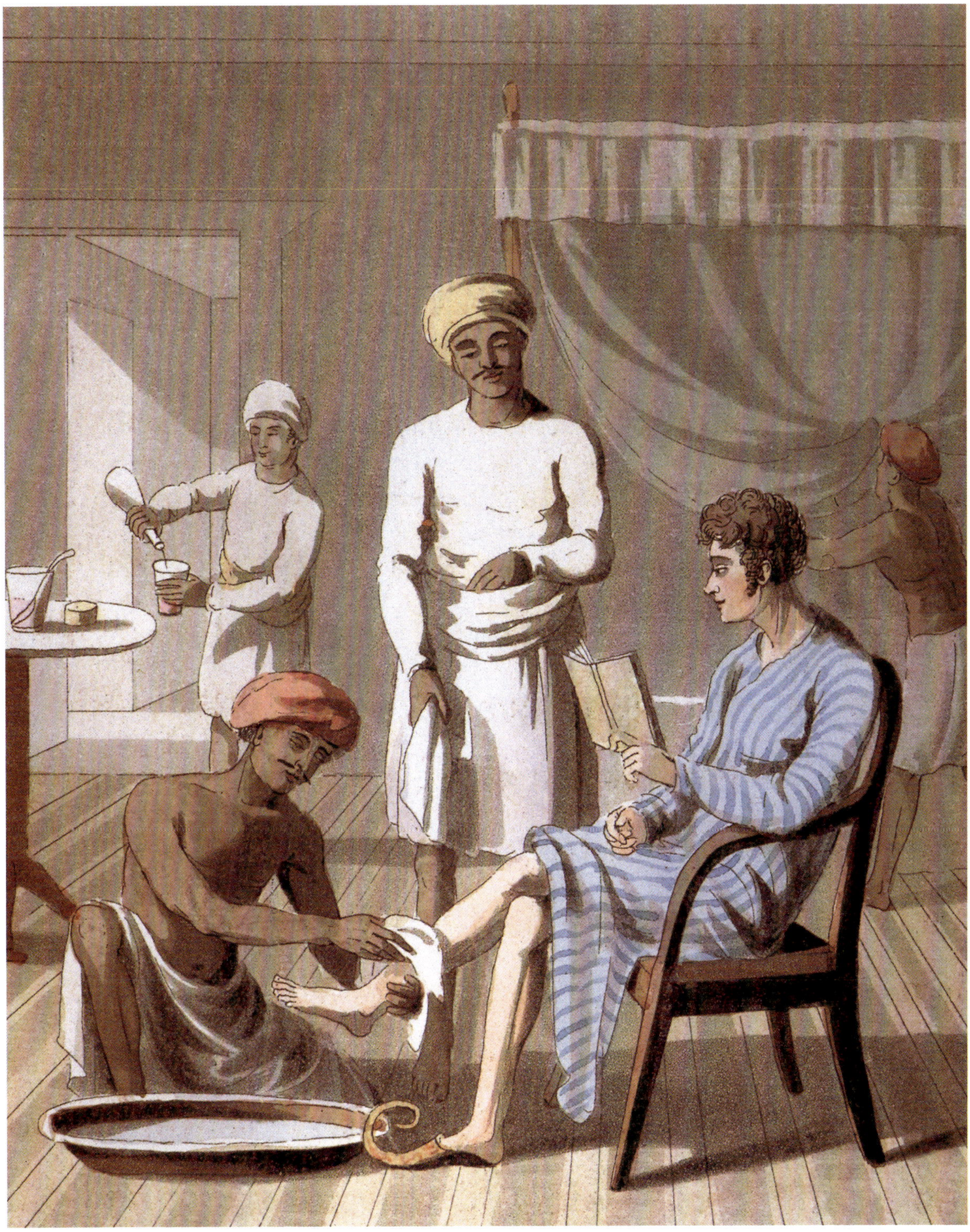

A Gentleman Dressing, attended by his Head-Bearer and other servants.
Hand-coloured aquatint engraving after a drawing by Sir Charles Doyly, 1813.

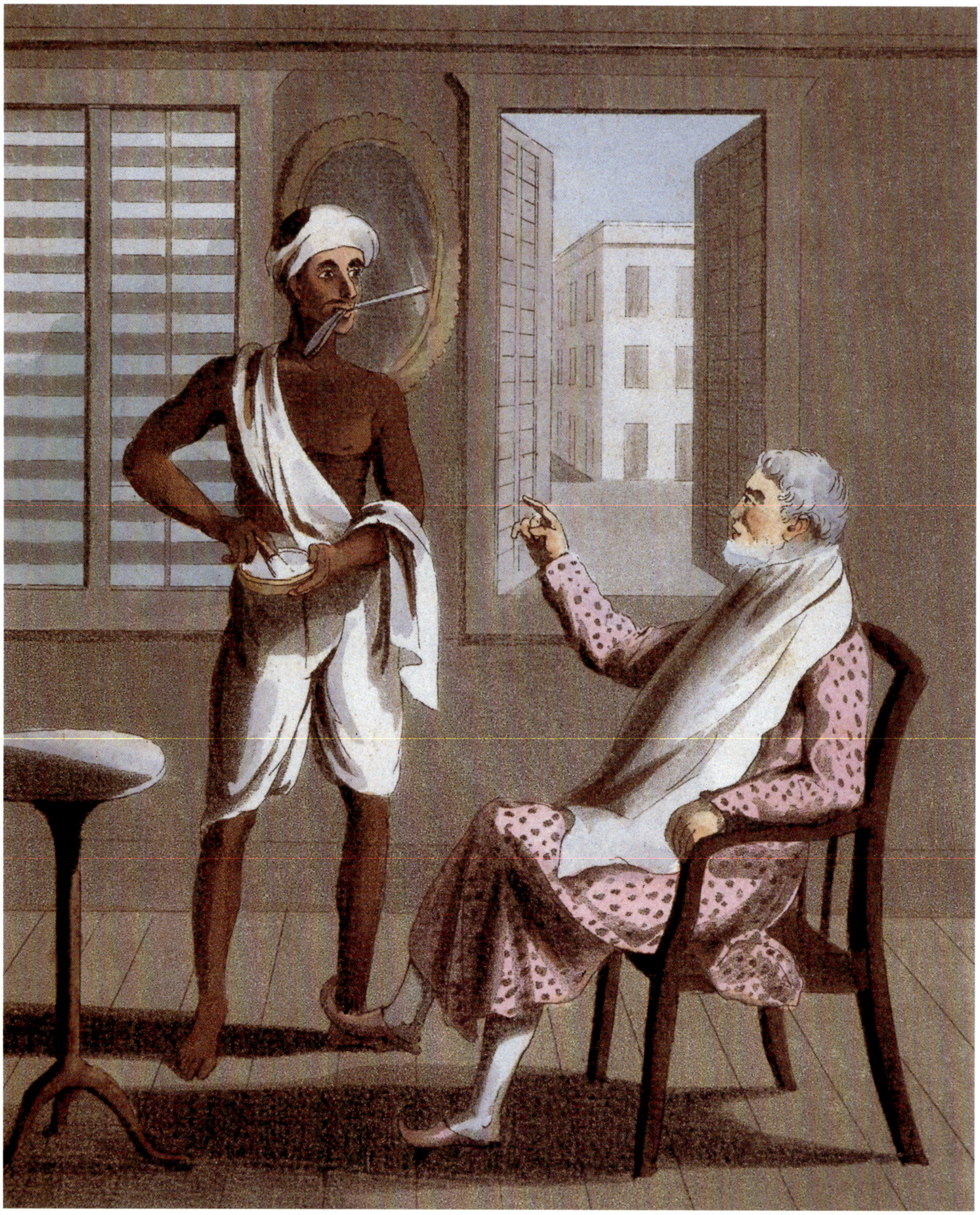

A Gentleman attended by his Hajaum, or Native Barber.
Hand-coloured aquatint engraving after a drawing by Sir Charles Doyly, 1813.

Facing page above: *The Palmer Family.* General William Palmer with his two bibis, Children and three female attendants. Unfinished oil on canvas by Francesco Renaldi, Calcutta, 1786.

Facing page below: *A swarm of admirers hover around Miss C's carriage at the bandstand.* Lithograph after a drawing by G.F. Atkinson, c.1856.

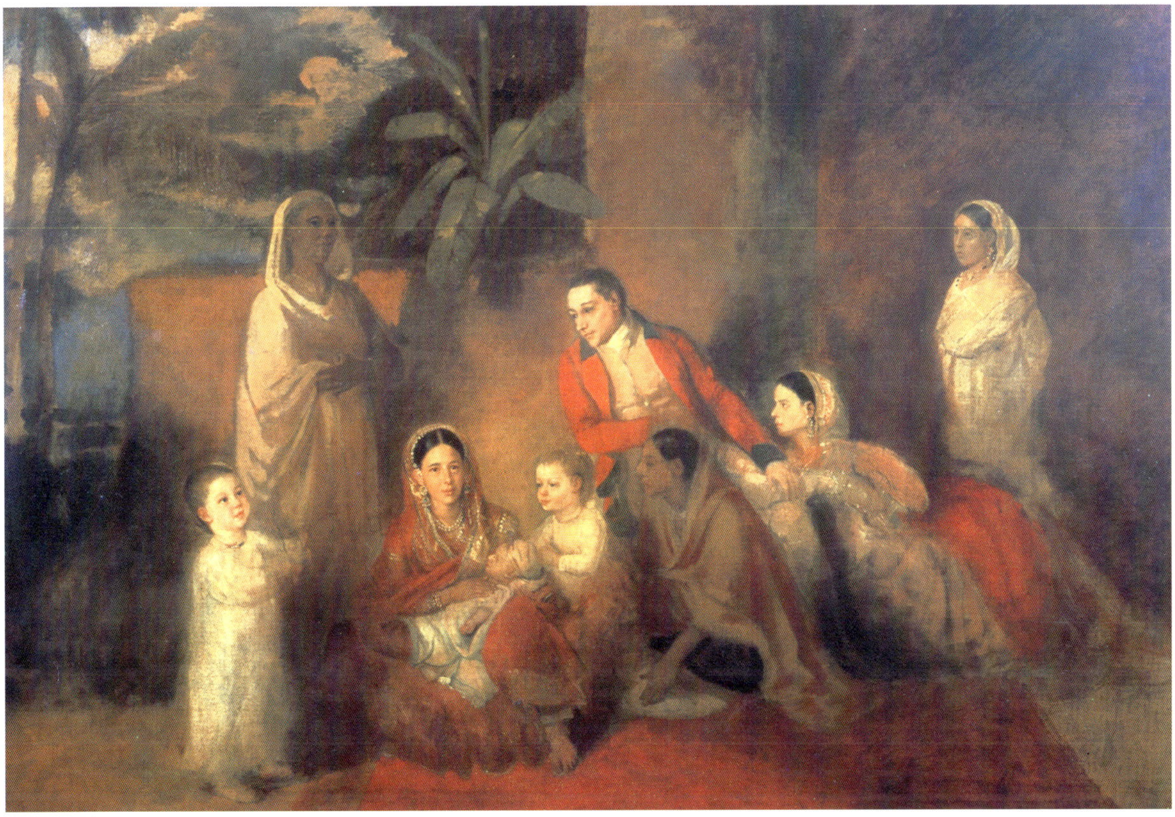

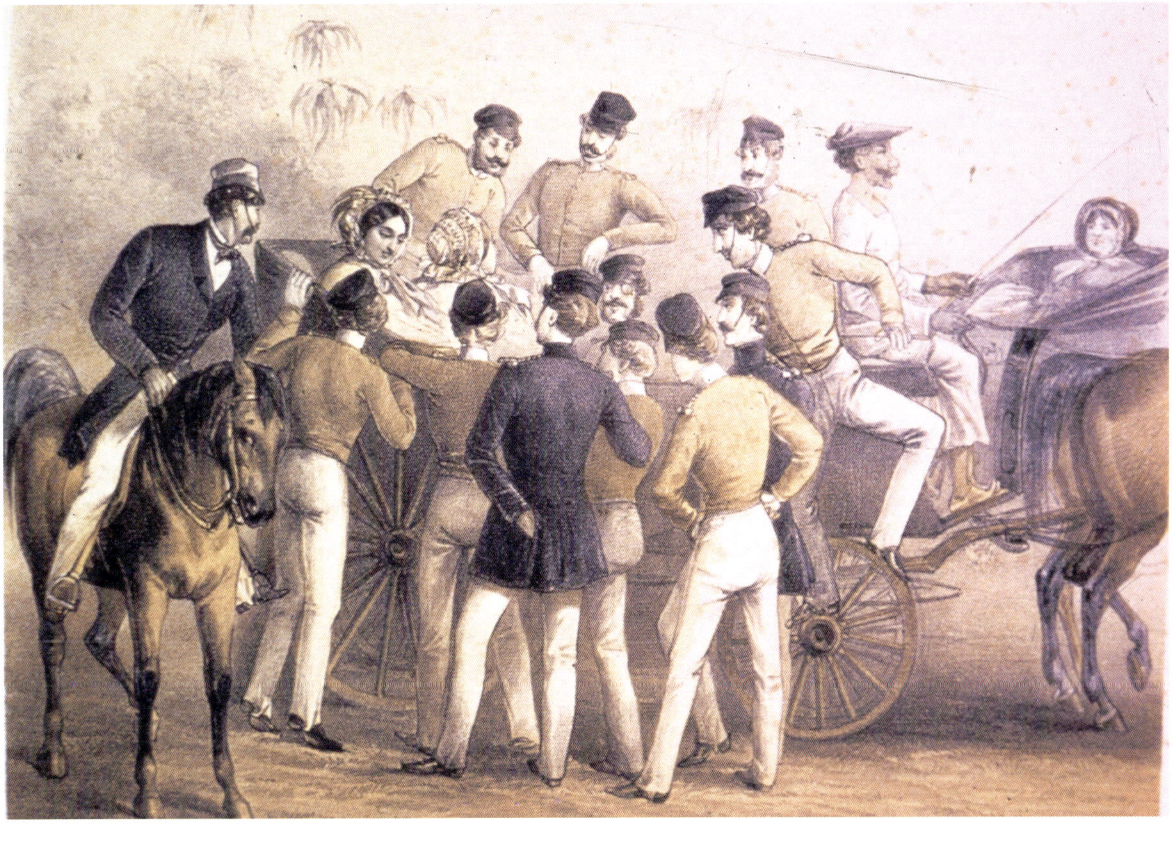

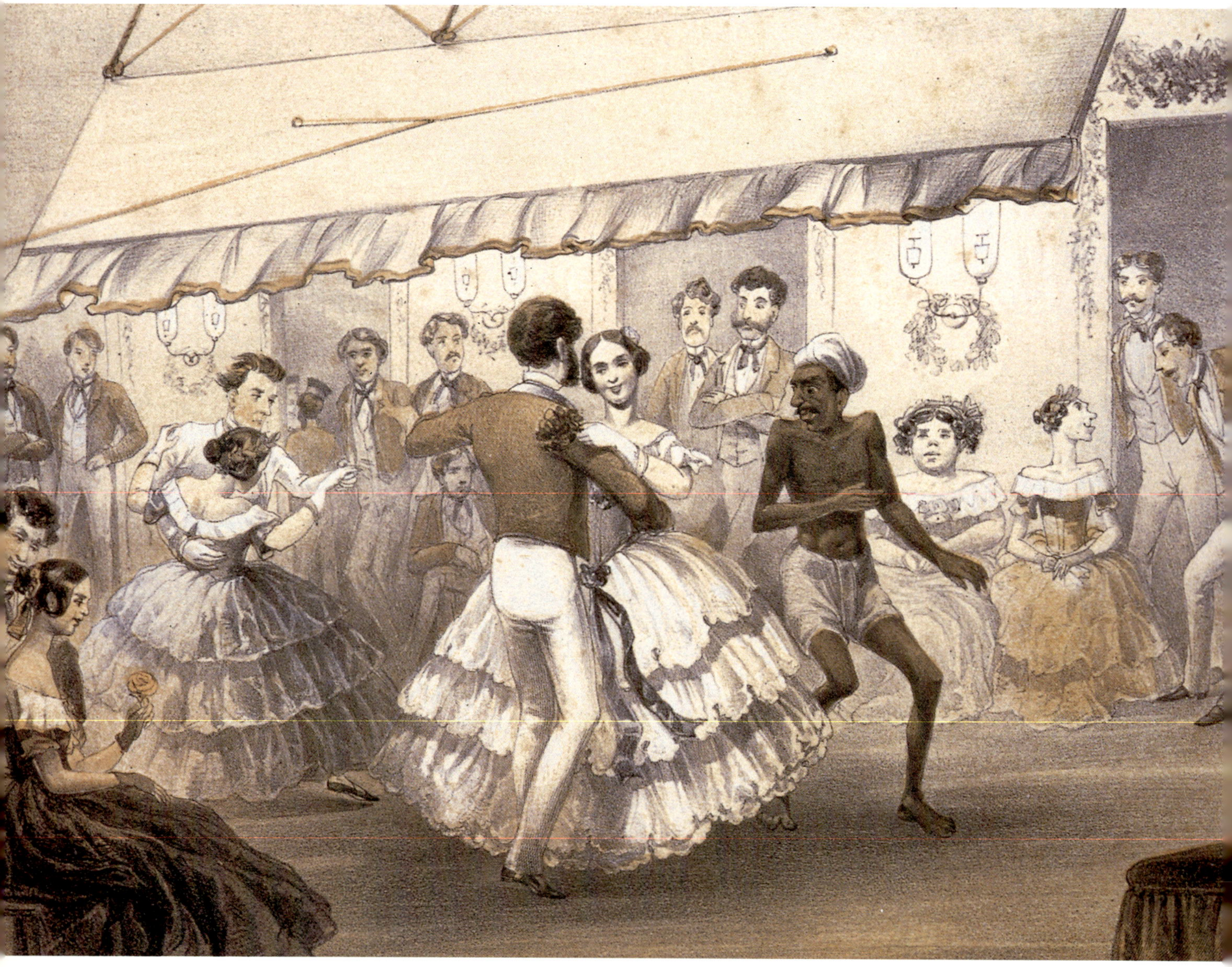

The Ball for new arrivals.
Lithograph after a drawing by
G.F. Atkinson, c.1856.

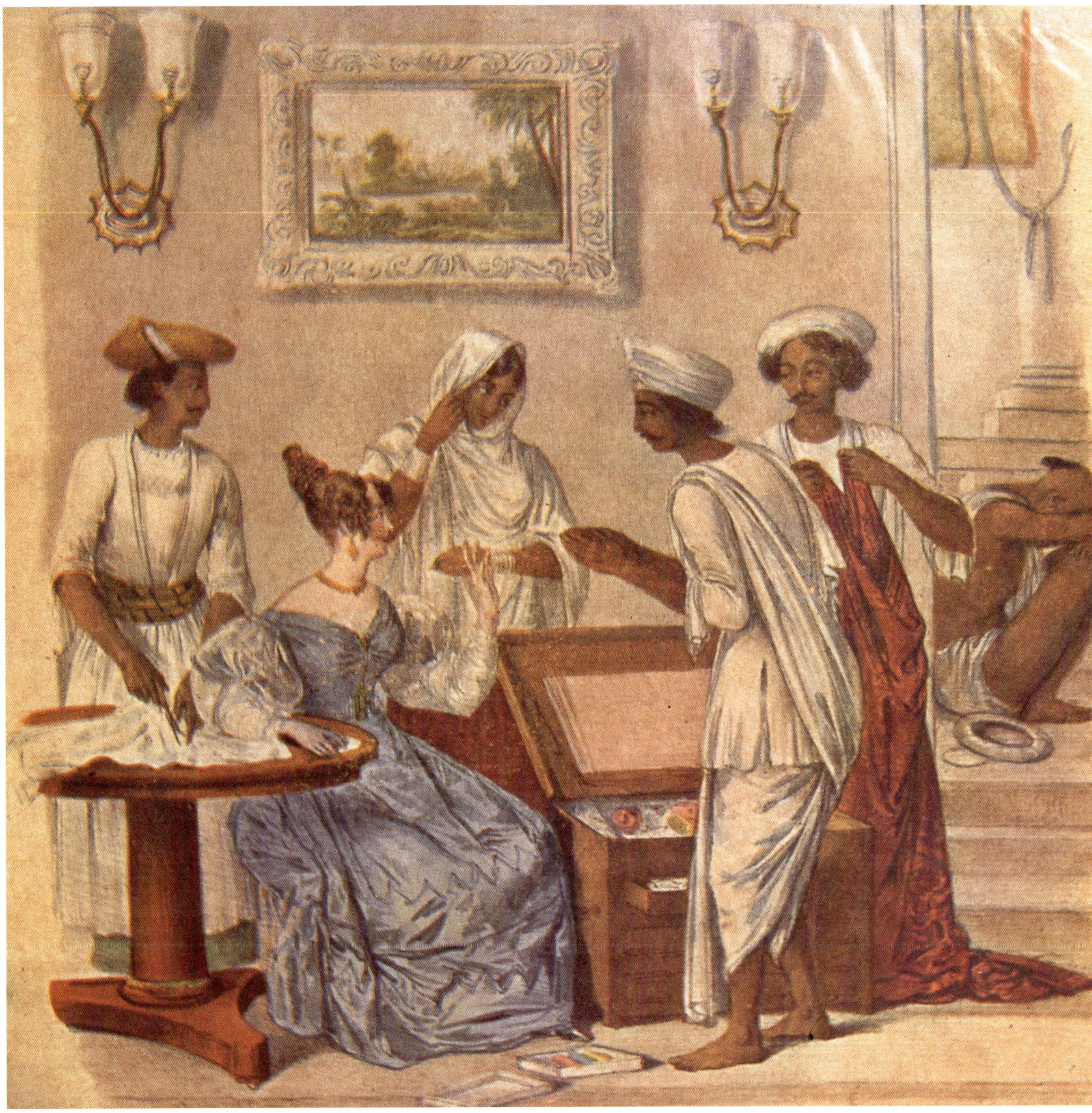

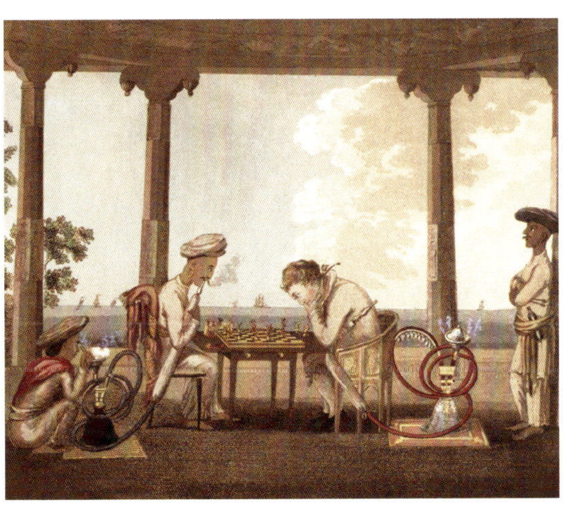

Above: *Pykars or Pedlars.*
An European lady is supposed to have purchased several articles from the two pedlars who have a wooden box filled with millinery, etc. Coloured lithograph after a drawing by S.C. Belnos, c.1820.

Left: *Smoking the Hooka,* over a game of chess, on the Coromandel coast. Hand-coloured aquatint engraving after a drawing by Captain Charles Gold, 1806.

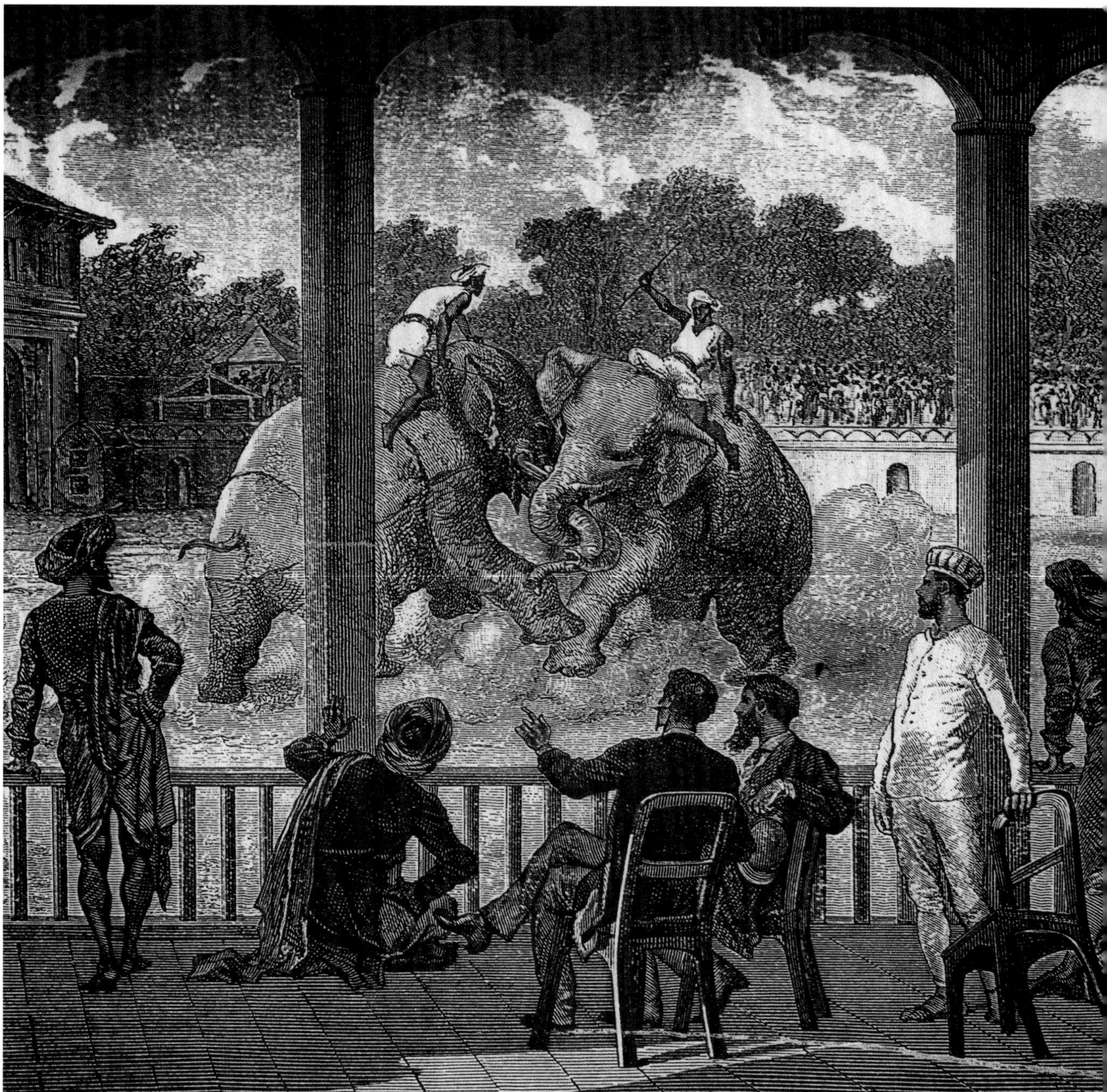

Elephant Fight at Baroda.
Engraving from 'India and its Native Princes', by L. Rousselet, London, 1875.

SHIKAR AND ANIMAL FIGHTS

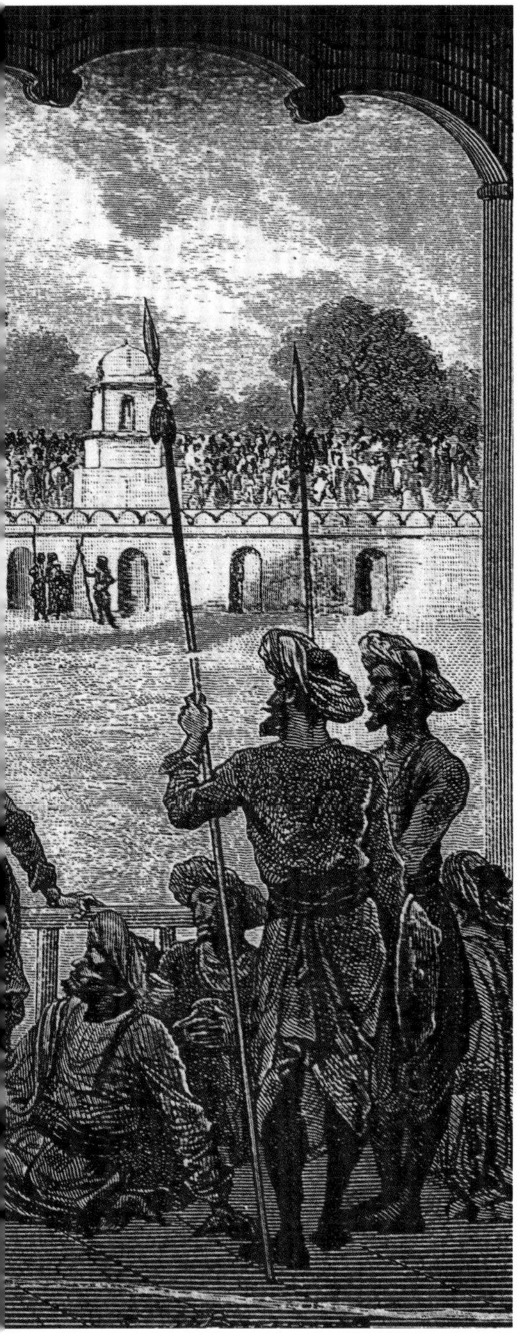

THE ENGLISH sahibs were introduced to big game hunting by Indian Rajahs and nawabs for whom it had been a traditional outdoor sport from time immemorial. Over the years, shikar (hunting) emerged as the most popular and adventurous sport both for civilians and soldiers in the East India Company. By the beginning of the nineteenth century, it dominated their outdoor life and no other subject occupies a more prominent place in Raj literature. There are countless accounts of hunting expeditions with stories of adventurous encounters with wild animals, including tigers, leopards, lions, hogs, and wild buffaloes. Hunting remained one of the favourite pastimes and principal diversions of the Englishmen throughout the Raj. It was also considered an essential exercise to enhance the Imperial image.

These lively accounts by English sportsmen seem to take the readers with them on their hunting trips and introduce them to the sights, sounds, and hazards of the sport. They bring alive the world of animals in the vast jungles of India from Mysore to the Himalayas. Amongst the many books written on the subject, perhaps the most comprehensive and informative is *Forty Years Among the Wild Animate of India* by F.C. Hicks of the Imperial Forest Service. The incidents narrated by him are the pick of his experiences from a long period spent almost entirely in pursuit of big game in dense jungles. It is both a scientific study and a guide for sportsmen. He shot more than 200 tigers.

Pigsticking and tiger shooting were the first two sports full of excitement and danger. Tiger hunts were grand affairs with dozens of elephants and a big base camp. The game of games, easily the most popular with both civilians and soldiers was pigsticking or hog-hunting, according to Bombay phraseology. Captain Williamson in his classic *Oriental Field Sports* (1819) gives a vivid description of hog-hunting expeditions and the courage and ferocity of the boars. Besides anecdotes, he offers advice to the hunters on "how to succeed as a pigsticker." Captain R.S.S. Baden-Powell was an authority on the subject. In his book *Pigsticking* (1889), which was a complete guide for pigstickers, he compares the game to a battlefield as both "demand the dash and keenness, the pluck and determination for ultimate victory."

Animal fights were a favourite royal pastime in India from historical times. The Indian princes and nawabs patronized animal fights on festive occasions and held special shows to entertain the British elite. Captain Mundy in his journal gives a graphic account of a series of animal fights organized in 1827 by the King of Oudh in honour of the Commander-in-Chief Lord Combermere in Lucknow:

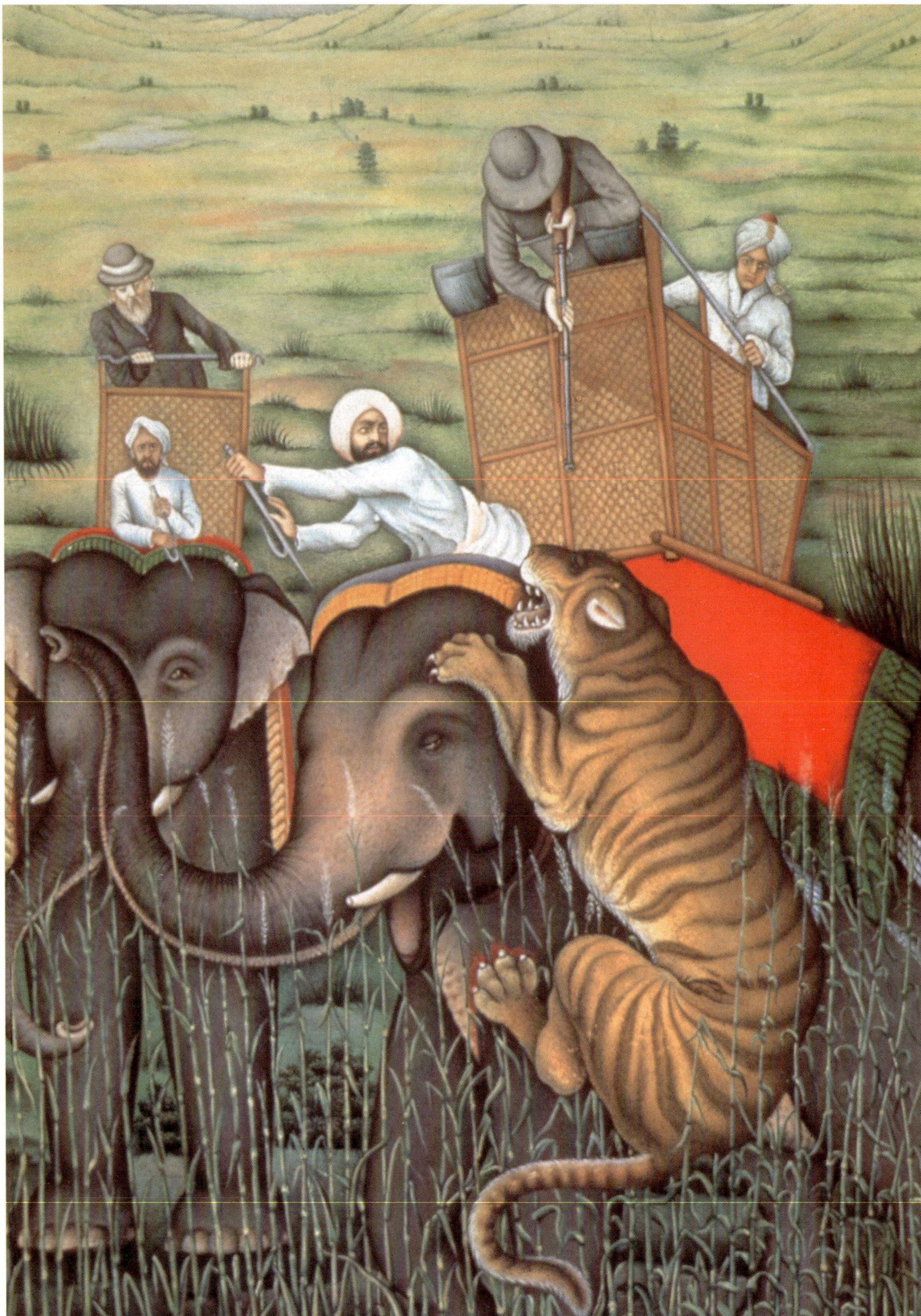

"A gigantic cage of strong bamboos, about fifty feet high, with the same diameter and roofed with a rope network was set up in the centre. Several wild animals were kept in small cells with sliding doors opening into the main theatre. In the large cage, crowded together, and presenting a formidable front, well armed with horns, stood a group of buffaloes sternly awaiting the conflict. As soon as the trap-doors were lifted, two tigers and the same number of bears and leopards, rushed into the cage. The buffaloes instantly commenced hostilities, and made complete shuttlecocks of the bears, who however, finally escaped by climbing up the bamboos beyond the reach of their horned antagonists. The tigers, one of which was a beautiful animal, fared scarcely better: indeed, the odds were much against them, there being five buffaloes. They appeared, however, to be no match for these powerful creatures, even single-handed, and showed little disposition to be the assaulters. The larger tiger was much gored in the head, and in return took a mouthful of his enemy's dewlap, but was finally bored to the ropes and floored. Throughout the conflict, the leopards remained on the sideline and avoided breach of peace. Thereafter, a rhinoceros was let loose in the open courtyard and the attendants tried to induce him to attack a tiger that was chained to a ring. The rhinoceros, however, considered a fettered foe as quite beneath his enemity. Having once approached the tiger, he quietly surveyed him, as he writhed and growled, expecting the attack, turned suddenly round and trotted awkwardly off to the yard gate, where he capsized a palanquin which was carrying away an English lady tired of witnessing these fearful sports. The concluding spectacle was of elephant fights on the sandy banks of the Goomty river. The well-trained elephants fed with exciting spices and led by two or three men armed with long spears advanced slowly from opposite sides of the plain. As they approached, their speed gradually increased, and at length they met with a grand shock, entwining their trunks, until one, finding himself overmatched, turned tail, and received his adversary's charge in the rear. This was so violent, that the mahout of the flying elephant was dislodged from his seat but fortunately he escaped with a few bruises."

Capt.T. Williamson describes a battle between a buffalo and tiger:

"The buffalo usually came out to fight with utmost confidence, conscious of his own prowess. With rapid and furious motions, he would charge the tiger giving it no respite and carry out a war of extermination. It was said that the buffalo would never quit until a tiger's death proclaimed his victory. In very rare instances, the tiger ever came out triumphant."

A Tiger Hunt.
A Sahib on an elephant leaning to shoot a tiger. Watercolour by a Punjabi artist, c.1892.

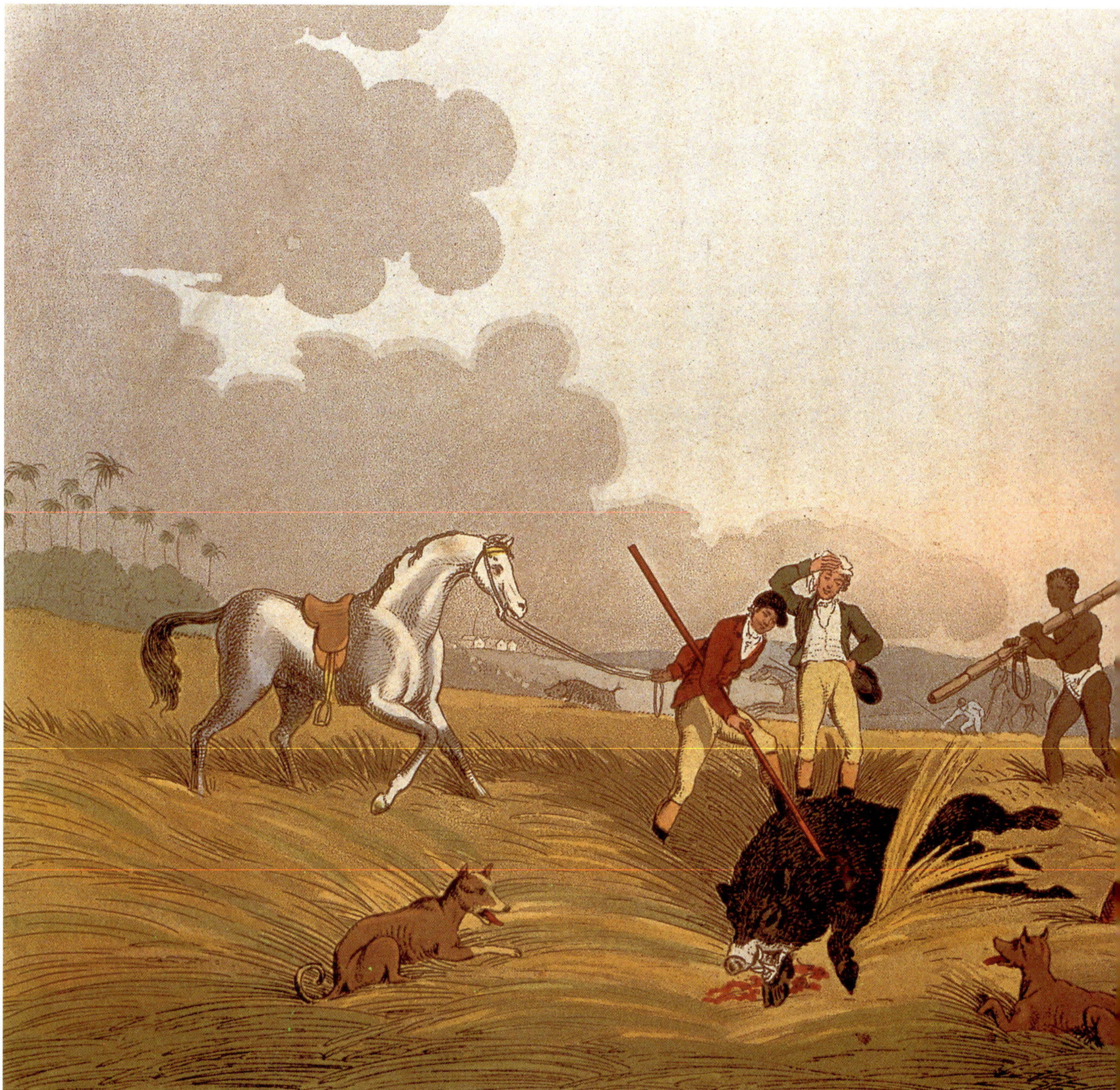

The Dead Hog.
Coloured aquatint after a drawing by T. Williamson, 1819.

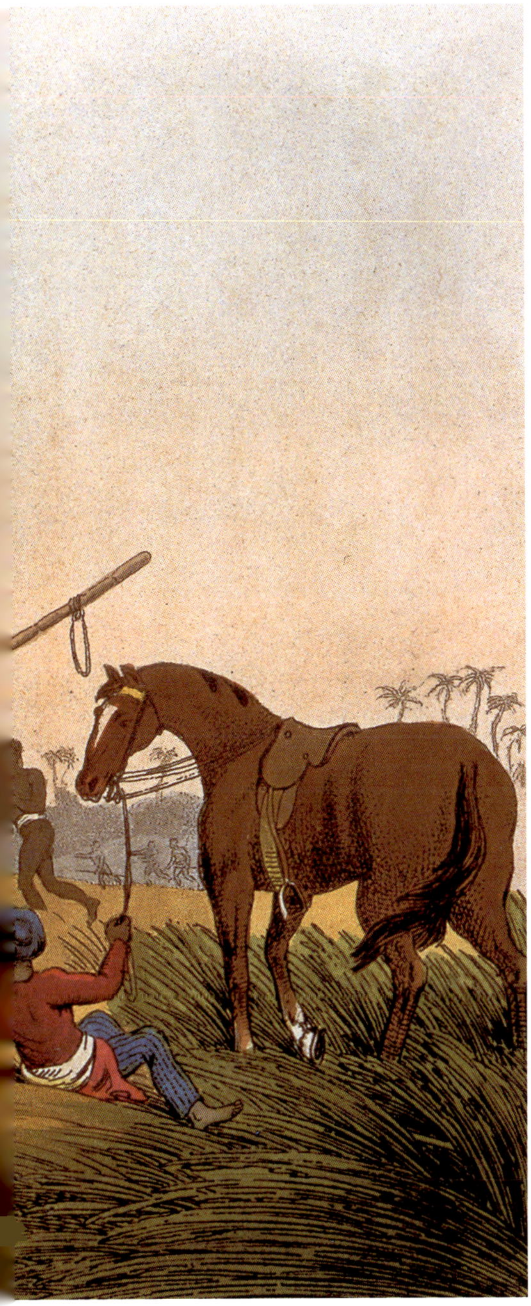

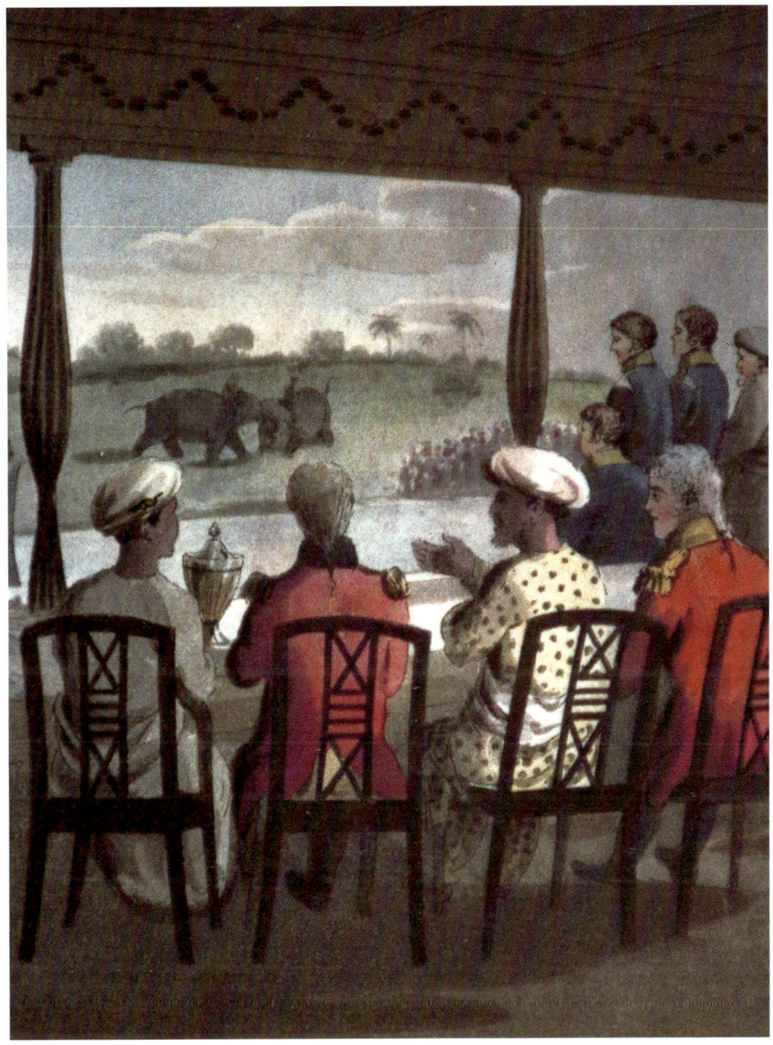

Above right: *Marquis Wellesley & his suite, at the Nabob of Oude's Breakfast Table Viewing an Elephant Fight.* Hand-coloured aquatint engraving after a drawing by Sir Charles Doyly, 1813.

Then there were also bird fights for entertainment. Murghabazi or cock-fights were one of the most popular pastimes of the royalty, nobility and commoners alike. Lucknow was the centre of this sport. Even some Europeans living in Lucknow became its devotees and participated in cock-fights with the princes and nobles. General Claude Martin was an expert at cock-fighting and Nawab Sadat Ali Khan used to bet his birds against those of the General. Colonel John Mordaunt, Commander of Nawab Asif-ud-daula's bodyguards and a leader of the court revels, was a specialist in the sport and regularly organized cockfights for the Nawab attended by the local European gentry. Lord Hastings is reported to have attended Mordaunt's cock-fight in April 1784.

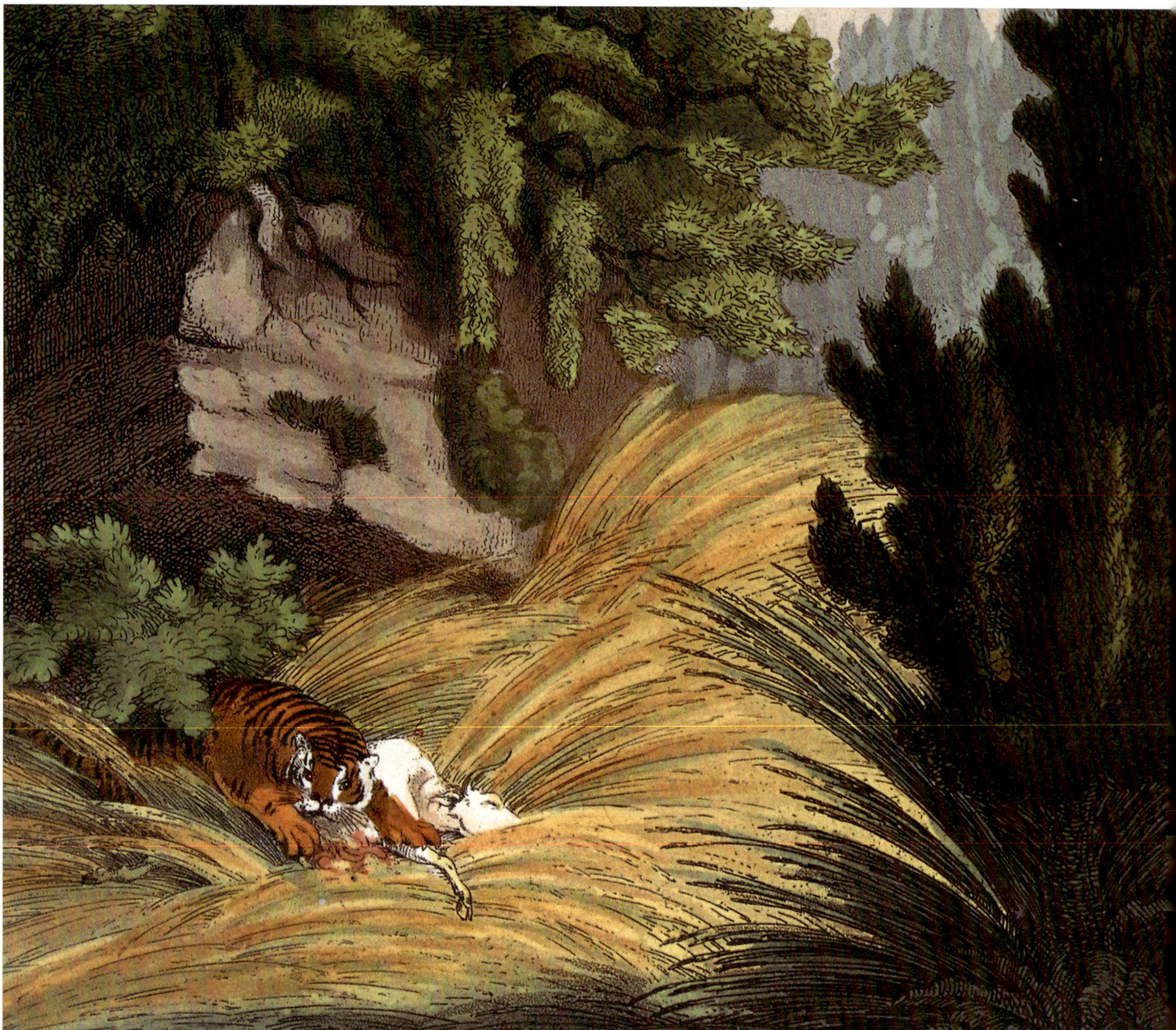

Shooting a Tiger from a Moychaun or Platform.
Coloured aquatint after a drawing by T. Williamson, 1819.

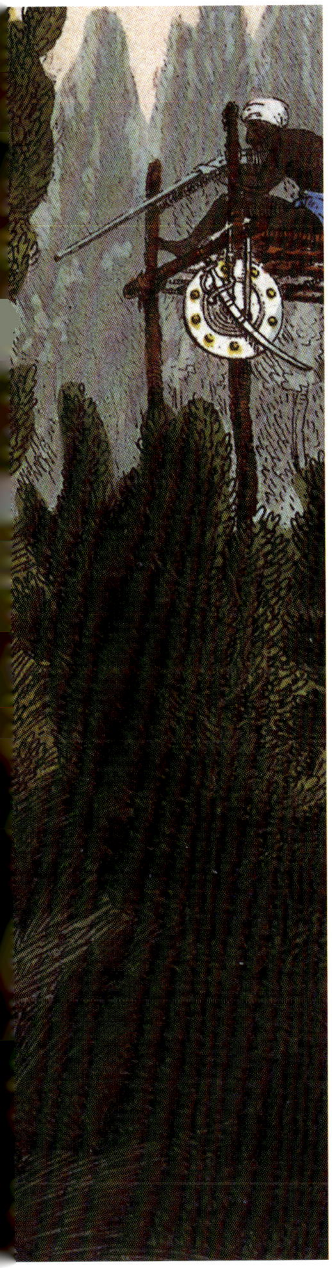

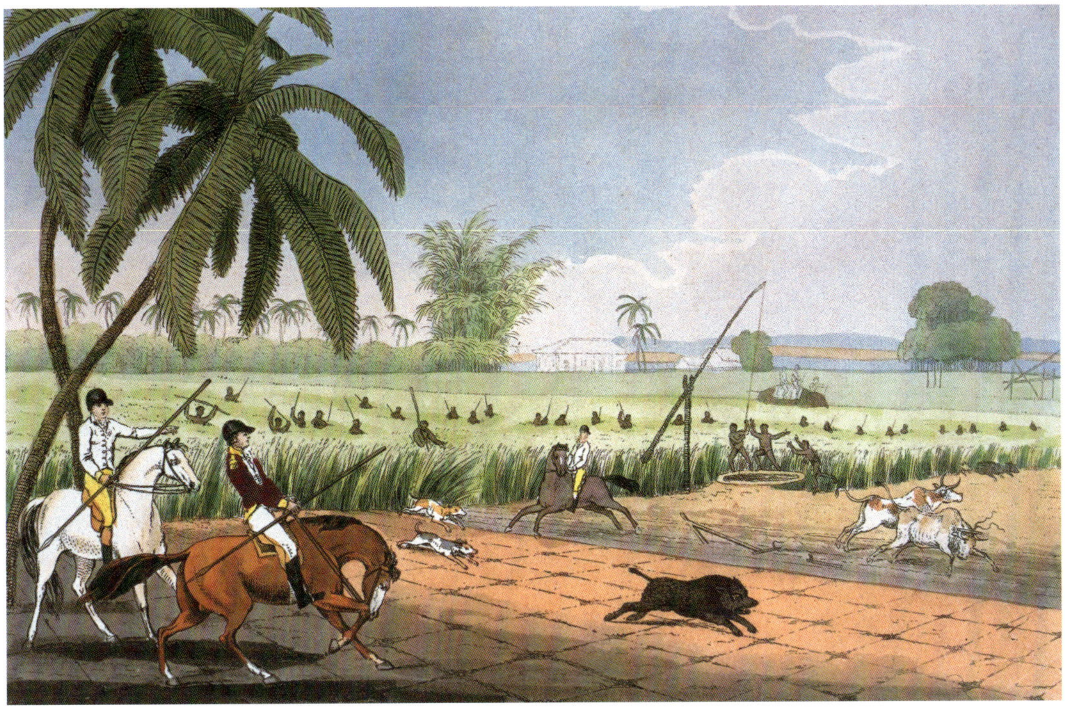

Beating Sugar Canes for a Hog.
Coloured aquatint after a drawing
by T. Williamson, 1819.

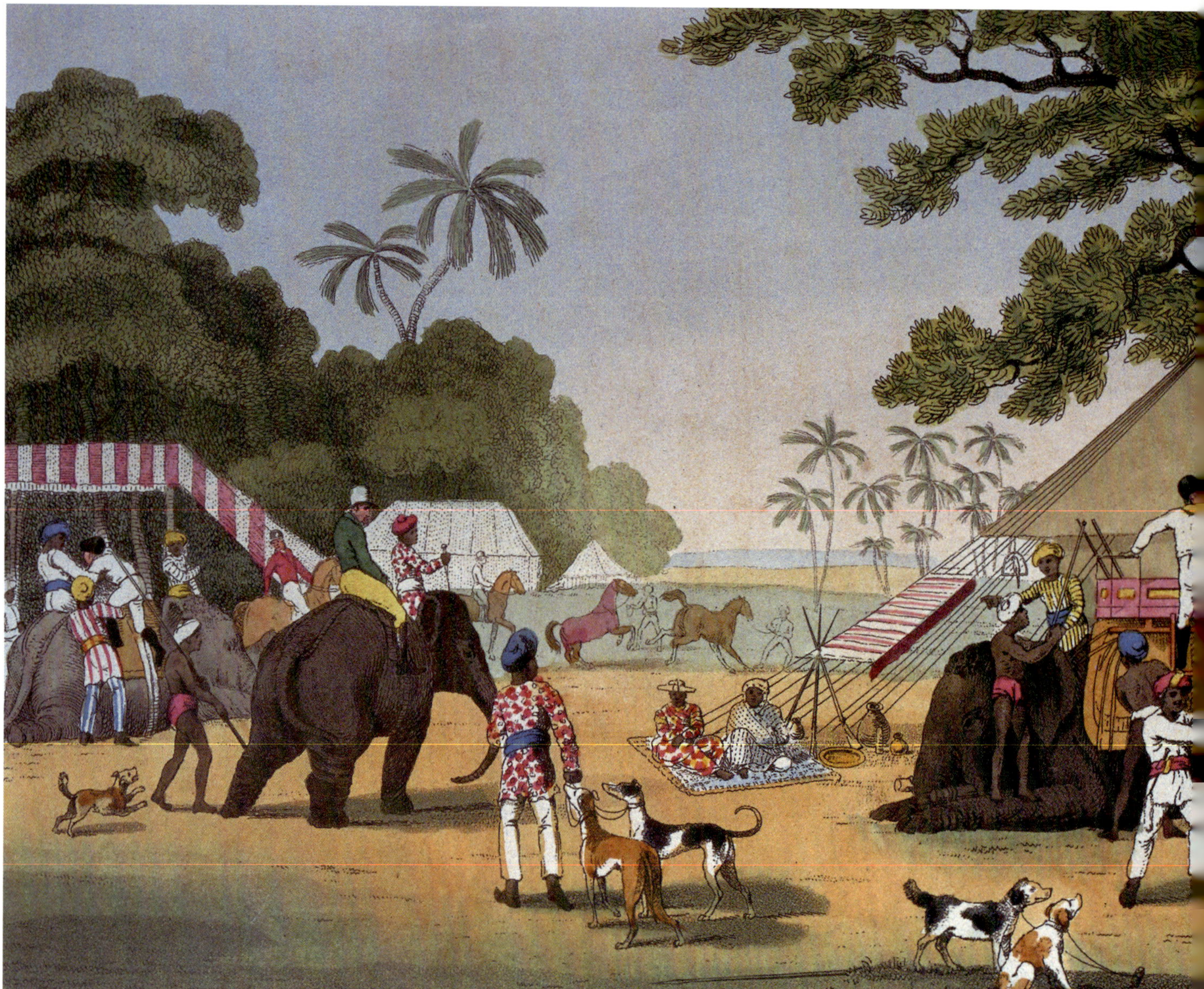

Hunters going out in the Morning.
Coloured aquatint after a drawing
by T. Williamson, 1819.

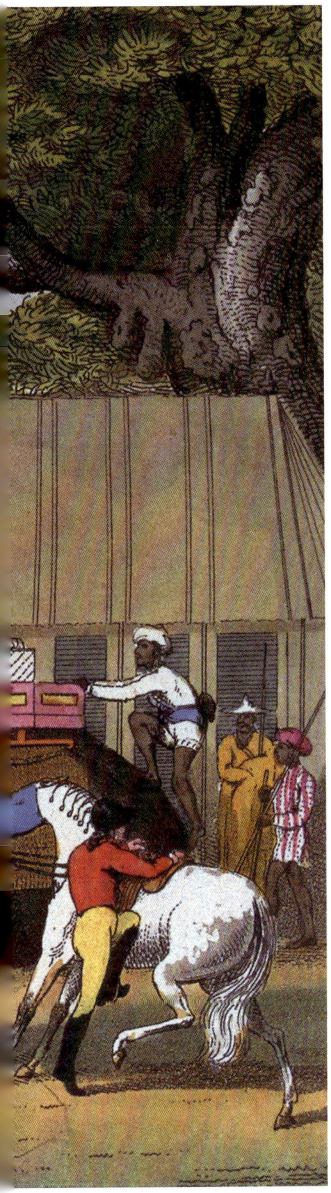

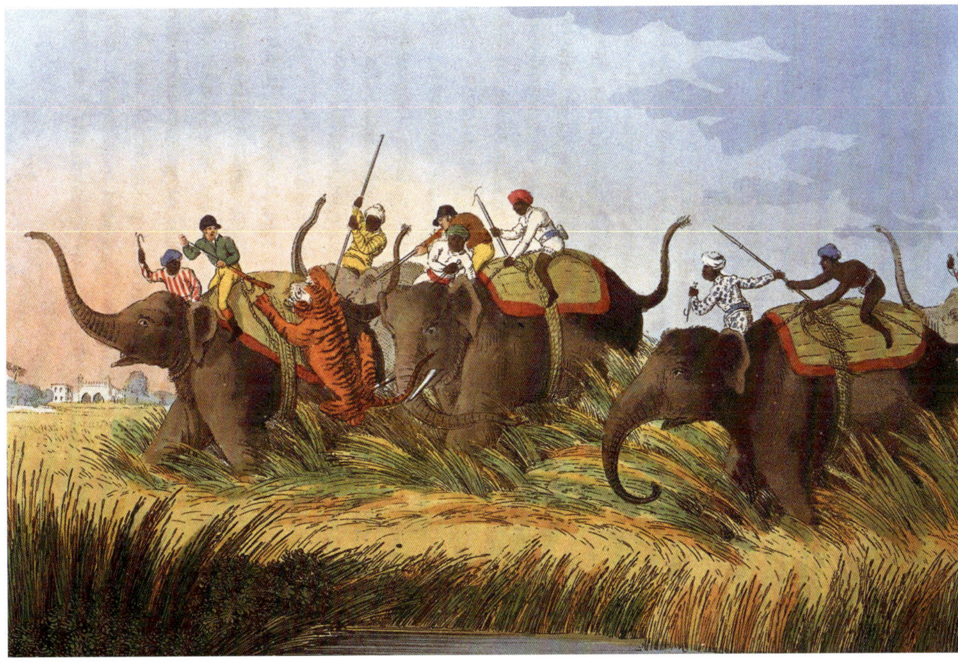

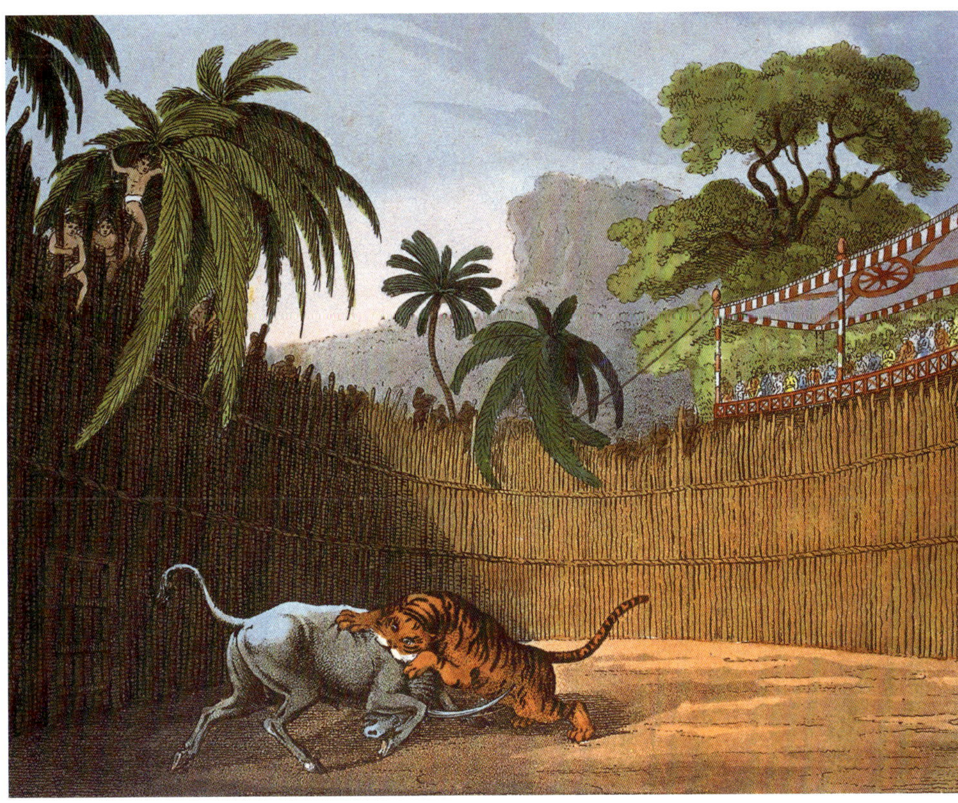

Above: *A Tiger springing upon an Elephant.*
Coloured aquatint after a drawing by T. Williamson, 1819.

Below: *A Battle between a Buffalo and a Tiger.*
Coloured aquatint by T. Williamson, 1819.

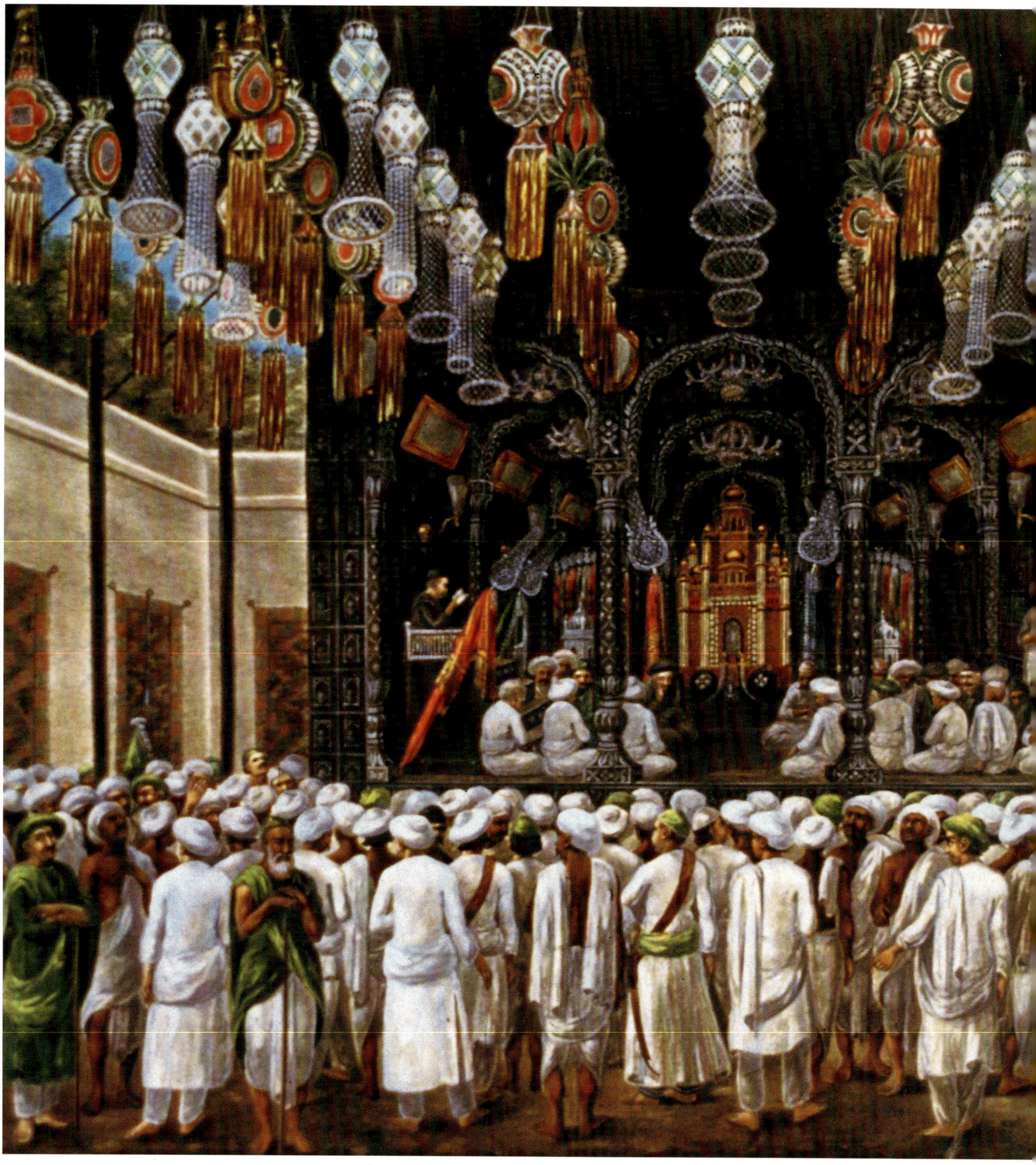

FESTIVALS AND AMUSEMENTS

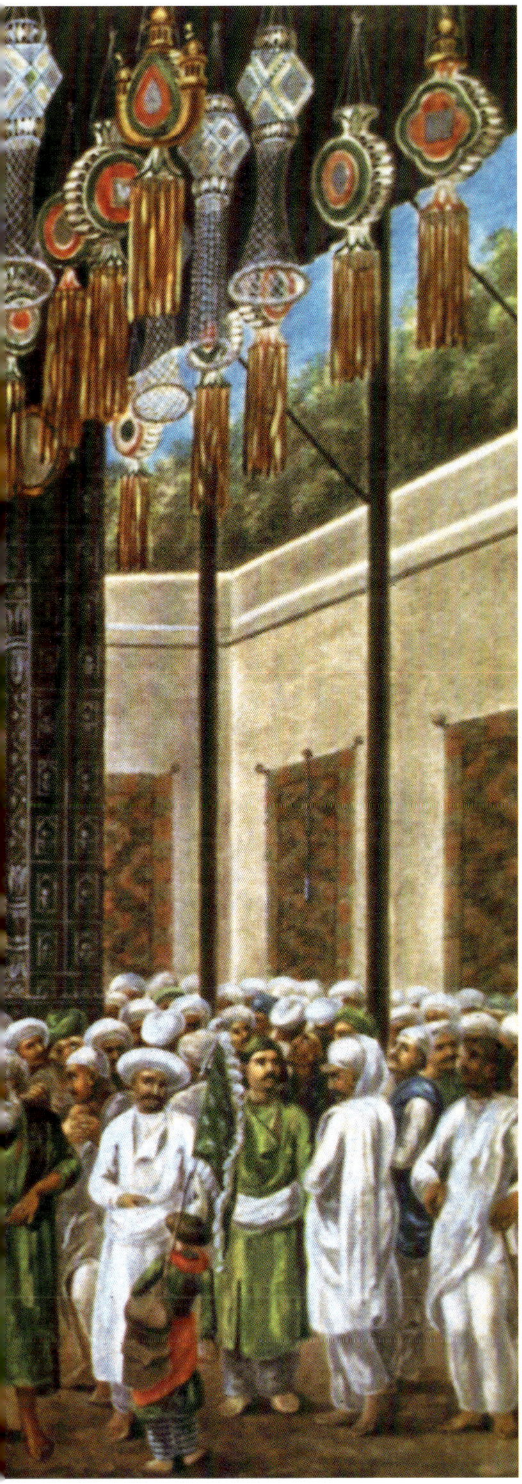

The Muharram Festival, Prayers being held in the Imambara.
Watercolour by Sewak Ram, a Patna artist, c.1807.

RELIGIOUS FESTIVITIES have always been an integral part of the life of Indians. British visitors were impressed by the hectic gaiety of the people at village fairs and festivals, singing and dancing with drums. The festivals imparted intensity to community life and inspired hilarity, feasting, and social contacts on a large scale. The major Hindu and Muslim celebrations were Holi, Diwali, Durga Puja, Muharram and Id. Among the regional events, a great deal has been written about the grand Jagannath Puri 'Rath Yatra' and the 'Charak Puja' or hook swinging, a form of ritual self-mortification.

The Hindu festival of spring, Holi, was easily the most popular for its colourful hilarity, fun and merry-making. It had a special attraction for the Sahibs. The British accounts of Holi describe it as a 'Carnival of the Hindus,' a sort of Hindu saturnalia, which was compared to the Portuguese Christmas. Contemporary writings document the European attendance at Indian festivals. In the East India Company's army, the participation of British officers at Holi was a matter of etiquette. The sepoys were delighted to see their British officers participate in their revelry and would often play practical jokes on unpopular officers.

Diwali or the 'Festival of Lights' held pride of place in North India. There are colourful descriptions of Diwali by several British authors. Diwali on the ghats of Kanpur comes alive in a fascinating account in *Wanderings of a Pilgrim*, (1830) by Fanny Parks:

> *"On reaching the ghat I was quite delighted with the beauty of a scene resembling fairyland….On every temple, on every ghat, and on the steps down to the river's side, thousands of small lamps were placed from the foundation to the highest pinnacle, tracing the architecture in the lines of light. The evening was very dark, and the whole scene was reflected in the Ganges."*

Durga Puja was the biggest Hindu festival in Bengal. There is frequent mention of the lavish entertainments and festivities on this occasion. Kali or Durga is described as the tutelary goddess of Calcutta and her images and those of some other deities were carried in procession and submerged in the Hooghly river, which being a

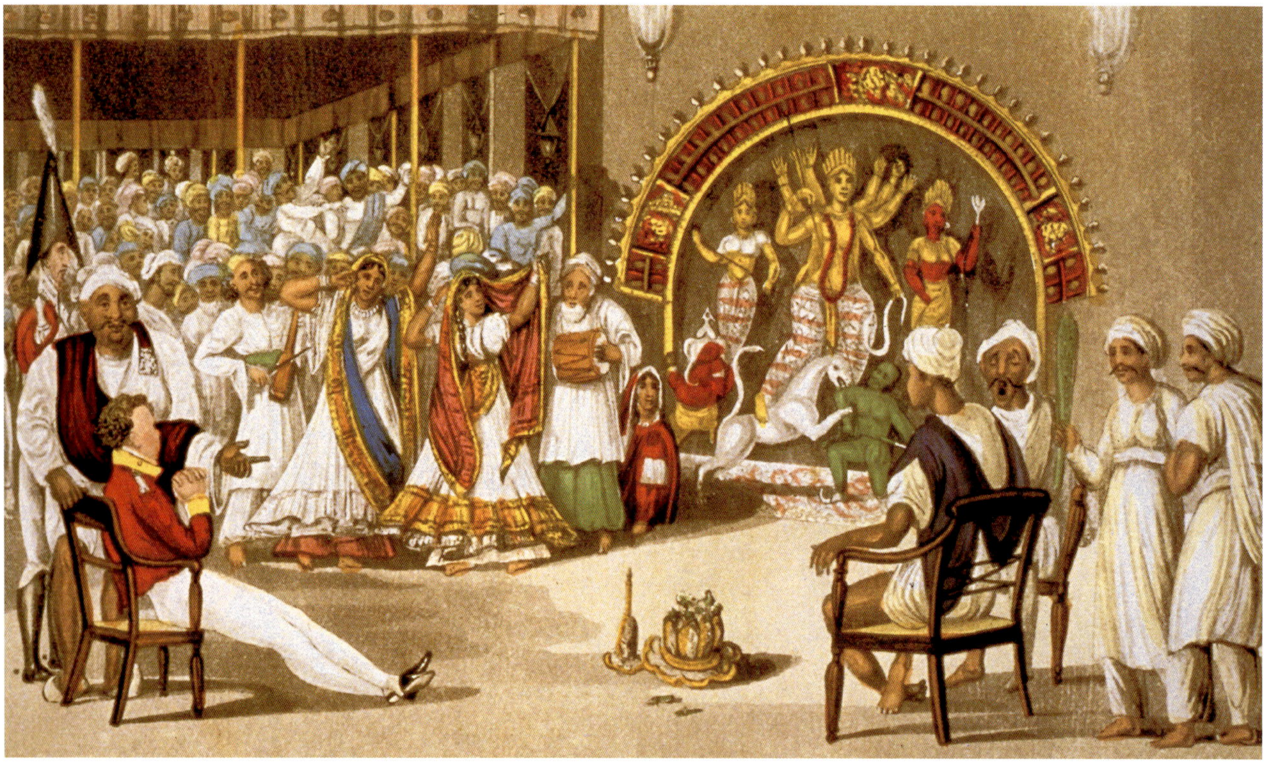

A Young British Cadet watching a Nautch at Durga Puja.
Aquatint after a drawing by Sir Charles Doyly, c.1810.

branch of the Ganges is considered to be sacred. The wealthy babus of Calcutta celebrated Durga Puja with great splendour and some of them succeeded in securing the presence of the Governor-General, the Commander-in-Chief, or other high dignitaries at these functions. A notable festival in Bihar which finds mention in contemporary accounts is the Harihar Kshetra festival at Sonepur, near Patna. People assembled from all parts of the region to worship Harihar Nath or Lord Shiva.

Another prominent festival was the Jagannath Puja in June-July at Puri. It was famous for its Rath Yatra when the temple images of gods were placed on their great cars or rathas, and taken through the city. This gigantic procession included dignitaries seated on elephants followed by the large crowds of pilgrims.

The lower classes of Hindu society tried to win the favour of gods through ritual self-mortification as depicted by the Charak Puja or the hook-swinging festival. Fanny Parks in her eye-witness account describes this "disgusting practice" of swinging by hooks.

For Muslims, Muharram was one of the most important religious occasions. It was a ten-day annual mourning for Husain, the son of Ali by Fatima, daughter of the Prophet. The Mughal emperor led a procession on the occasion of the Muharram festival followed by the British Resident, Indian nobles and large crowds of people. According to one account, they carried a finely ornamented model of the tomb of their ancestors, made of light bamboo and paper, for three days and nights, and were attended by people dressed in ridiculous costumes, shouting and dancing to the country music. The festival of Id was marked with cheerful bustle and amusement when the princes offered camels in sacrifices. On the occasion of Id-ul-Fitr at the end of the fasting month of Ramzan, there was rejoicing all around and the nawabs and other chieftains led splendid processions to the mosques for prayers. All accounts emphasise the fact that Muslims celebrated their festivals just like the Hindus, with the same earnestness and ostentation and amused themselves with dance and song and other entertainments, including feasts and sports.

The greatest festival for the British was Christmas celebrated with full exuberance. Eliza Fay wrote in 1780 to her friends in England that "Keeping Christmas, though sinking into disuse at home prevails here with all its ancient festivity." She found that large plantain trees were placed on each side of the principal entrances and the gates and pillars were ornamented with wreaths of flowers, fancifully disposed, which greatly beautified the scene. She also wrote about the public dinner at the government house and an "elegant ball and supper" in the evening. These were repeated on the New Year's Day. Another festive occasion for the sahibs was the celebration of the King's birthday that was observed with equal gaiety and grandeur.

Religious ceremonies, processions and diverse rituals were observed by the different classes of society from cradle to grave. The wedding ceremonies with their colourful celebrations offered a fascinating sight to British observers. Fanny Parks attended a noble Muslim family wedding and gave a colourful account of the marriage procession with elephants, musicians and dancing girls and various rituals and customs. Indian women in some parts of the country also observed the ceremonies of tree worship, especially trees invested with divine attributes such as the banyan and peepul, and also some plants like the Tulsi.

The celebration of festivals was also an occasion for public entertainment as they watched the amazing feats and tricks of jugglers, street performers and snake charmers. The most awe-inspiring were the legendary rope trick and the basket trick involving the mysterious disappearance of girl contained in the latter. Even more amazing was the feat of swallowing a sword blade. Then there was the mind boggling 'levitation show' where a performer was seen poised in the air about four feet from the ground in a sitting attitude. Among other clever tricks there are descriptions of jugglers changing pebbles into birds, joining cotton pieces into one long cord, and throwing cannon balls with their toes. Sahibs were equally dazzled by the skills of women acrobats, particularly when one of them turned backwards on her feet to pick up straws with her eyelids. Finally there was the common bunderwallah who made the monkeys dance to the beat of his hand drum.

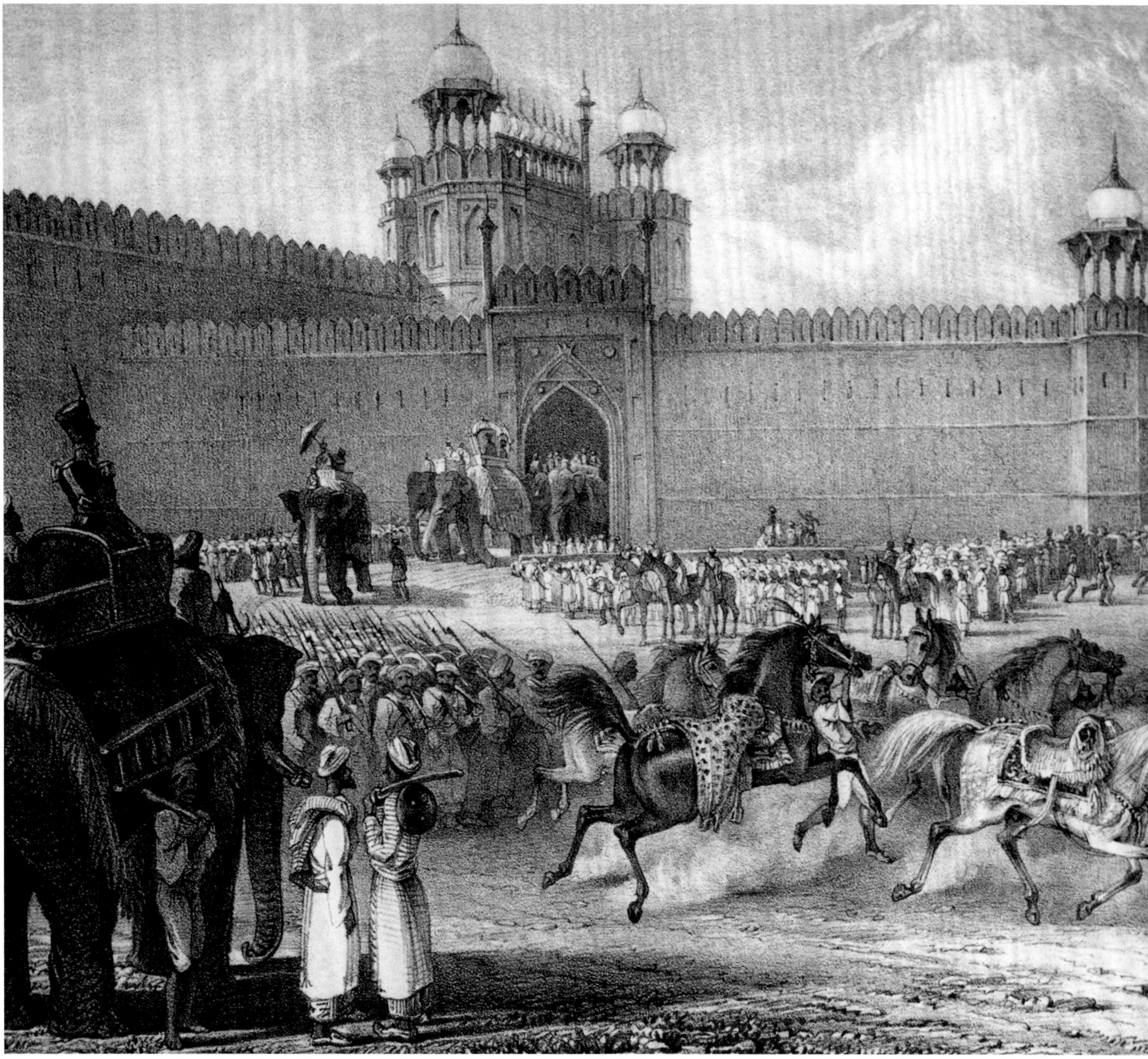

Festival of Buckrah Eade, Dhele.
Lithograph by Major John Luard, c. 1833.

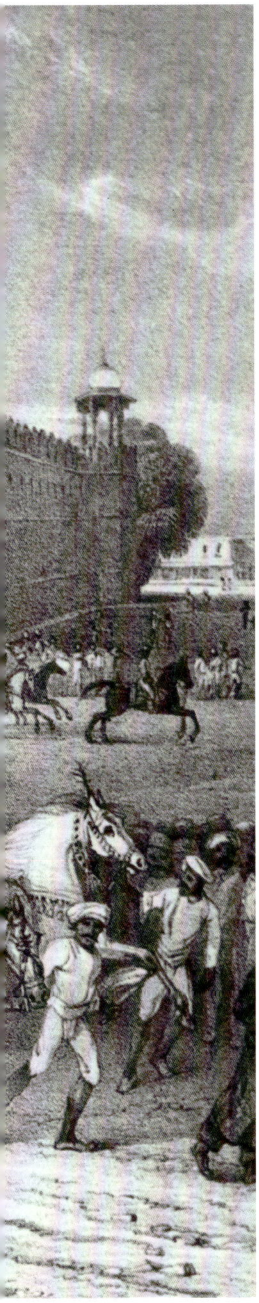

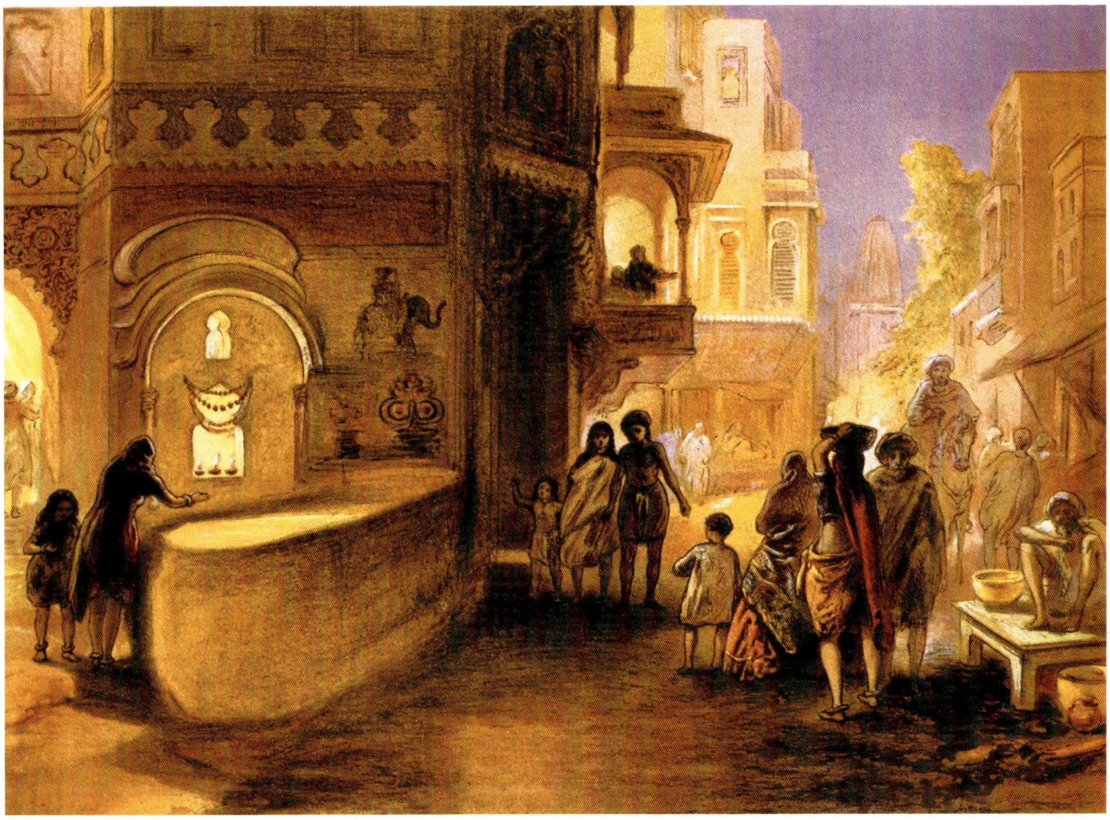

The Diwali or Feast of Lamps, Rajpootana.
Chromolithograph after a drawing by
William Simpson c. 1860.

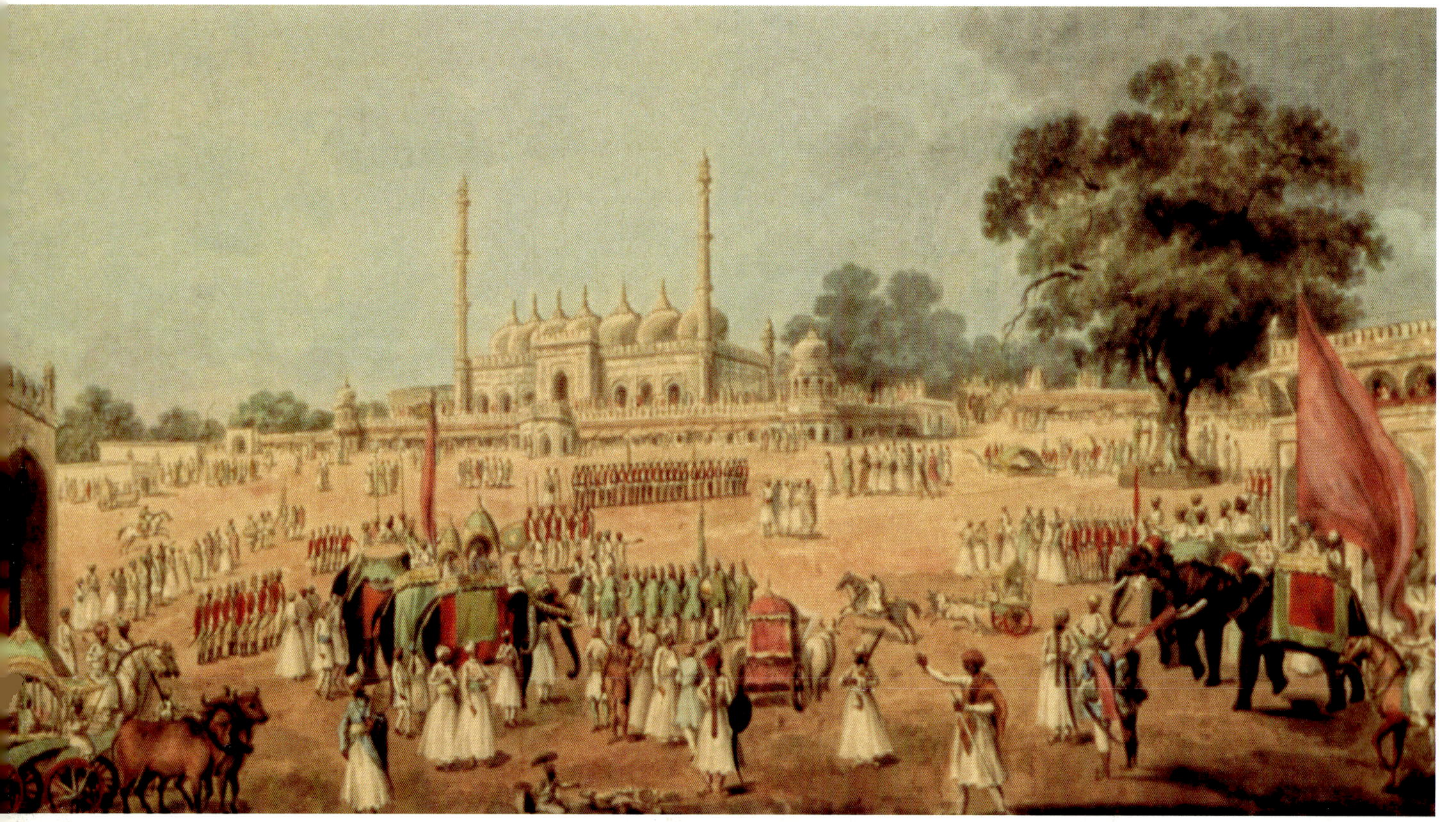

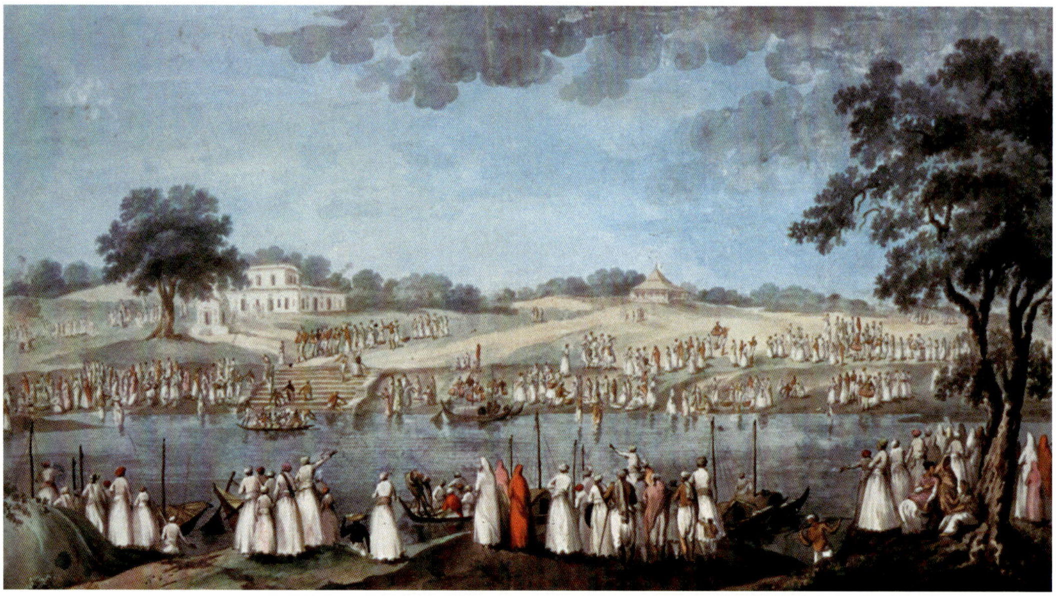

Above: *Mubarak-ud-Daula, Nawab of Murshidabad proceeding to the mosque for the Festival of Bakar Id.* Watercolour by a Murshidabad artist, c.1800.

Below: *Chat Poojah at Moorshedabad.* The Chail Festival, the Hindu New Years' Day. Men and women bathing in the river. Watercolour by a Murshidabad artist, c. 1800.

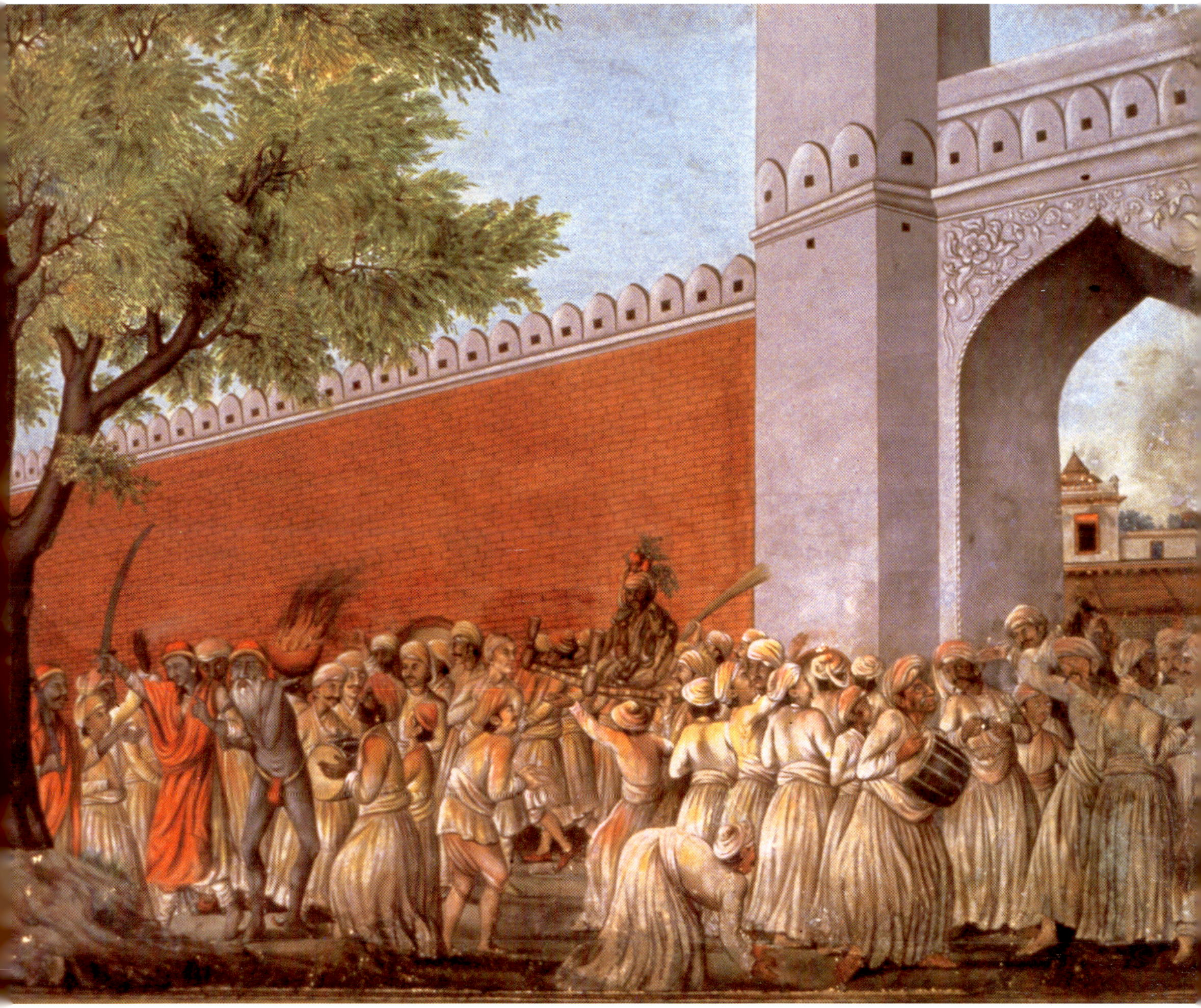

The Holi Festival Lucknow.
A man garlanded and crowned with shoes is being carried by a dancing and surging crowd. Water colour by a Lucknow artist, c. 1800.

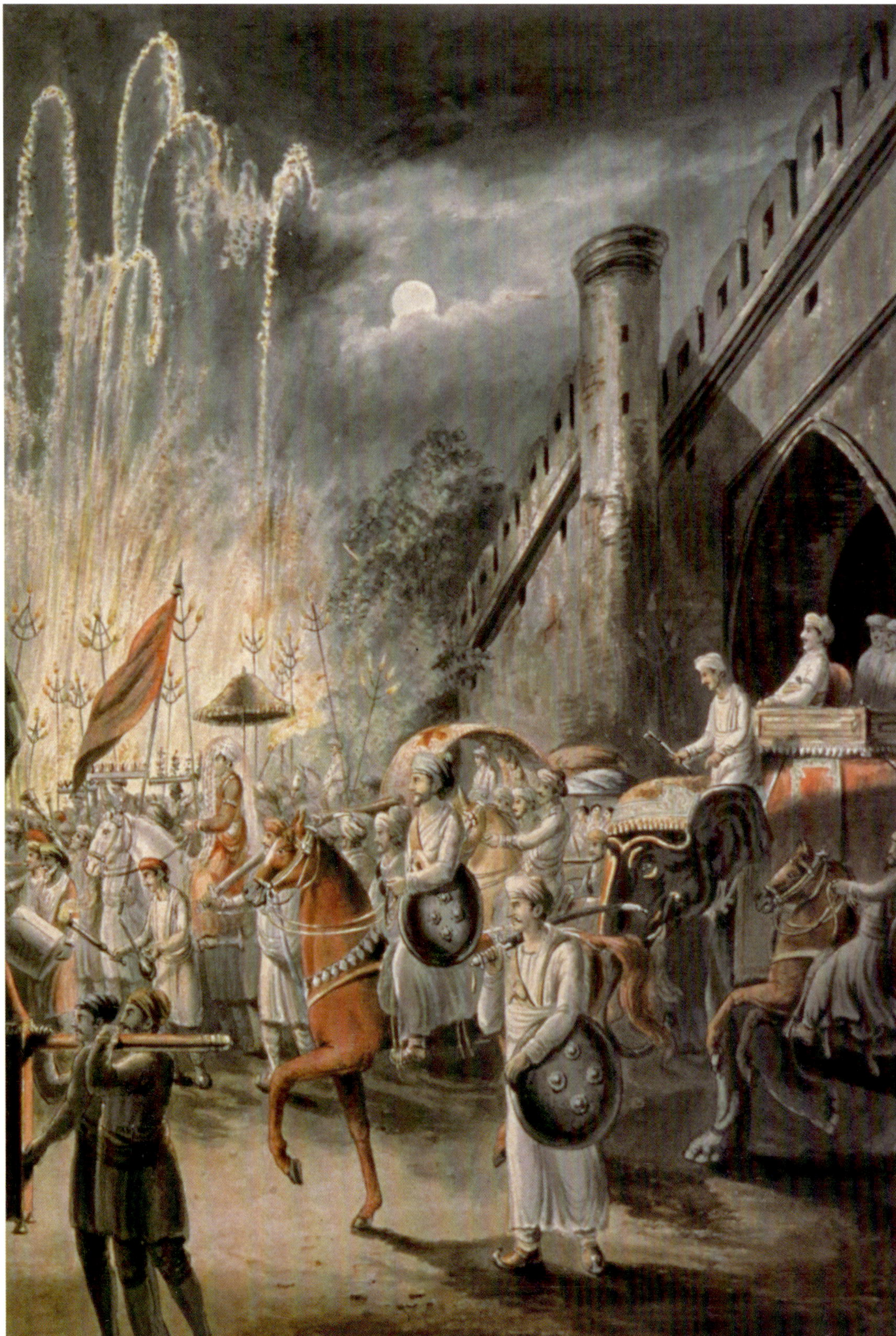

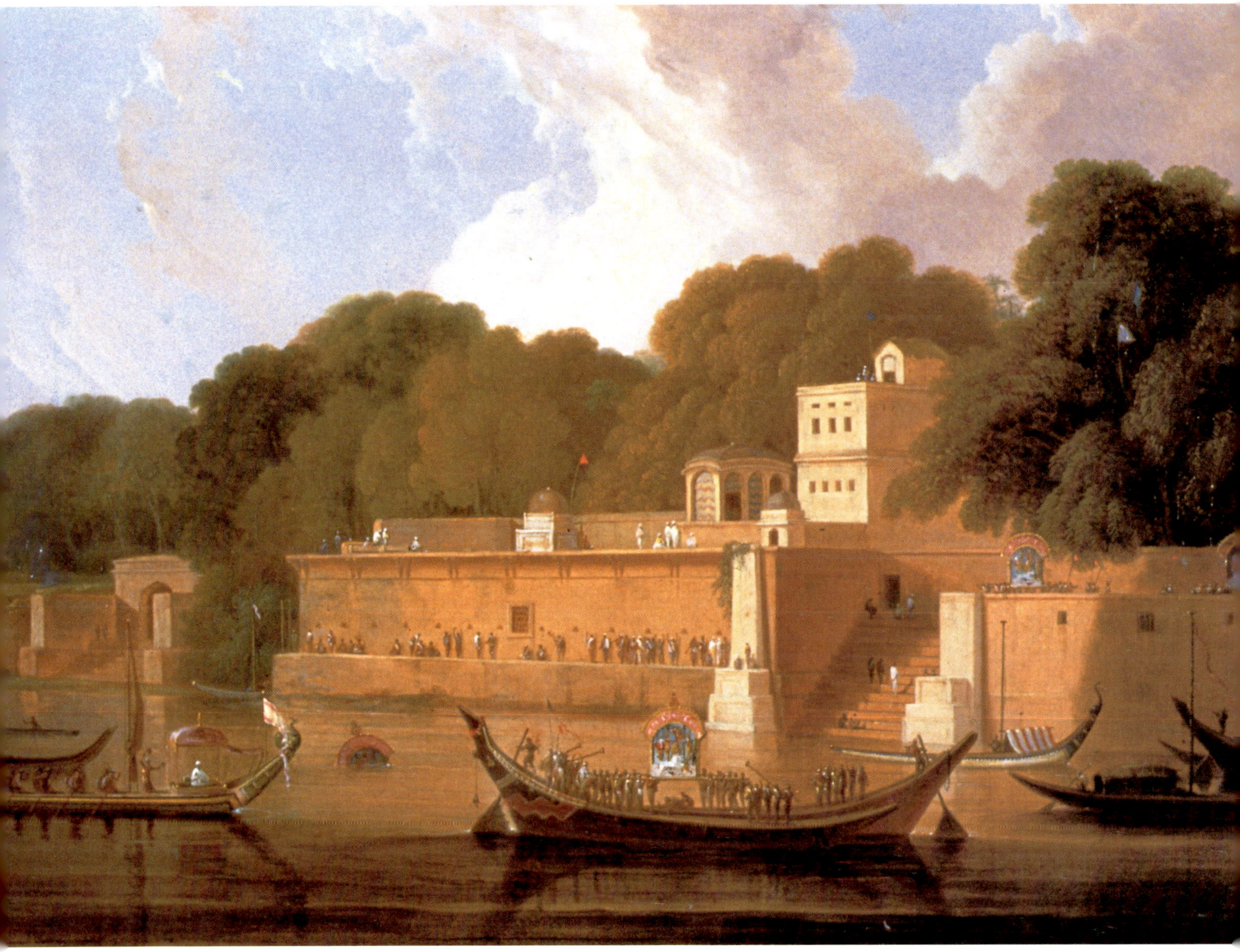

Facing page: *Mahomedan Wedding at night.*
The bridegroom and his party riding by moonlight in a Muslim wedding procession with fireworks around, watercolour by a Murshidabad artist, c. 1810.

Above: *Ceremony of the Goddess Durga in The River.*
Durga puja immersion, oil on canvas by Thomas Daniell, 1810.

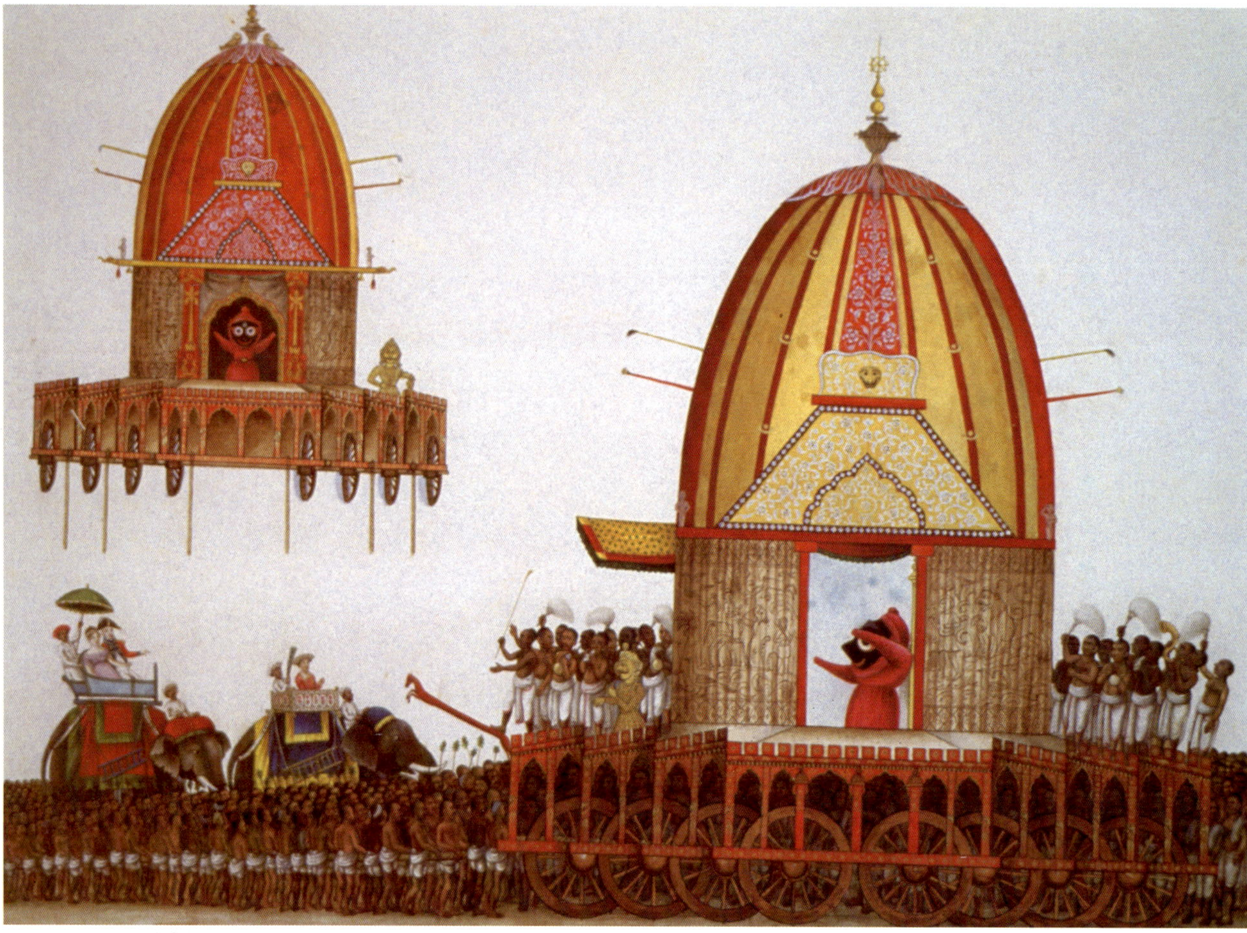

The Idol Juggernaut on his car taken during the Rath Jatra of 1822, Puri. The Jagannatha Procession showing a British couple on an elephant following a crowd of pilgrims. Above is a front elevation of the car. Water colour by a local artist, 1822.

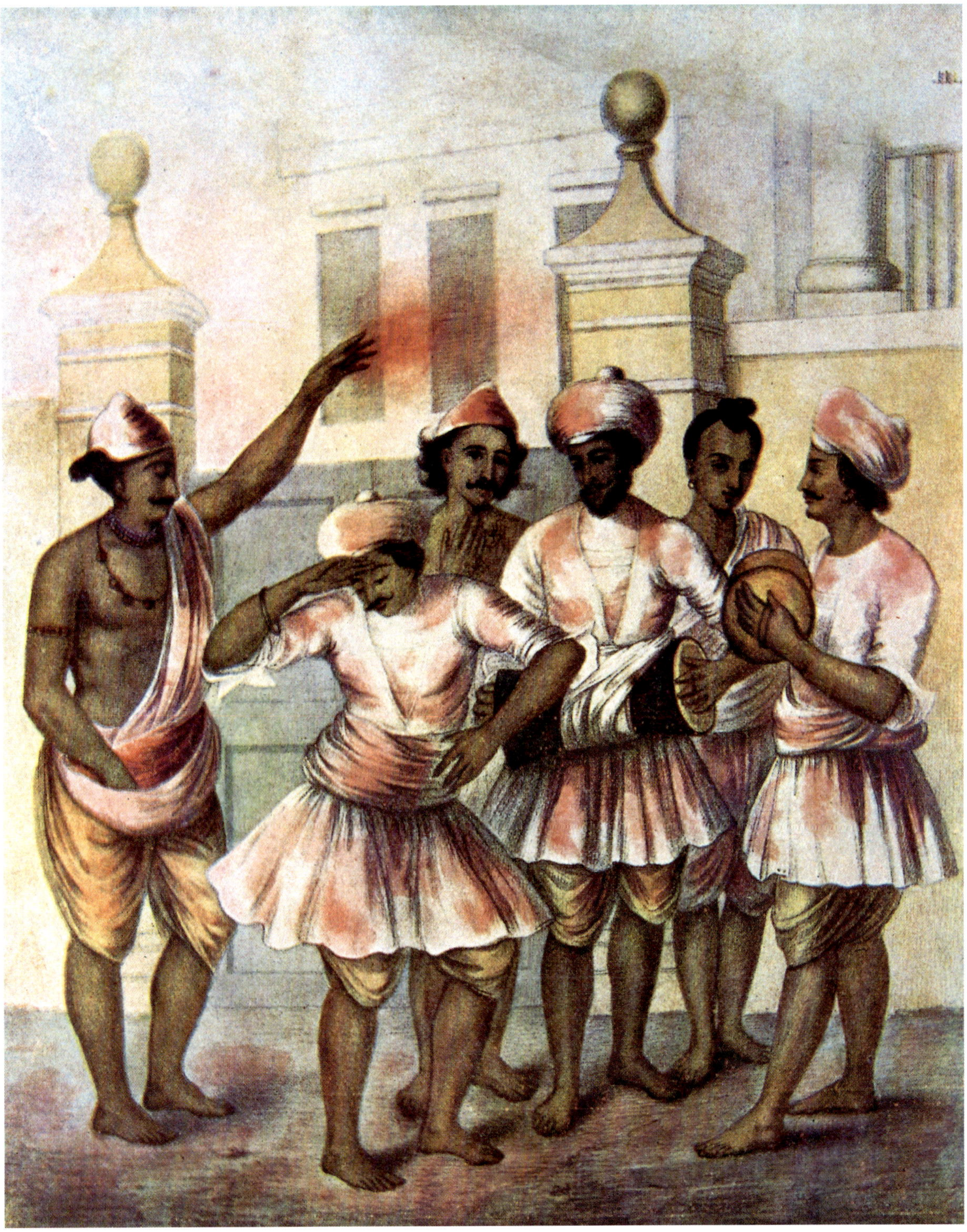

The Hooly Festival.
A set of Rowaney bearers dancing about the streets in celebration of this festival at Calcutta. Lithograph after a drawing by S.C. Belos. c. 1820.

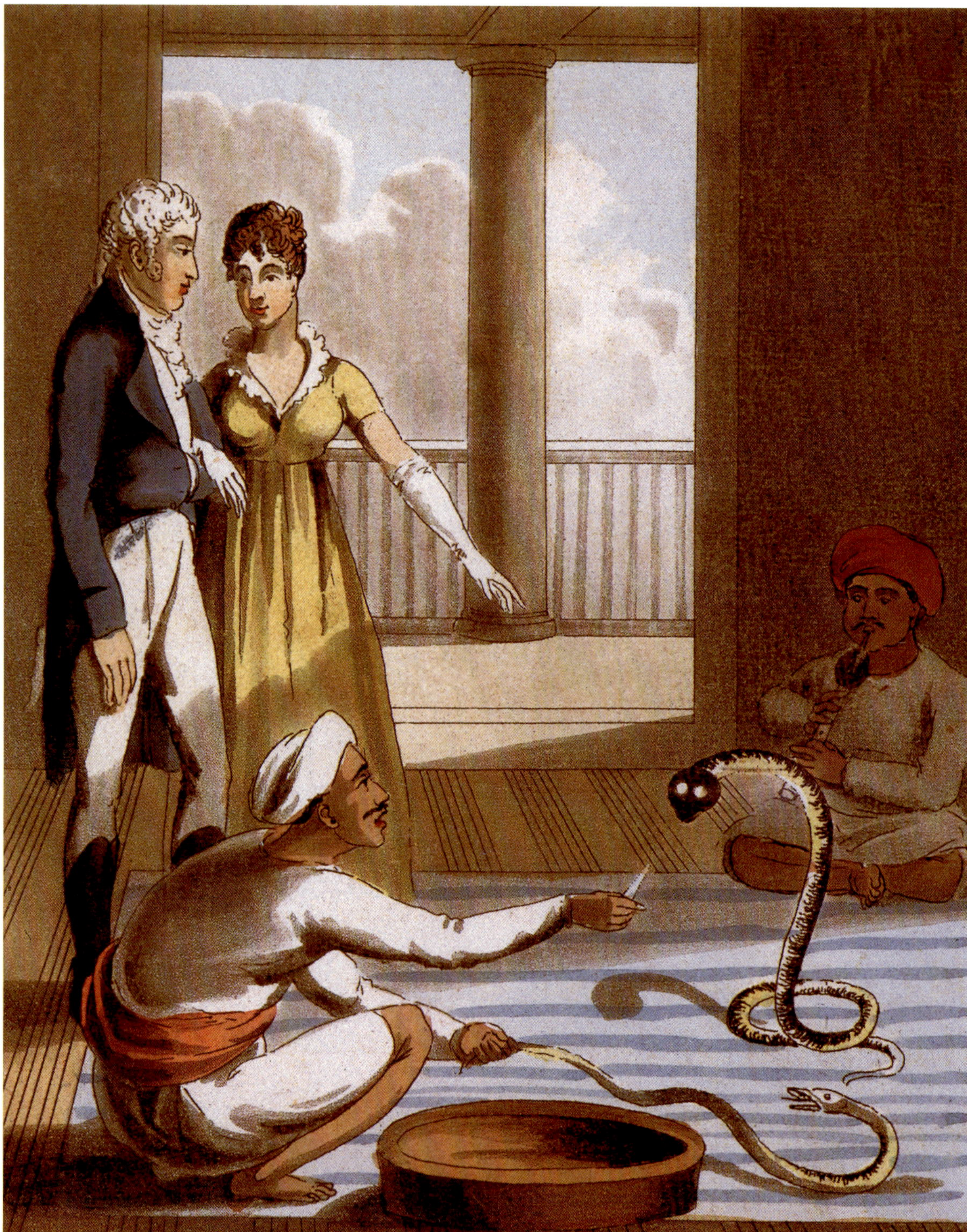

A Saumpareeah.
Snake-Catcher, exhibiting snakes before Europeans. Hand-coloured aquatint engraving after a drawing by Sir Charles Doyly, 1813.

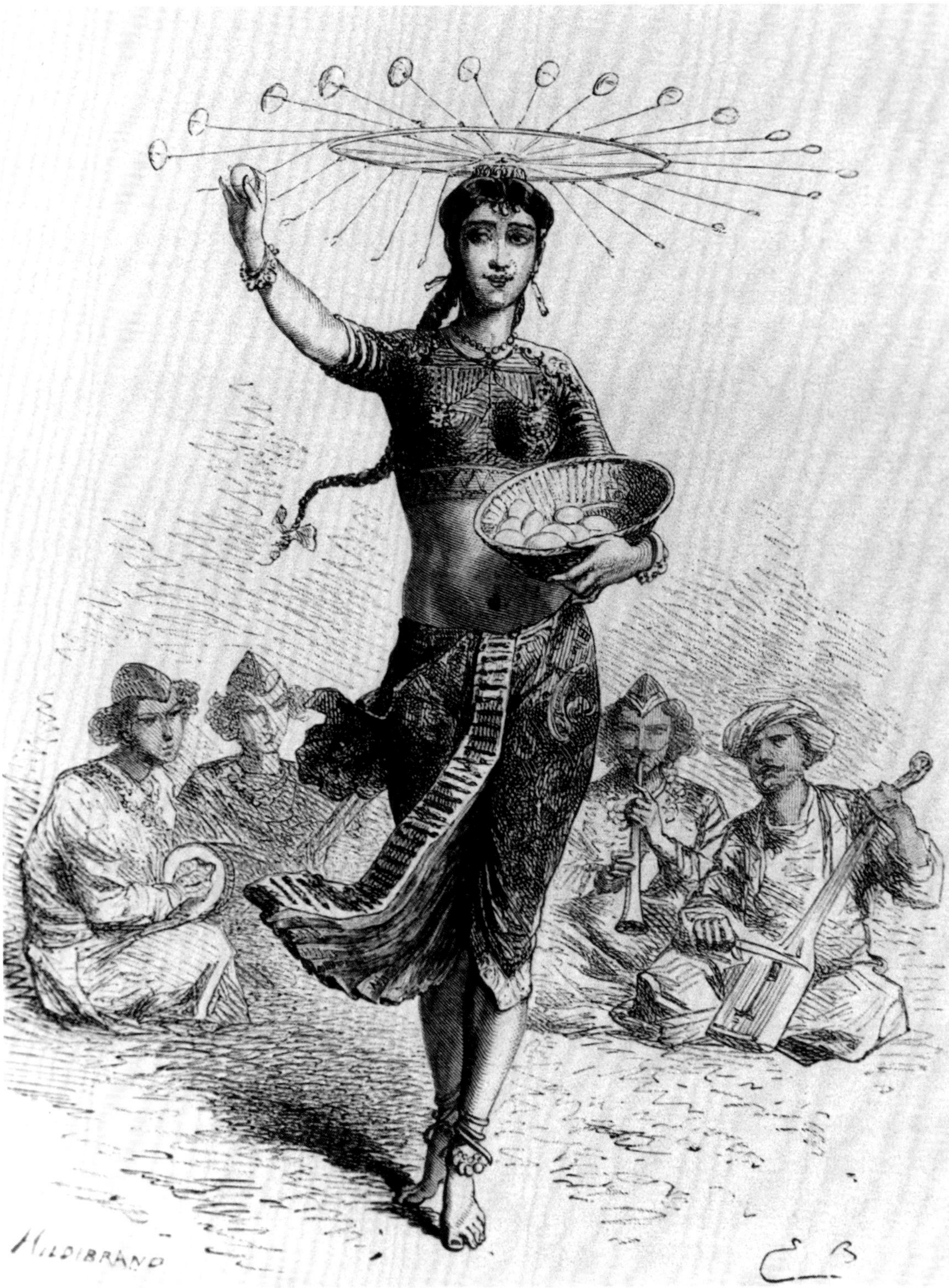

The Egg Dance by a Woman Performer.
Engraving from 'India and the Princes' by L. Rousselet, London, 1875.

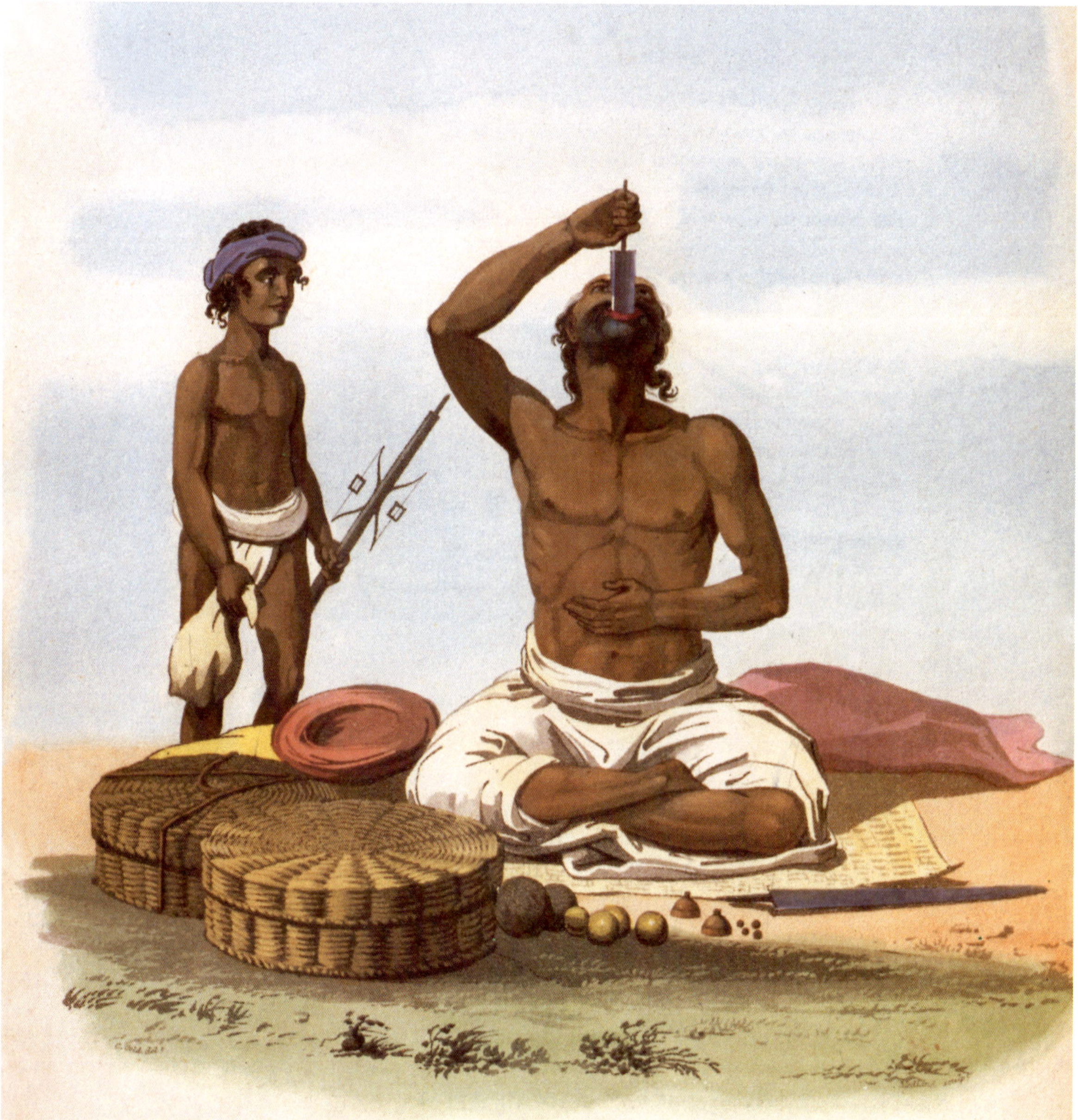

A Juggler Swallowing a Sword Blade.
Hand-coloured aquatint engraving after a drawing by Captain Charles Gold, 1806.

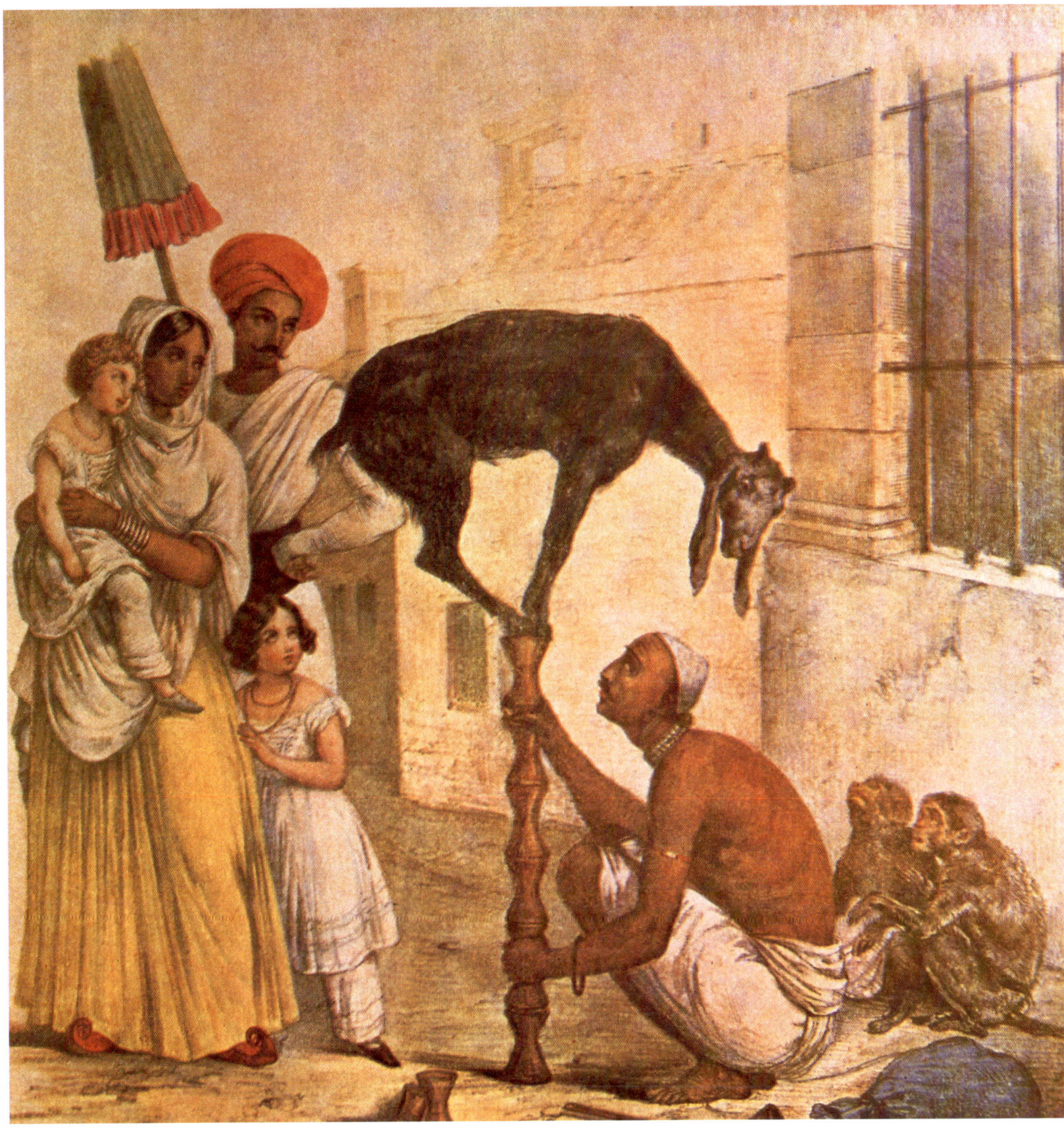

A Bunder Wallah.
Lithograph after a drawing by
S.C. Belnos, c. 1820.

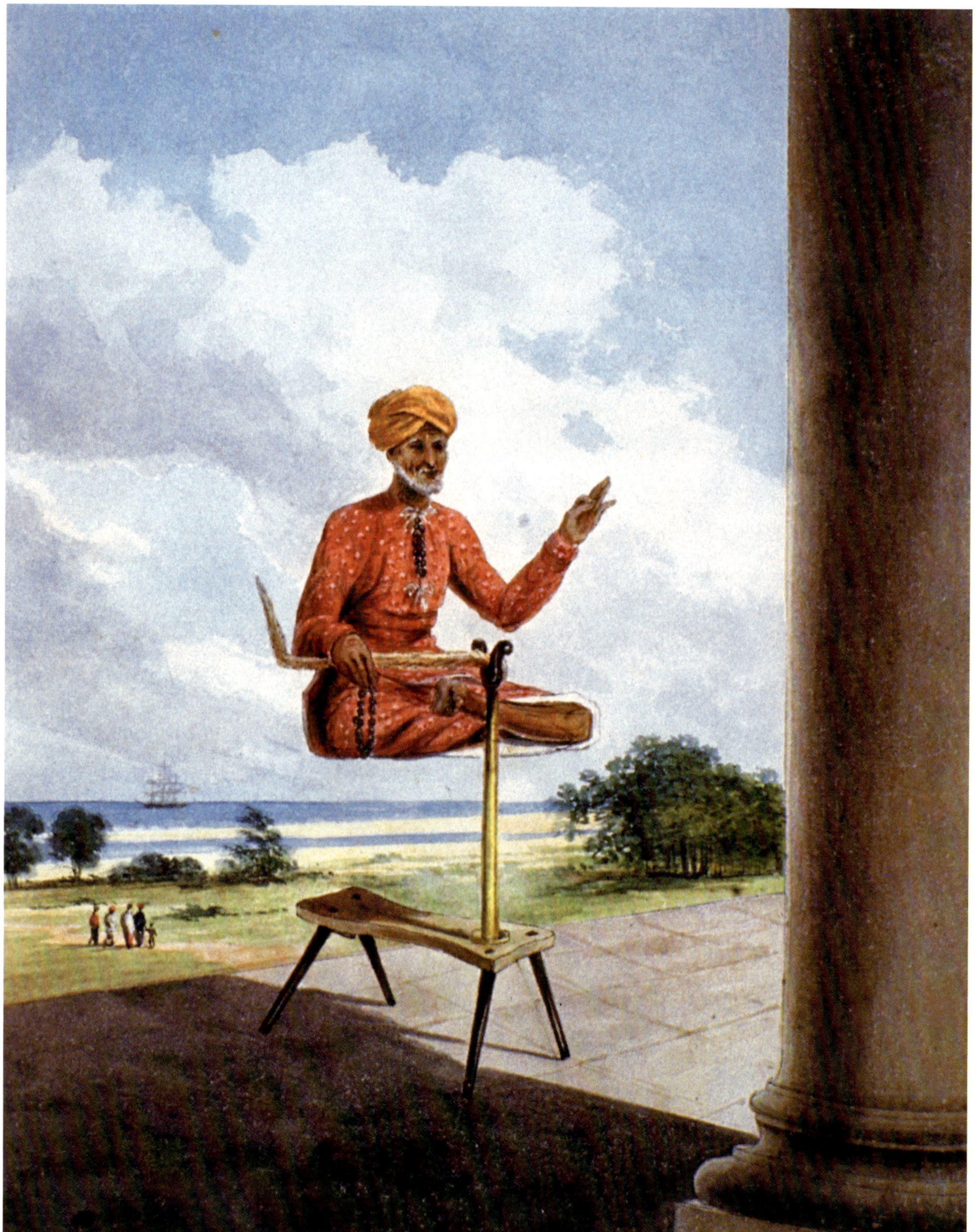

A Man showing Levitation.
Lithograph by John Gantz after his own drawing, c. 1820.

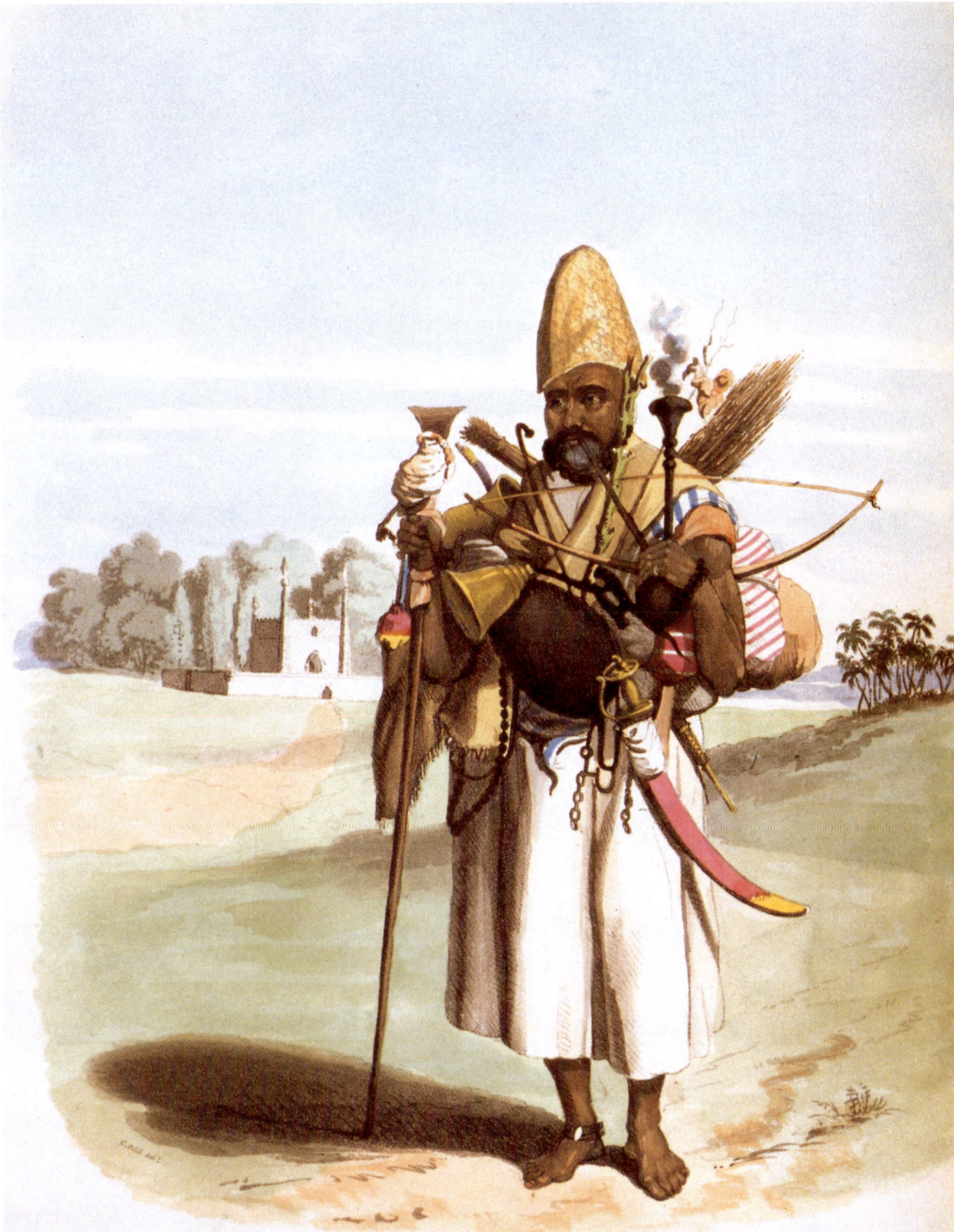

A Moorish Fakir, decorated for the festival of Hussian and Hussam, at Trichinopoly.
Hand-coloured aquatint engraving after a drawing by Captain Charles Gold, 1806.

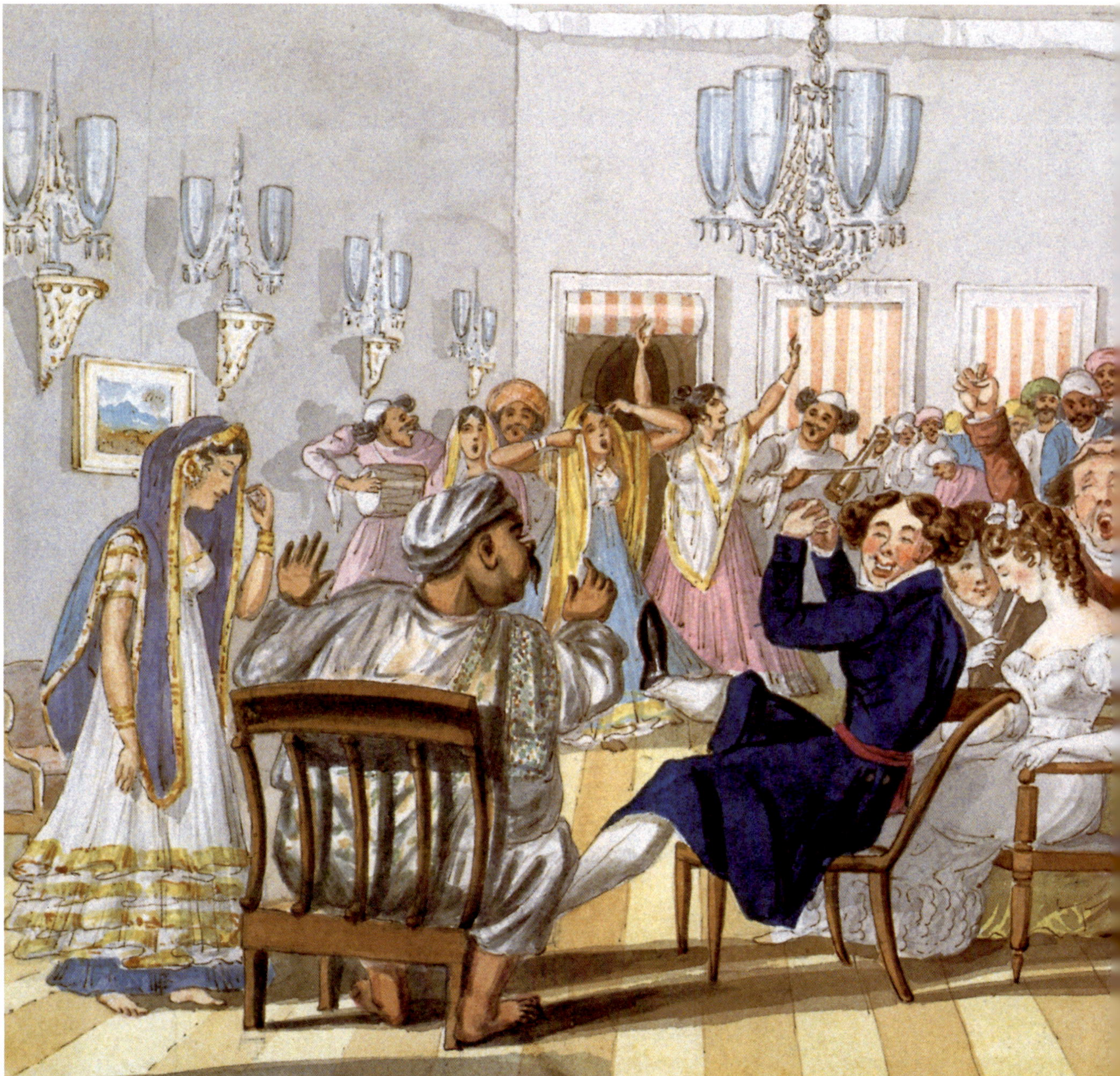

Raja Nob Kishens nautch party at Calcutta.
Nob Kishen seen from behind sitting in a European chair is entertaining a fashionable party of Europeans to a nautch performance. Watercolour by Sir Charles Doyly c.1825–28

DANCE AND MUSIC

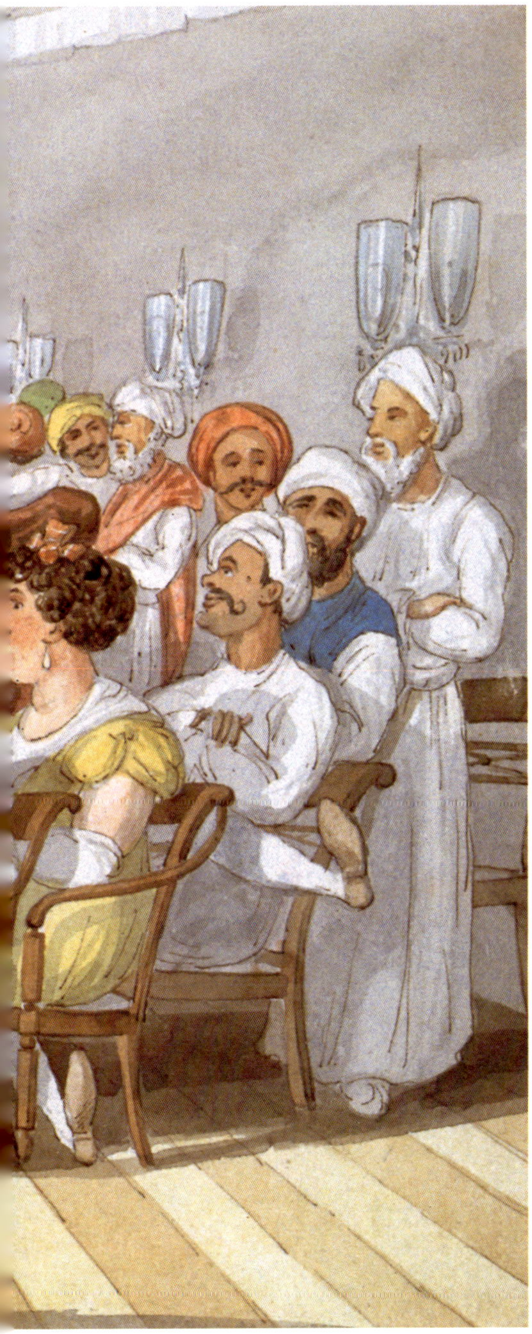

DANCE AND music have universal appeal and represent the celebration of life. Indian music goes back to ancient times. According to renowned violinist and conductor Yehudi Menuhin, the roots of world music lie in Indian music. Through the ages the Indian performing artiste of dance and music has appeared in different incarnations, from ganika to devadasi, nartaki, kanchani and then as Nautch girl during the Raj.

The Sahibs were introduced to the world of Indian dance and music through nautch entertainment by their Indian hosts. Very soon, the enraptured Sahibs turned into patrons of nautch girls. With a tradition spanning centuries, the nautch girl, described by James Forbes as "delicate in person, soft in her features, perfect in form" captivated the English elite by her grace and charm. Some of them found her song and dance "superior to all the operas of the world." No wonder that some of the fun-loving post-Plassey English Nabobs followed local custom and maintained their private troupes of nautch girls and musicians.

Over the years, the nautch emerged as the most popular form of entertainment with the Company officials. Raj literature abounds with fascinating accounts of glamorous and bejewelled nautch girls in their glittering costumes. A dinner in the English community was usually followed by a nautch performance. So were festive occasions such as the King Emperor's birthday and the visits of dignitaries to civil and military stations. So popular was this entertainment, especially with the soldiers, that nautch girls began to move enmasse to British cantonments. They would also accompany the British troops when on march providing them enroute entertainment. The Bengal gentry organized fabulous nautch parties to entertain their British guests in Calcutta, which was the capital of the Raj.

The songs sung by the nautch girls were usually in Persian. Their themes ranged from the amorous escapades of popular gods or conventional romantic tales, usually expressing the lover's yearning for the beloved. Lily S. Anderson, an American visitor, was so deeply impressed by a nautch girl's performance that she eloquently admires the fantastic coordination of music and motion that merged the dancer's entire physical frame with music. Their charming poses and glittering robes of the nautch girls as portrayed in many paintings underline their physical beauty and sensuous appeal.

Sir Charles Doyly, a leading amateur artist, had nautch portraits made by his Indian assistants. He gives a singularly interesting description of the nautch scene:

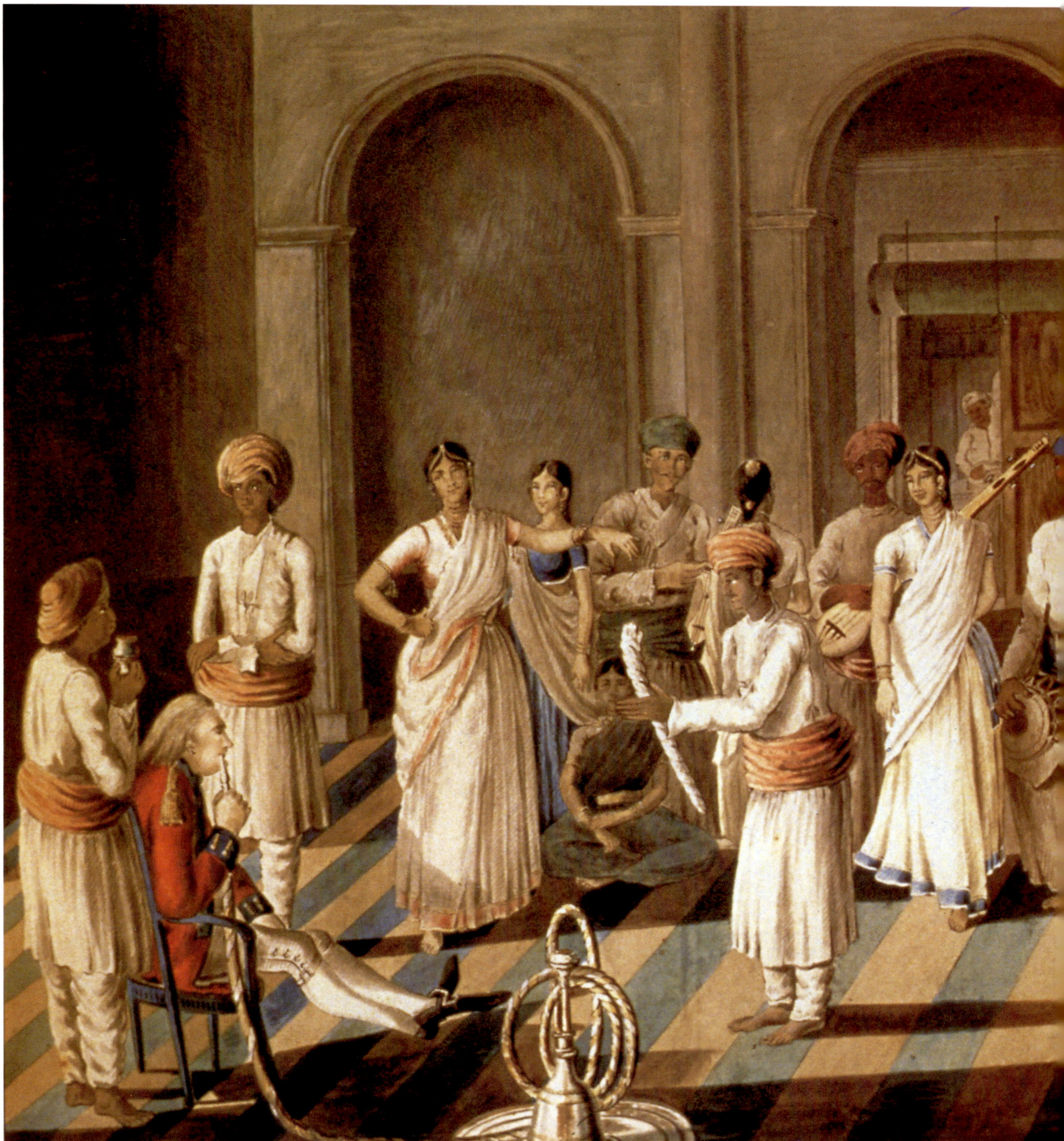

A nautch by native dancers at Vizagapatam being watched by Capt Lyons of Bengal Infantry. Watercolour by Captain Crockatt of Bengal Engineers Establishment, c.1800.

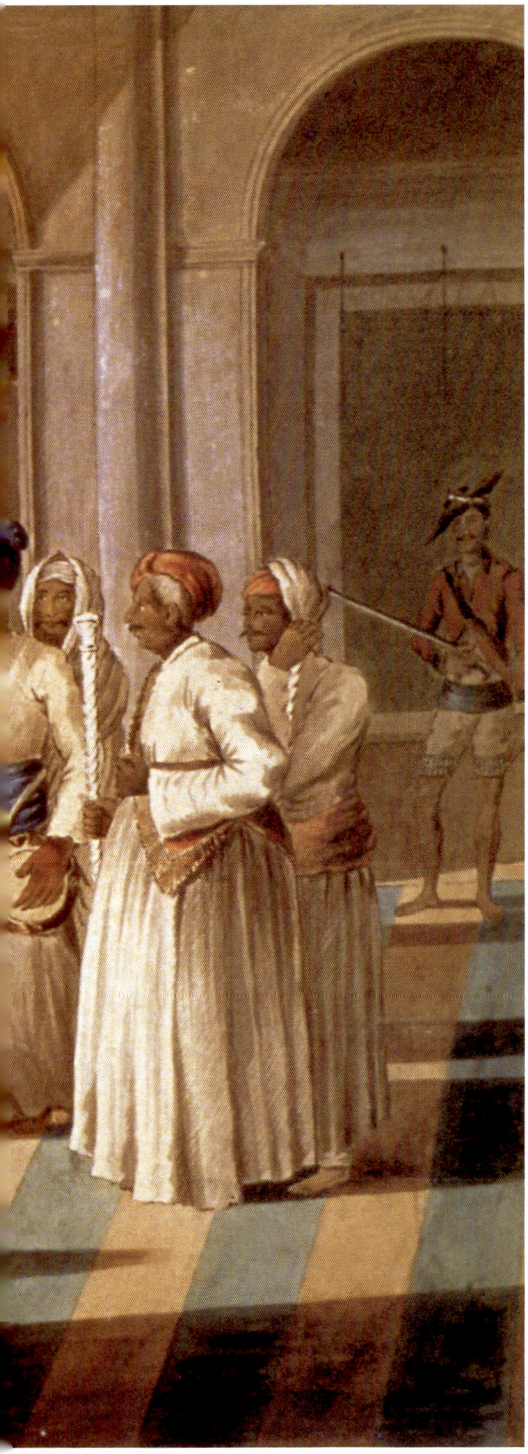

See! How invitingly the creatures dance!
What elegance and ease in every motion!
Not as the ladies do at home, or France,
So turbulent and full of strange commotion;
Of this our Indian fair has an odd notion;
Their step is slow and measured — not a caper
That lifts them from the ground, — but grave devotion
To time, and suppleness of figure's taper,
It is no doubt the modestest — at least on paper!

* *

Or how describe the graceful play of arms,
Which, beautifully waving, as they move,
Reveals, at every step, a thousand charms;
Expressing terror, languishment, or love;
While their dark, speaking eyes, unceasing rove

The British professional artists were struck by the charm and beauty of the nautch girls who had no inhibitions and freely gave sittings for their portraits. Some Sahibs even commissioned Indian artists to make their pictures in different poses. A number of British officials in Delhi in the early nineteenth century were flamboyant characters who held lavish nautch parties at their mansions. One such notable character was Sir David Ochterlony (1758–1825) nicknamed 'Loony Akhtar.' In one of the paintings he is shown in Indian dress smoking a hookah and watching a nautch in his mansion. Another such person was William Fraser, who had striking portraits of his favourite nautch girls in the well-known *Fraser Album*. The most famous patron of Indian art and culture was the legendary Col. James Skinner (1778–1841) who lived in a lavish Indian fashion at his palatal mansion at Kashmiri Gate. He threw extravagant nautch parties popular with both Indian and British guests, and he would take great delight in presenting his guests with miniature paintings of nautch girls, at times of the very same who were entertaining them.

In South India, devadasis attached to the temple were the professional dancers who were invited to entertain the Sahibs. They are described as "very good looking with large sparkling eyes, regular features and an intelligent pleasing appearance."

The institution of nautch dominated the entertainment scene until the middle of the nineteenth century. After the mutiny of 1857 came the dawn of the 'Age of Memsahibs'. Their strong influence combined with the zeal of Christian missionaries served to downplay and denigrate native art and culture. Their anti-nautch campaign finally dealt a death blow to this form of traditional Indian dance.

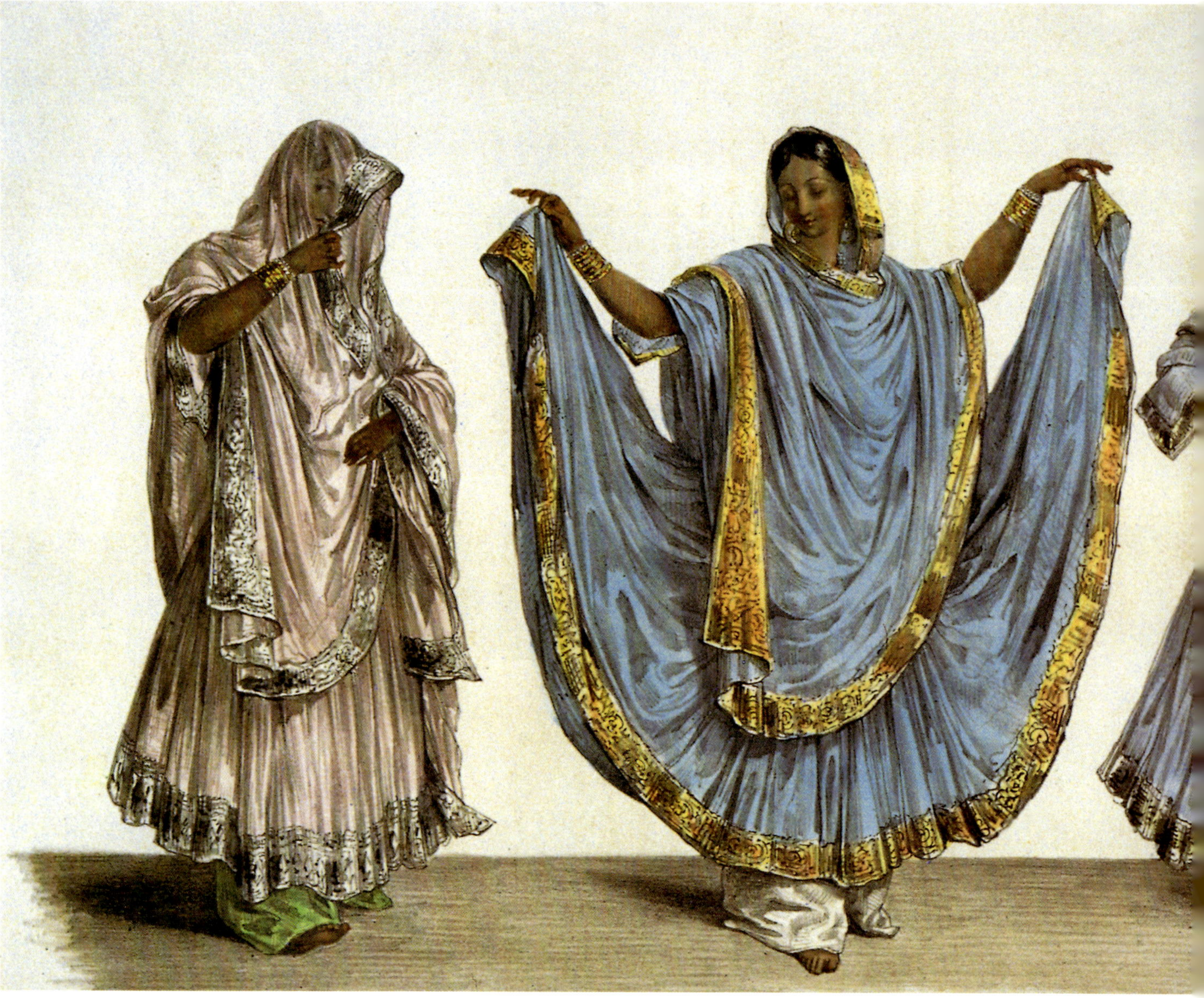

Three Dancing Girls of Hindostan. They represent different styles of the Eastern Nautch. Coloured lithograph after a drawing by S.C. Belnos, Calcutta, c.1820.

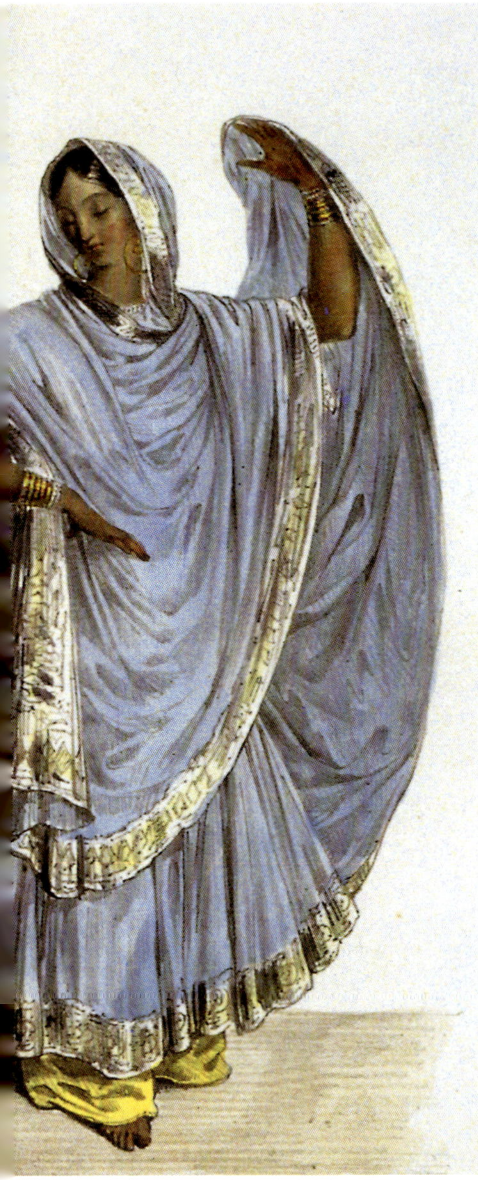

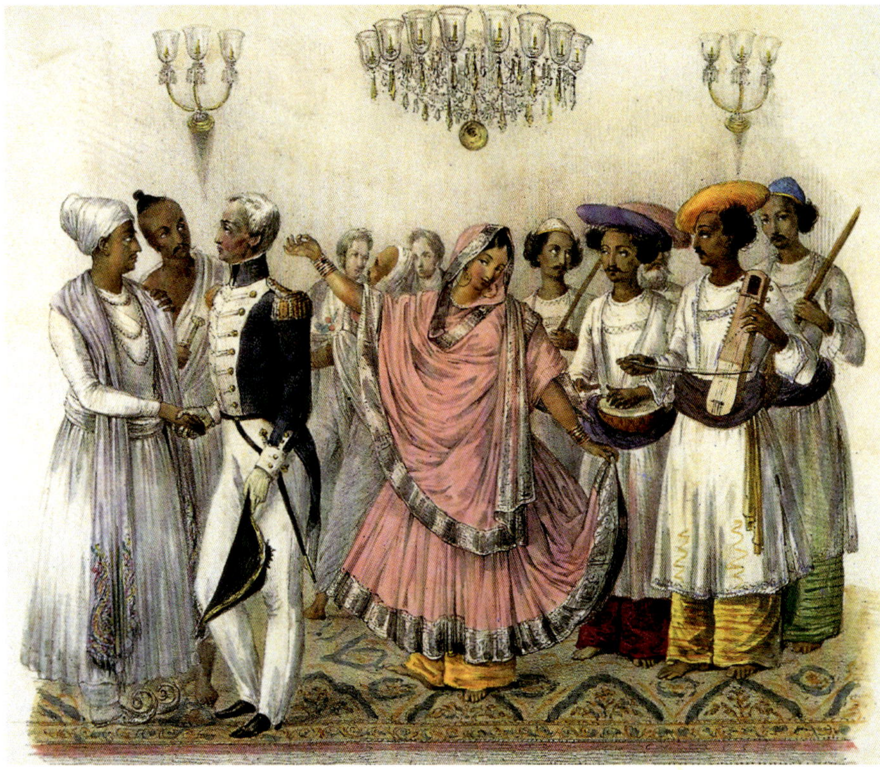

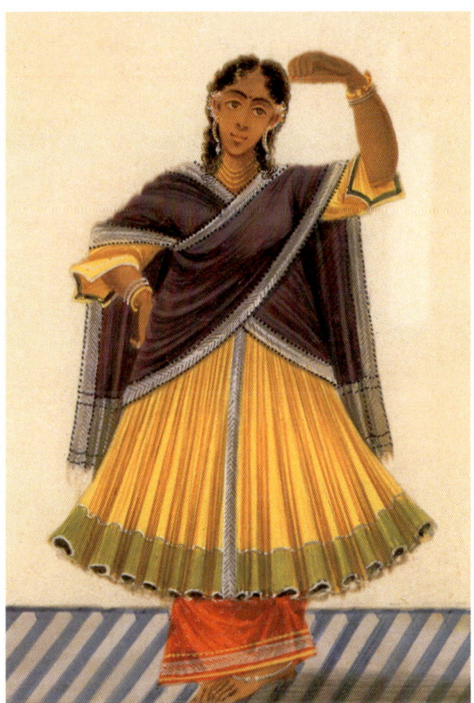

Above: *A Nautch during the Puja festival at the house of a Hindu Raja at Calcutta with European guests.*
Coloured lithograph after a drawing by S.C. Belnos, c.1820.

Left: *Nautch Girl.*
Mica painting by a Benaras artist, c. 1800.

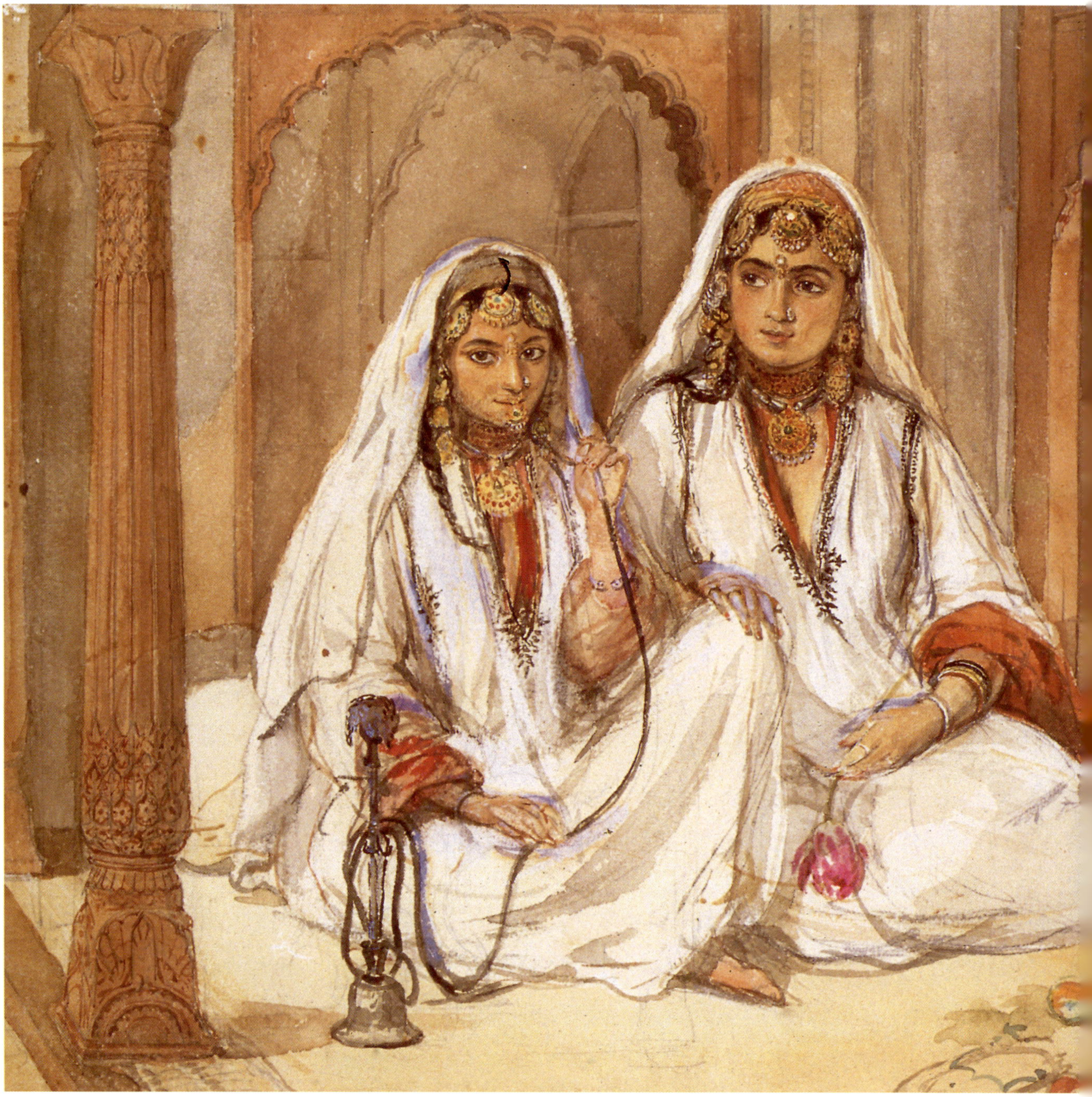

Kashmiri Nautch Girls.
Watercolour by William Carpenter,
Serinugger, August 1854.

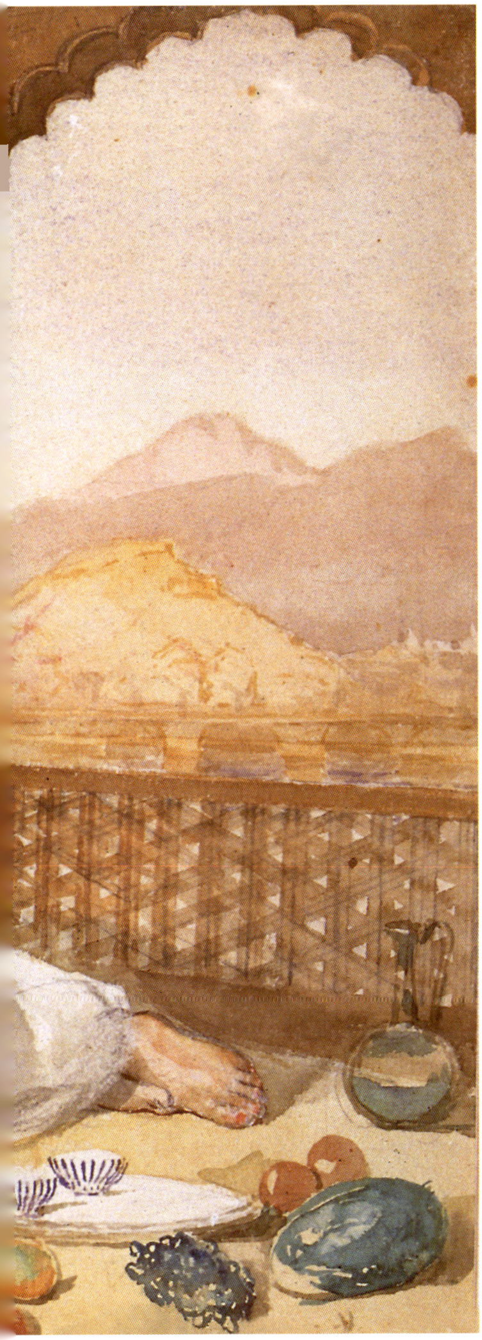

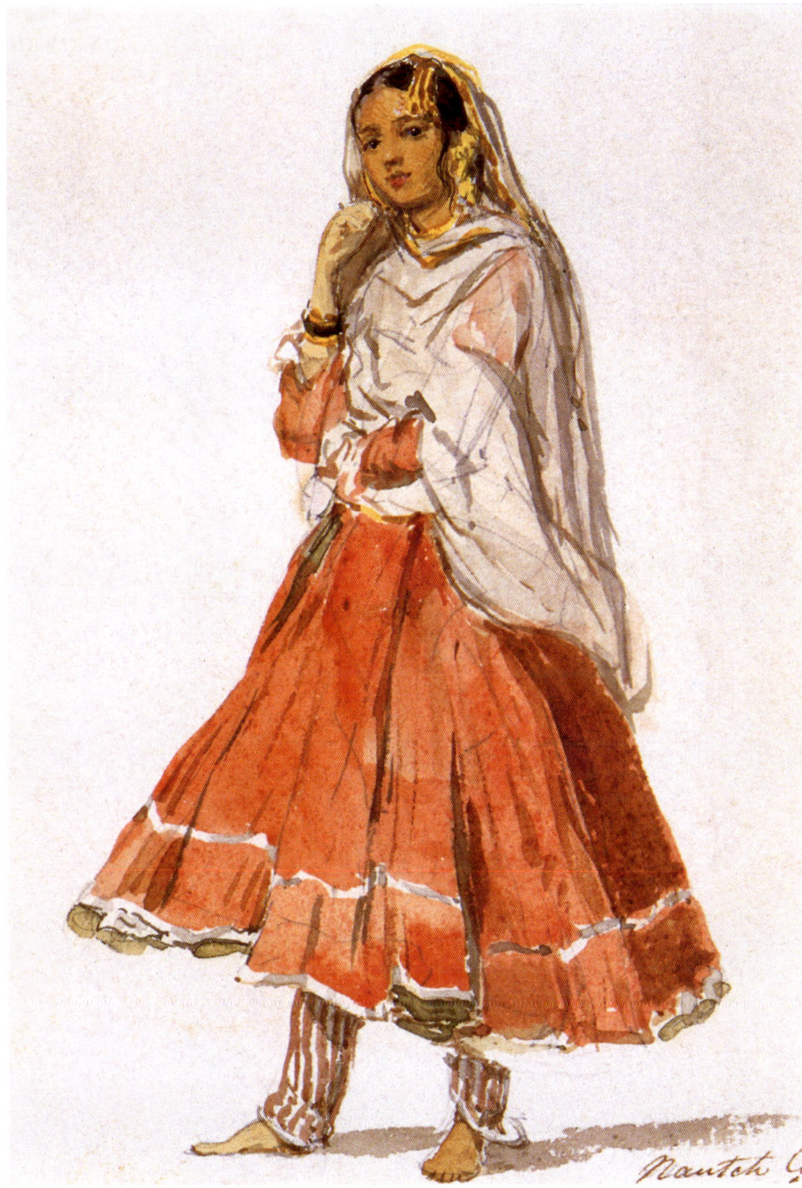

Nautch Girl of Udaipur.
Watercolour by William Carpenter, c. 1850.

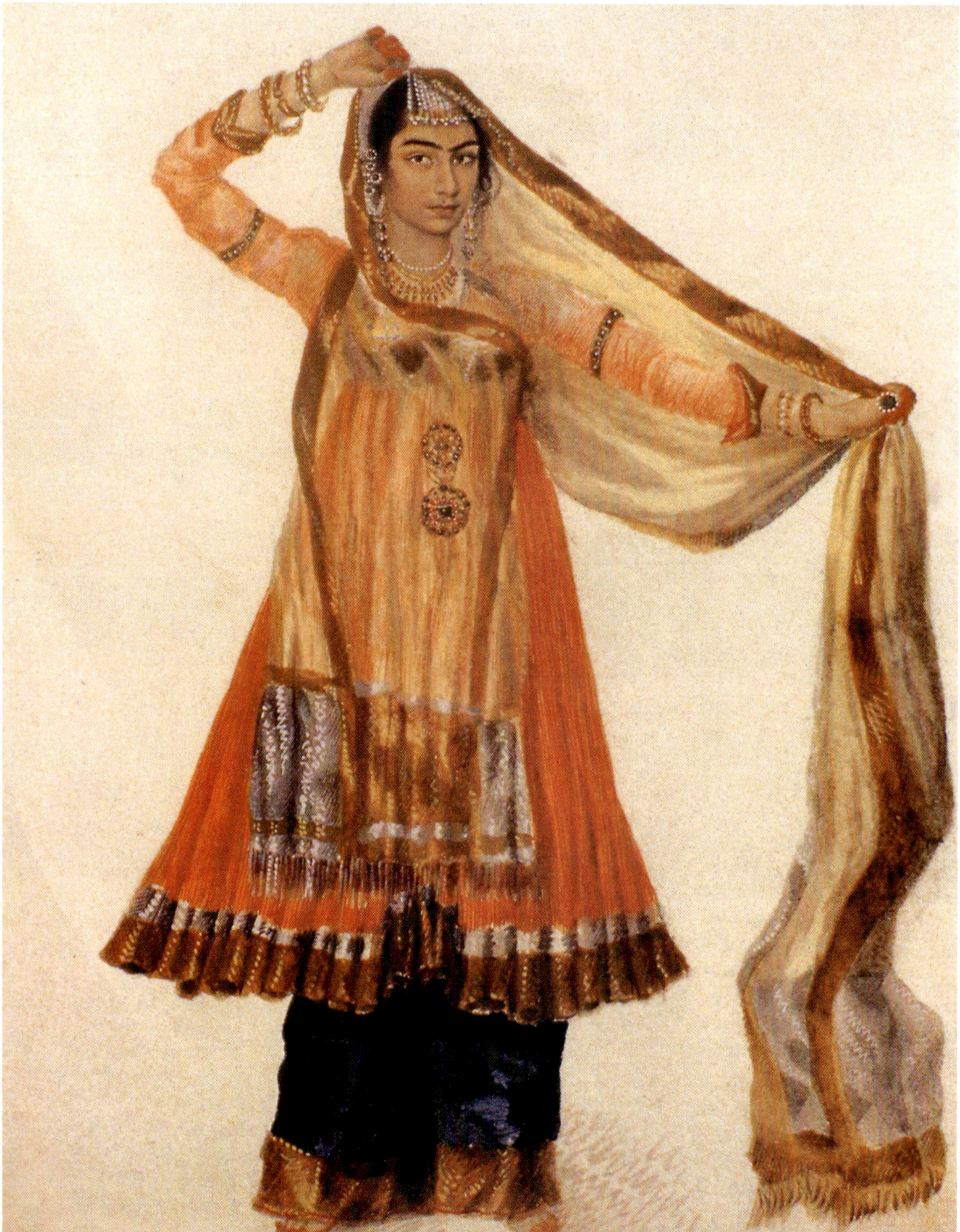

Inscribed in Persian: *Picture of Malliyagir, dancing girl – On the date 3rd September, year 1815, by Lallji, a Delhi artist.* Malaguire was a celebrated dancing girl of Delhi seen here in her nautch dress. Identified in transcription by E. S. Fraser.

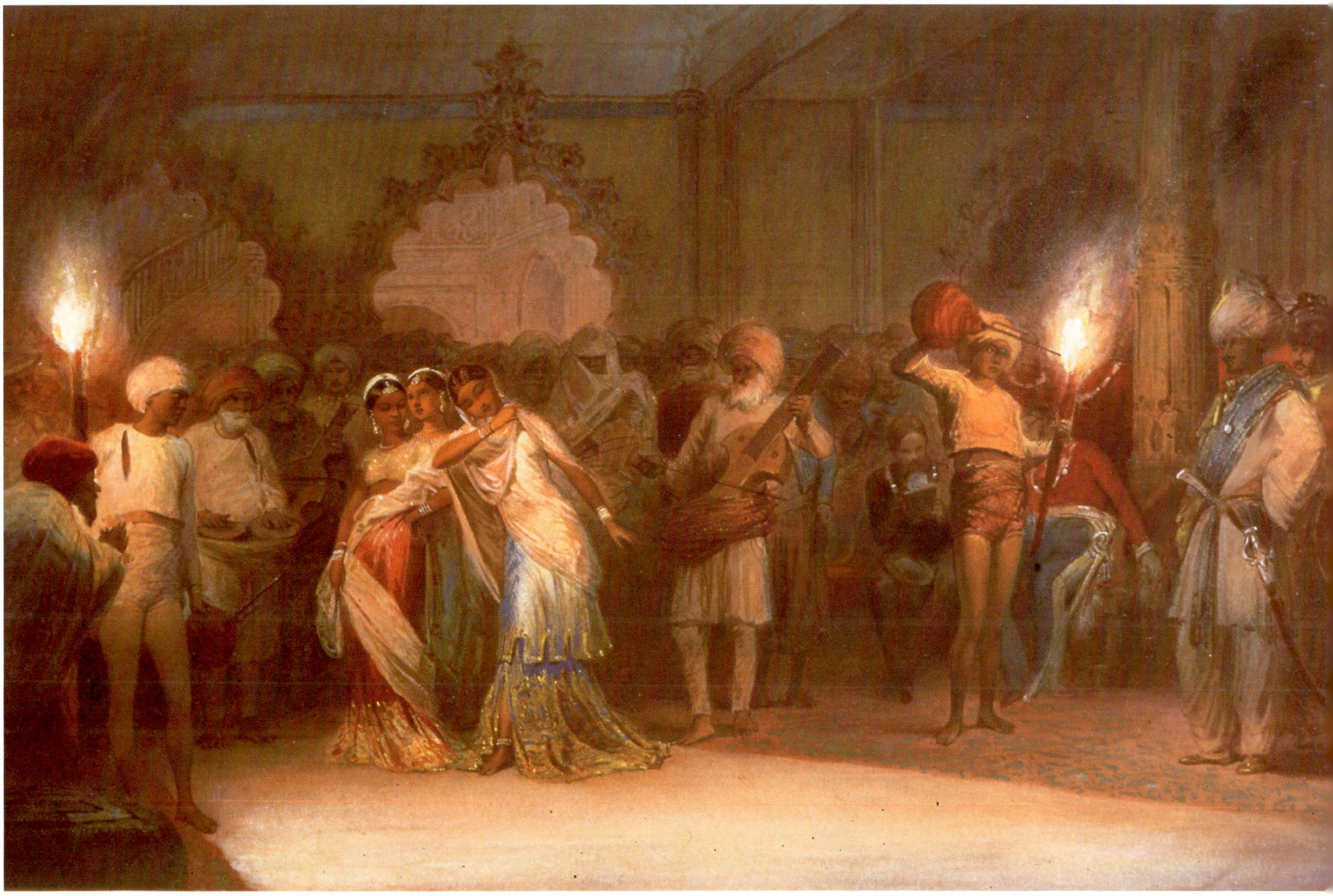

Nautch entertainment by Man Singh in honour of Lord Clyde, the C-in-C in Lucknow, March, 1859.
Watercolour by Egron Lundgren.

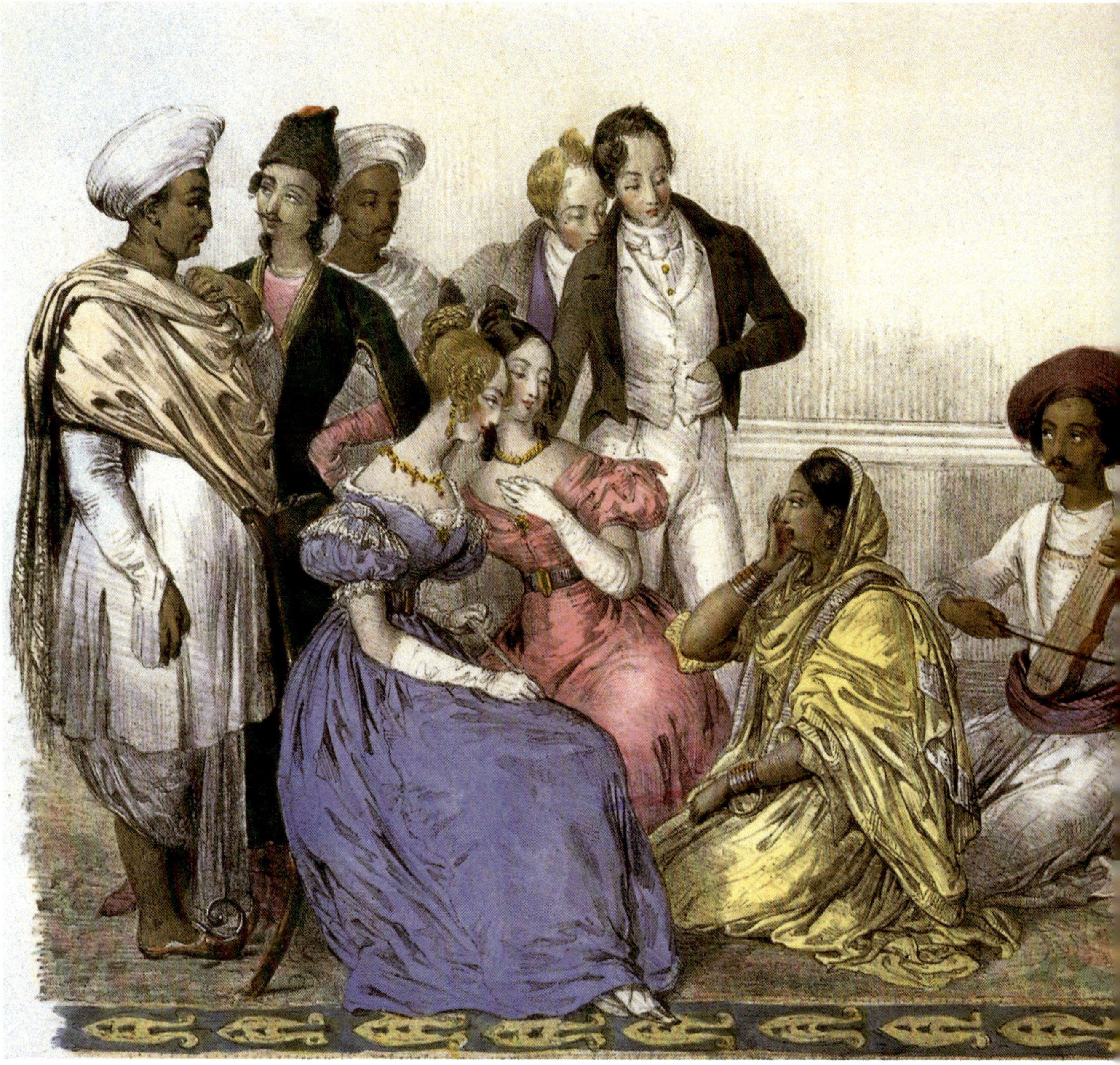

Nautch girl sitting at the feet of two memsahibs and singing.
Coloured lithograph after a drawing by S.C. Belnos.

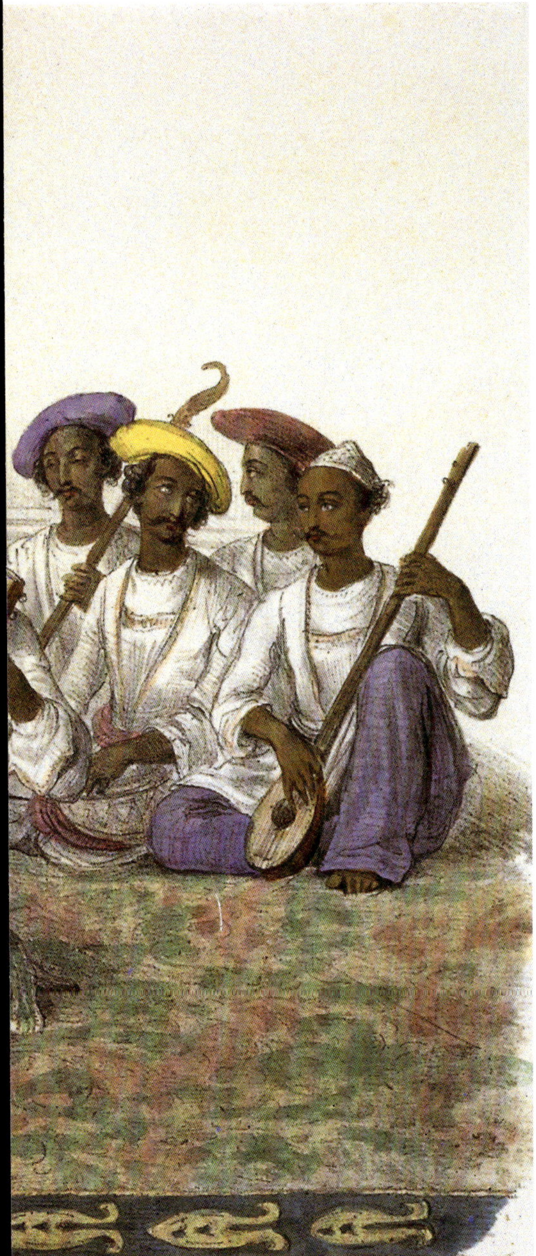

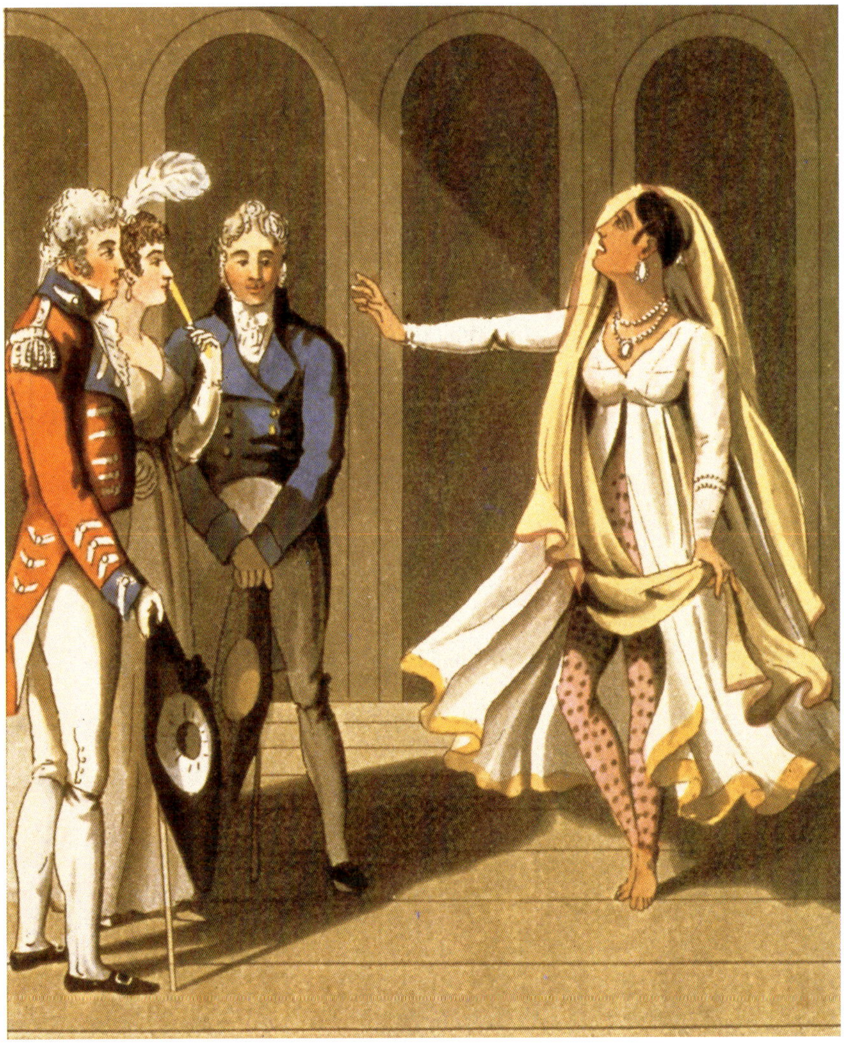

A Dancing woman, of Bengal, exhibiting before an European Family.
Hand-coloured aquatint engraving after a drawing by Sir Charles Doyly, 1813.

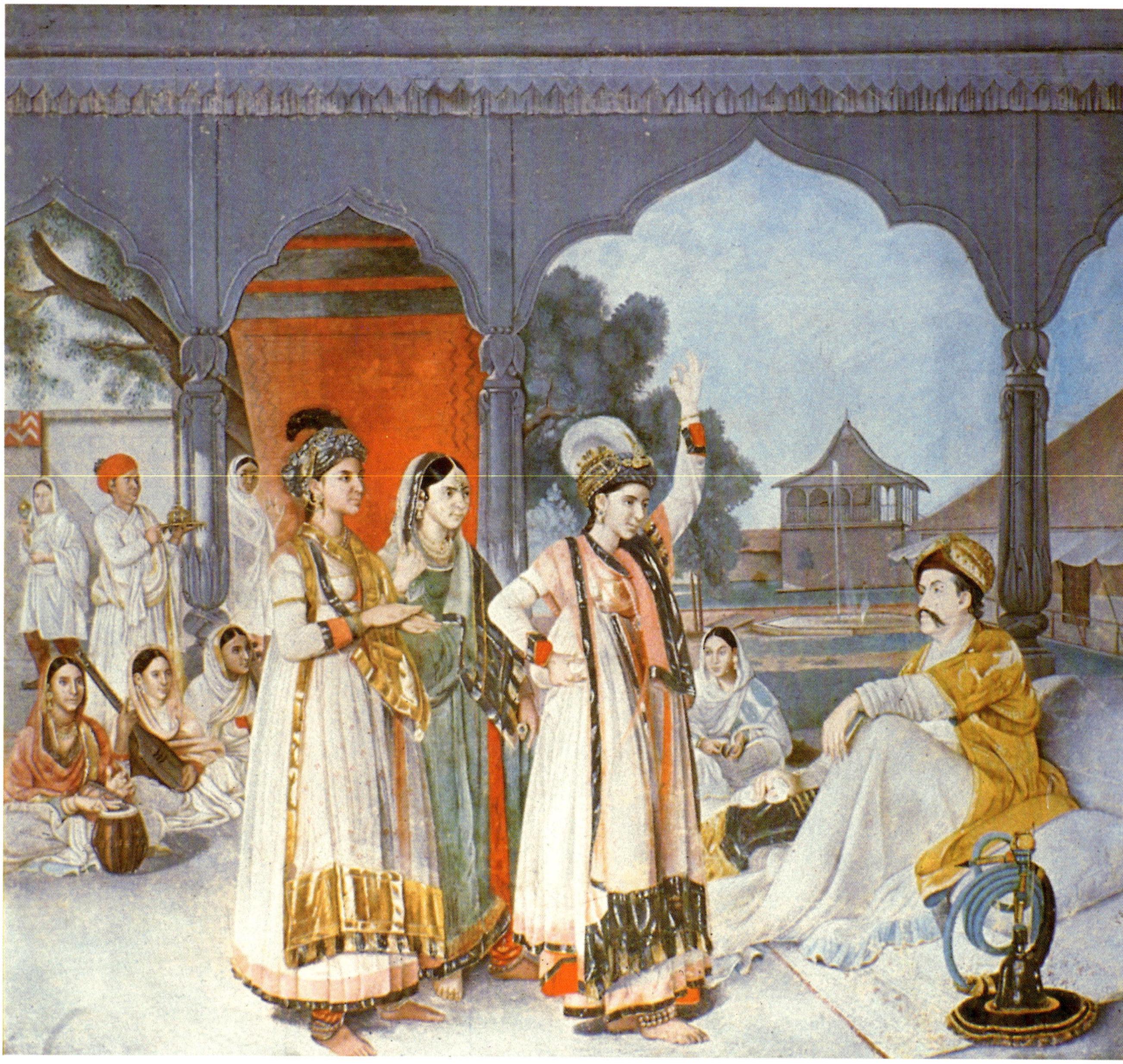

Col. Antoine Louis Henri Polier watching a nautch.
Watercolour by an Indian artist, Lucknow, c.1780 after a presumed painting by Tilly Kettle, Faizabad, 1772.

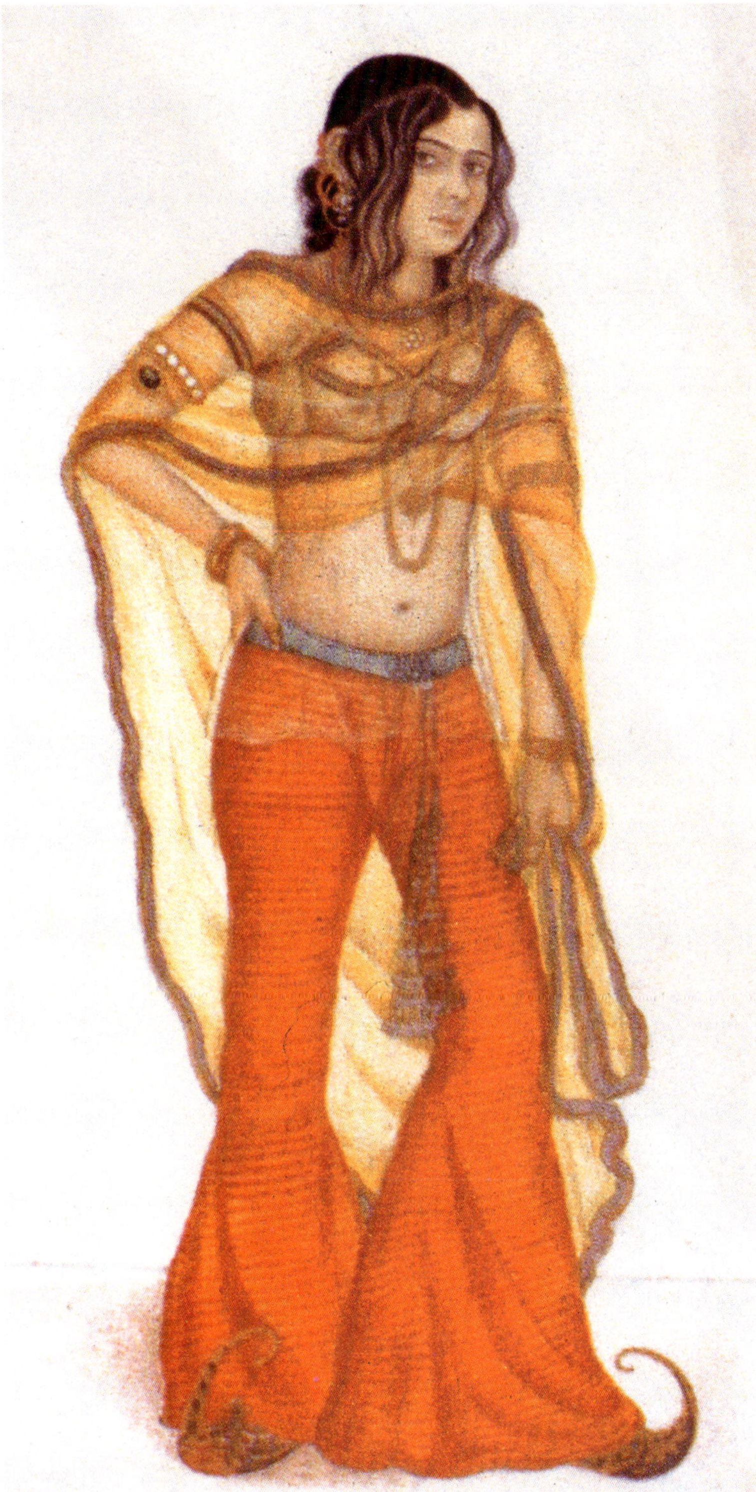

Inscribed in Persian: *Piyari Jan Khanagi (in indoor costume).* Identified by E.S. Fraser*: Peeare Jan, a dancing woman of Dehlee in the usual undress.* Watercolour by a Delhi artist, c.1815.

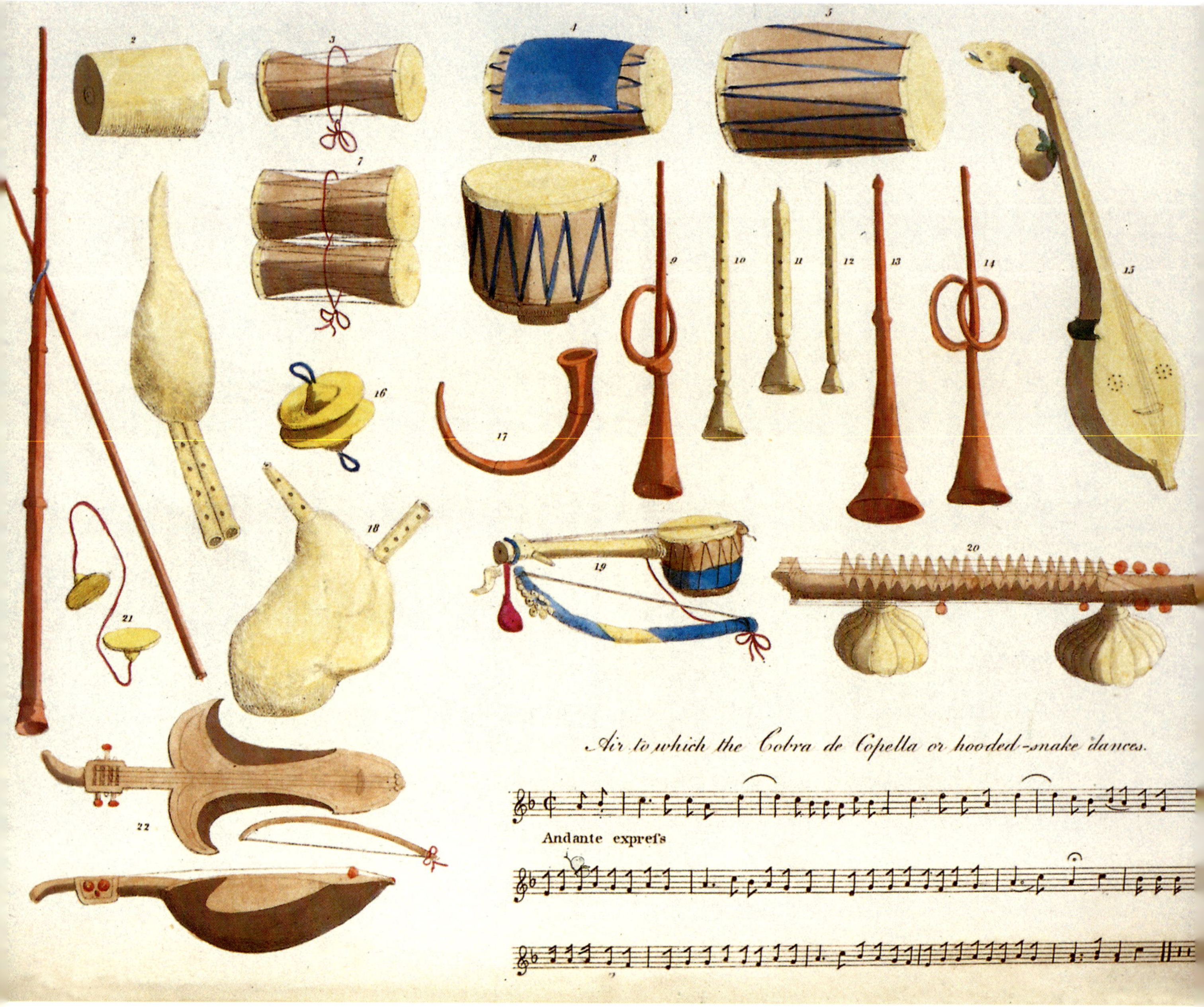

Musical Instruments.
Hand coloured aquatint engraving after a drawing by Captain Charles Gold, 1806.

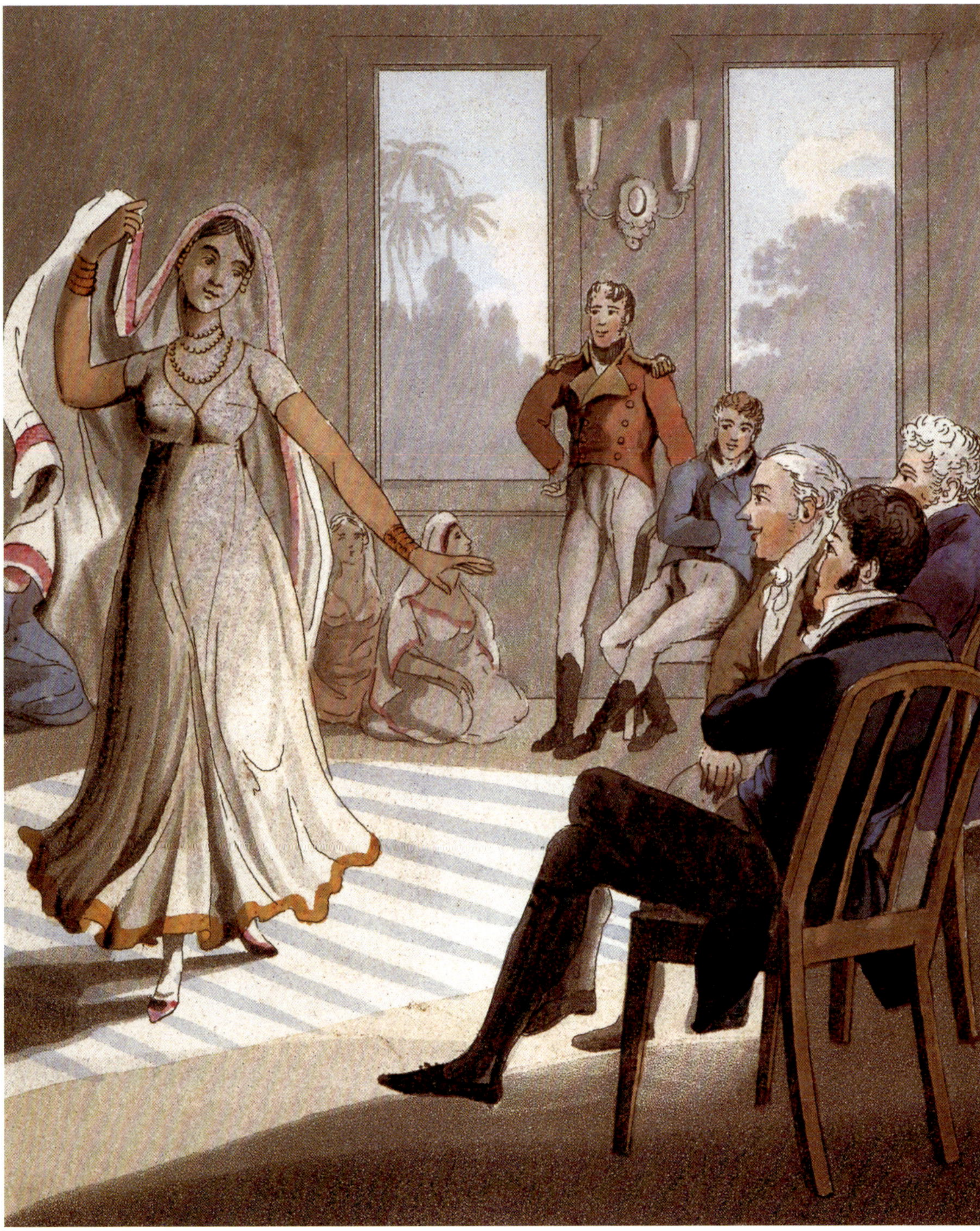

A Dancing Woman of Lucknow, exhibiting before an European Family
Hand coloured aquatint engraving after a drawing by Sir Charles Doyly, 1813.

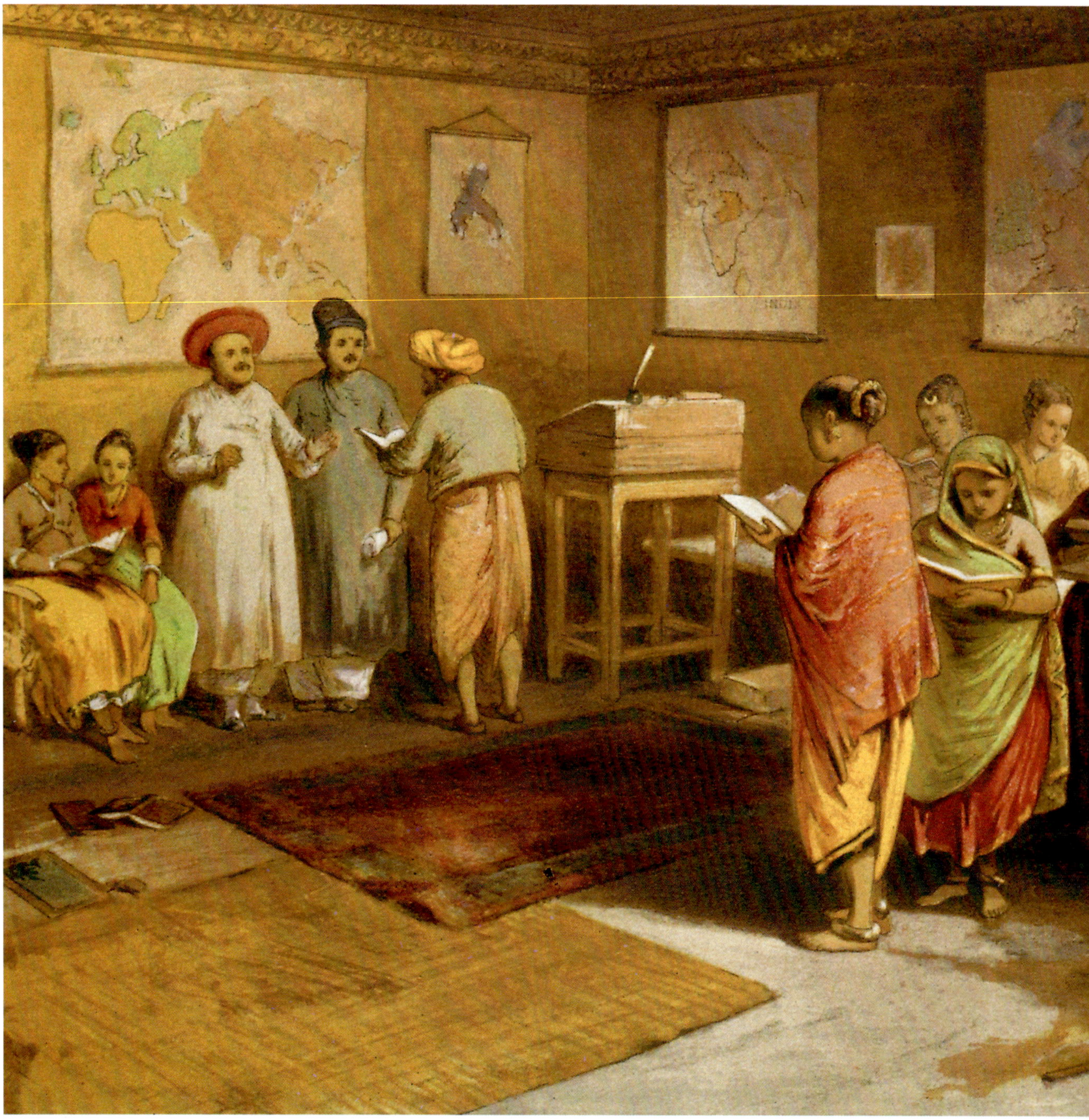

Marathi school.
Chromolithograph after a drawing by
William Simpson, c. 1860.

CASTE AND OCCUPATIONS

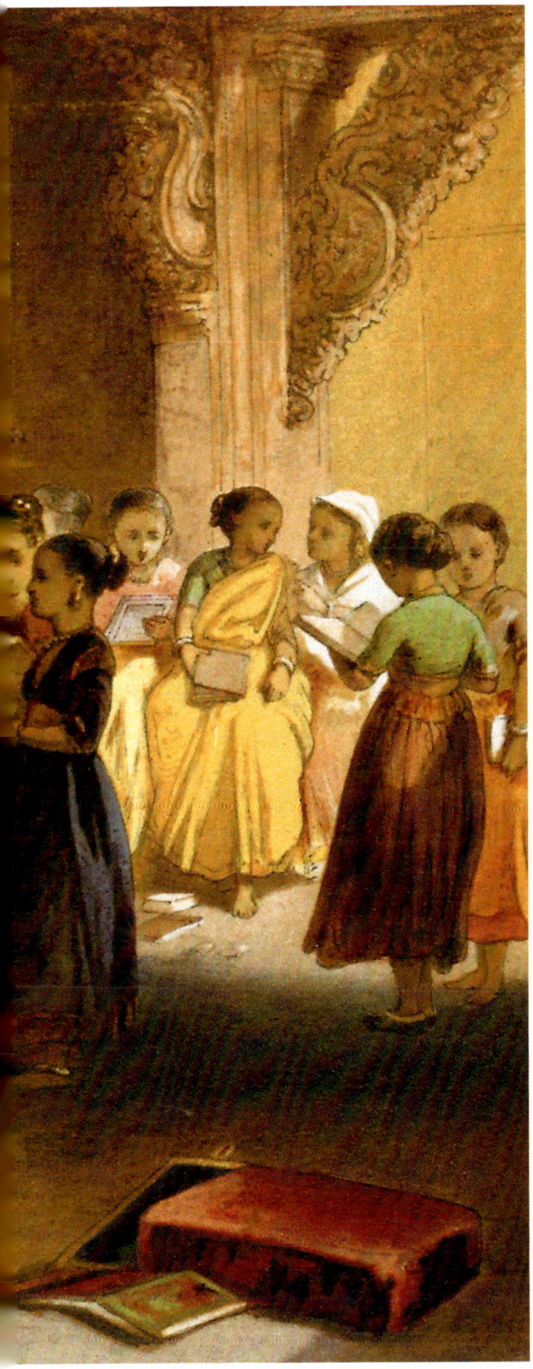

"MANKIND HAS a passion for classifying itself," wrote Lord Meston, "and ever since the days of Plato and Herodotus, ancient societies have been described as being divided into classes which had no inter-marriage or community of interest. It was left to India to develop this ancient idea into a system of incredible complexity."

No other people have erected a social structure comparable to the caste system of India. The origin of the system has been much debated but it is believed that the great law-giver Manu defined the laws of castes to be incorporated into a system of Hindu Law. The word caste is derived from the Portuguese word 'casta' meaning purity of breed. It was used by the early Portuguese settlers in India. The ancient Indian word for caste was 'varna.' According to Hindu belief, the supreme god Brahma, the Lord of Creation, caused the Brahmin to spring from his mouth, the Kshatriya from his arms, the Vaishya from his thighs and the Shudra from his feet. To each one of them, the Lord assigned separate duties and occupations. The Brahmins were required to teach and study the scriptures. He commanded the Kshatriya to protect the people, the Vaishya to till the land, tend cattle and engage in commerce, and ordered the Shudra to serve the three higher castes. It was generally believed that the whole structure of Hindu life had the sanction of the gods.

In Indian society, the Hindu was always known by his caste. The Hindu's attachment to caste, both high and low, was so forceful that it proved to be one of the chief hurdles for Christian missionaries to convert them.

Referring to the pride of caste, H.H. Wilson (1861) says:

> *"The lowest native is no outcaste, he has an acknowledged place in society, he is the member of a class; and he is invariably more retentive of the distinction than those above him. In depicting the horrors of the system, European writers lose sight of the compensations. The veriest Chandala who is one of a community is less miserable, less unhappy, than many of the paupers of the civilized communities of Europe, with whom no man owns companionship or kindred. They are the true outcastes, not the Pariah or Chandala."*

Abbe J.A. Dubois, the famous French missionary, counters criticism of the Hindu caste system and highlights its advantages:

> *"I believe caste division to be in many respects the chef d'oeuvre or the happiest effort, of Hindu legislation. I am persuaded that it*

Hindu Couples of Brahmin, Kshatriya, Vaishya and Shudra castes. Hand-coloured etchings by and after F.B Solvyns, (1808–1812).

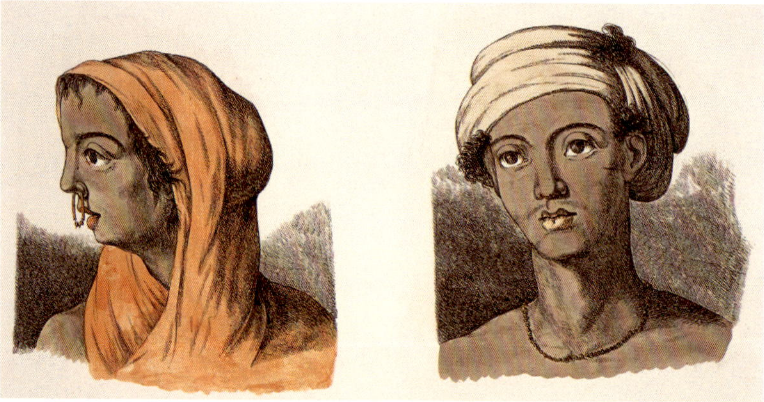

A Shudra couple

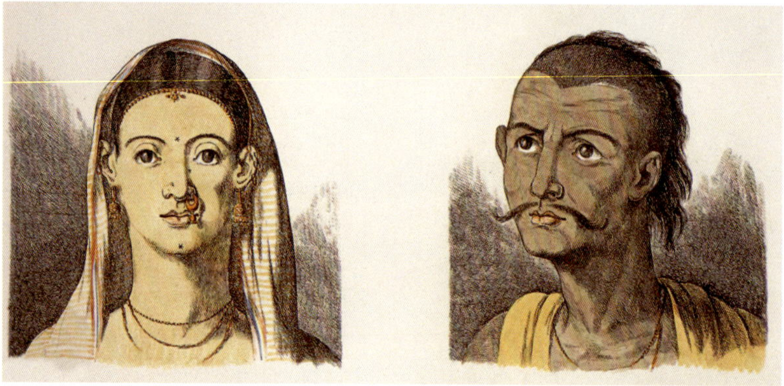

A Kshatryia couple

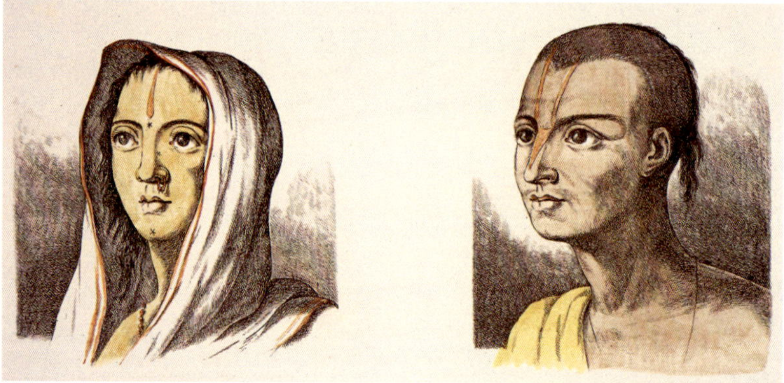

A Brahmin couple

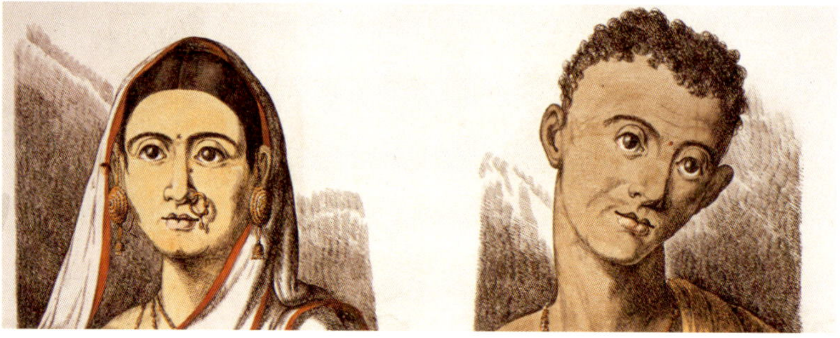

A Vaishya couple

is simply and solely due to the distribution of people into castes, that India did not lapse into a state of barbarism, and that she preserved and perfected the arts and sciences of civilization whilst most other nations of the earth remained in a state of barbarism. I do not consider caste to be free from many great drawbacks, but I believe the resulting advantages, in the case of a nation constituted like the Hindus more than outweigh the resulting evil..."

Caste assigns to each individual his own profession or calling and the handing down of this system from father to son from generation to generation, makes it impossible for any person or his descendents to change the conditions of life which the law assigns to him for any other. Such an institution was probably the only means that the most clear sighted prudence could devise for maintaining a state of civilization amongst a people endowed with the peculiar characteristics of the Hindus.

Social sanction for a profession or calling was based on the sheer accident of birth. According to Sir Charles Doyly, prejudices pertaining to professions were also wedded to social distinctions of castes. Few would normally accept work which lowered the traditional repute and dignity of their caste. This was the reason why the English residents had to employ an army of servants for different kinds of duties in their households.

Caste governed the code of conduct, religious rituals and practice and even food habits and clothing. Indian women lost their caste when they married Europeans or established a liaison with them. That is why their progeny were called half-castes or Eurasians and later Anglo-Indians who were disowned by Indian society. In order to defend its honour, caste exercised close control over its members. Every caste had its own customs and traditions and those deviating from them were duly punished. The greatest punishment for anyone was to be excluded from the caste by its members and it was not easy to regain his original position without obeying specific prescribed conditions. Incidentally, many a victim of this harsh treatment was welcomed by missionaries into their flock.

Muslim society, though not strictly divided like the Hindu castes, adopted a scheme of social gradation based on birth. Contemporary writings refer to two main social divisions, Sharaf or the high-born, and Razil, the low-born. The former constituted the gentry or classes which claimed high extraction and could be compared to the Brahmins and Kshatriyas of the Hindu society. The latter group included menial workers and those engaged in lower professions like barbers, butchers and potters.

By the beginning of the nineteenth century, the growing power and prestige of the British brought about several changes in the

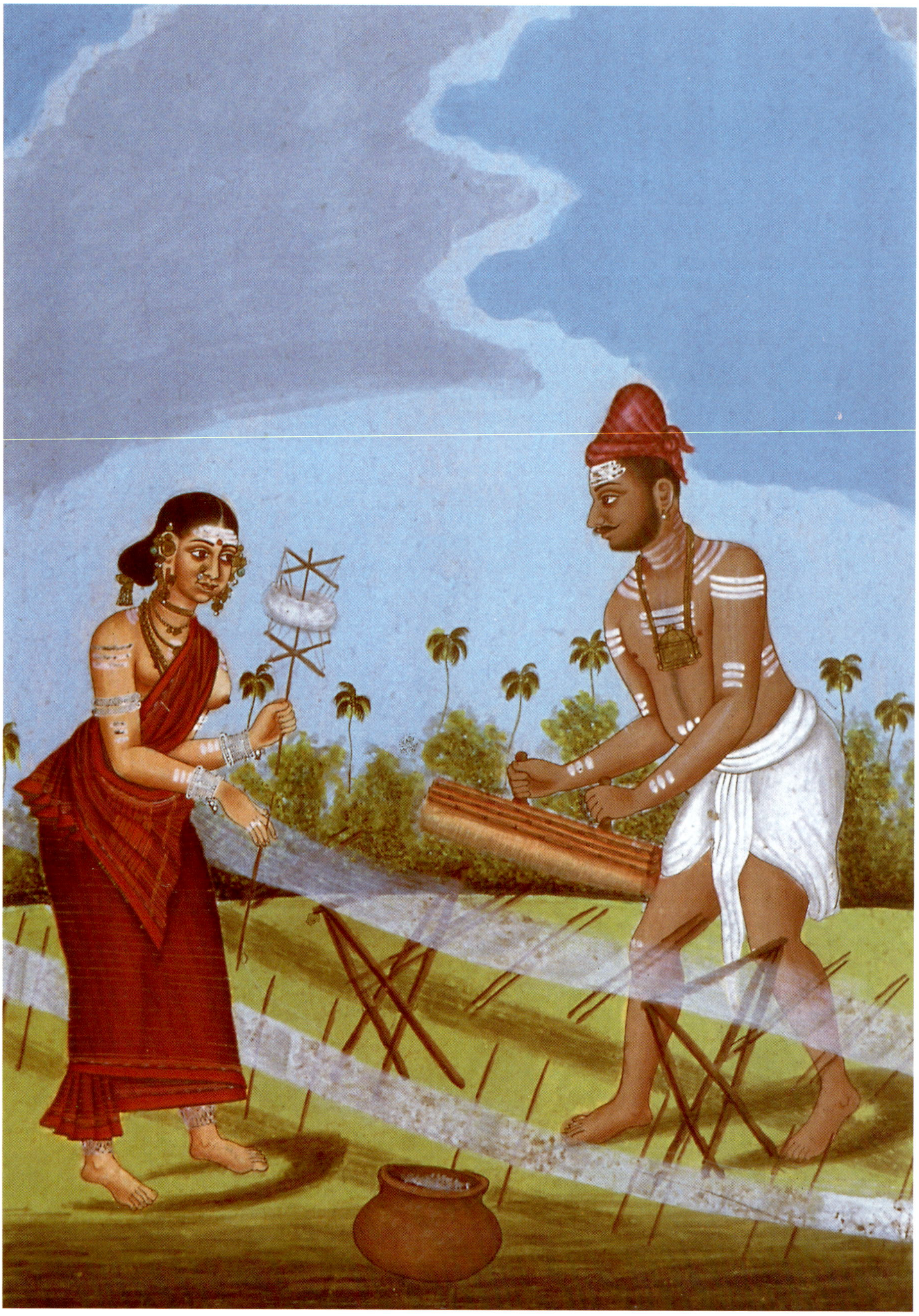

Indian economic scene. The vested interests established by castes started disintegrating and the spectre of poverty and starvation often compelled some high caste Hindus to humble themselves by lower professions. At the same time, some lower castes intruded into superior professions. The overall impact of these developments on the institution of caste system was, however, quite marginal and the entire Indian social structure continued to be dominated by the caste system which was the basis for social stratification not only among the Hindus but also among the Muslims.

It is interesting to observe how the British community developed a class system that was far more brutal than the one they had left behind. This system of social stratification has often been compared to the more rigid Indian caste system which the British found objectionable and frequently blamed for social problems and race relations in particular. Following this analogy the Brahmins were the Government civilian officials followed by the army officers, the warriors or Kshatriyas. The merchants constituted the Vaisyas group called box-wallahs who were socially kept at a distance by the former. The last in the social strata were the ordinary soldiers, tailors, barbers, half-castes or Eurasians corresponding to Indian Shudras.

Facing page: *A weaver and his wife.* A Tanjore artist, c.1800.

Below: *A silversmith and his wife.* Mica painting by a Trichinopoly artist, c.1820.

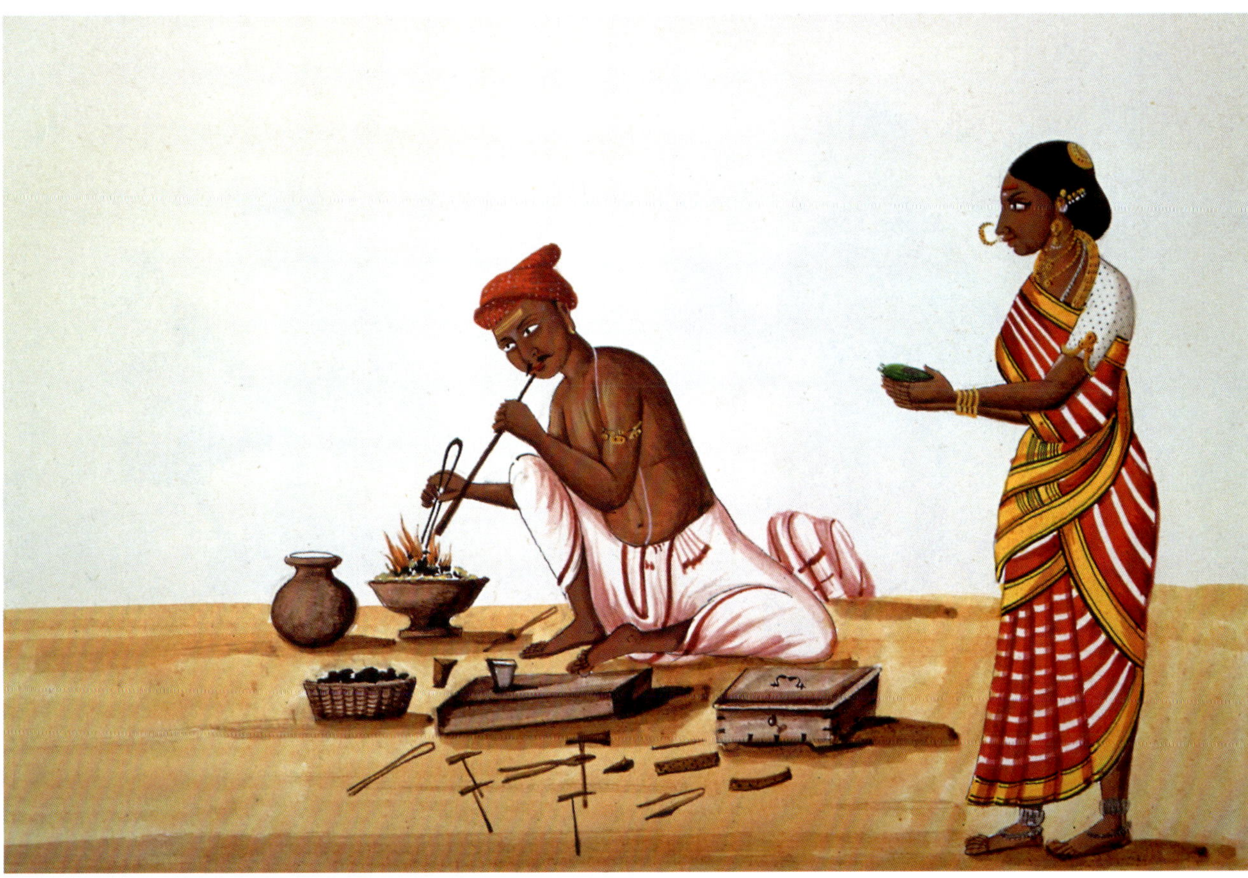

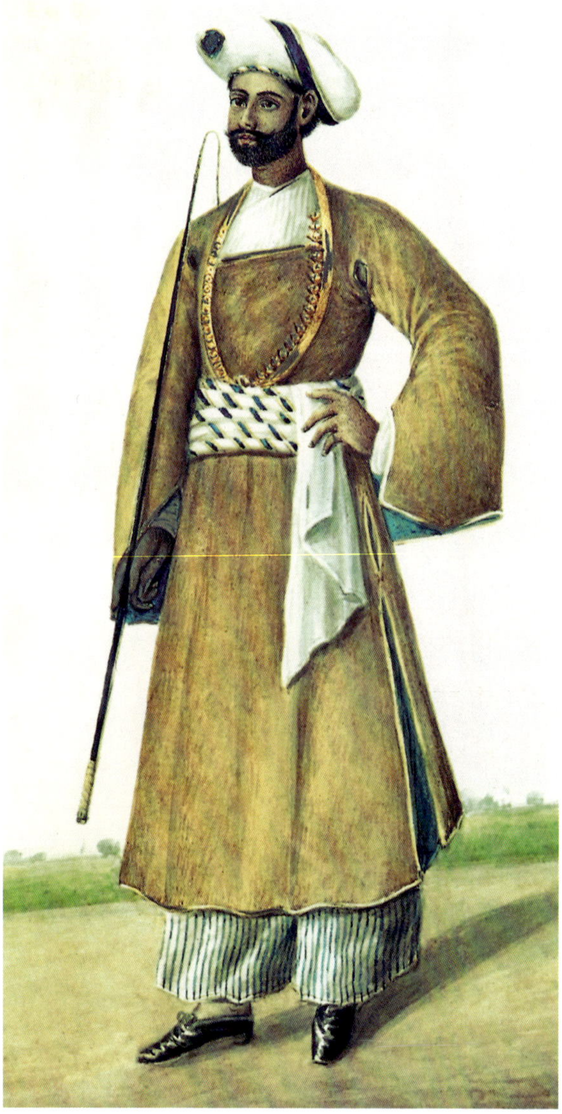

A Coachman.
Watercolour by Sheikh Muhammad Amir of Karaya, Calcutta, c. 1830

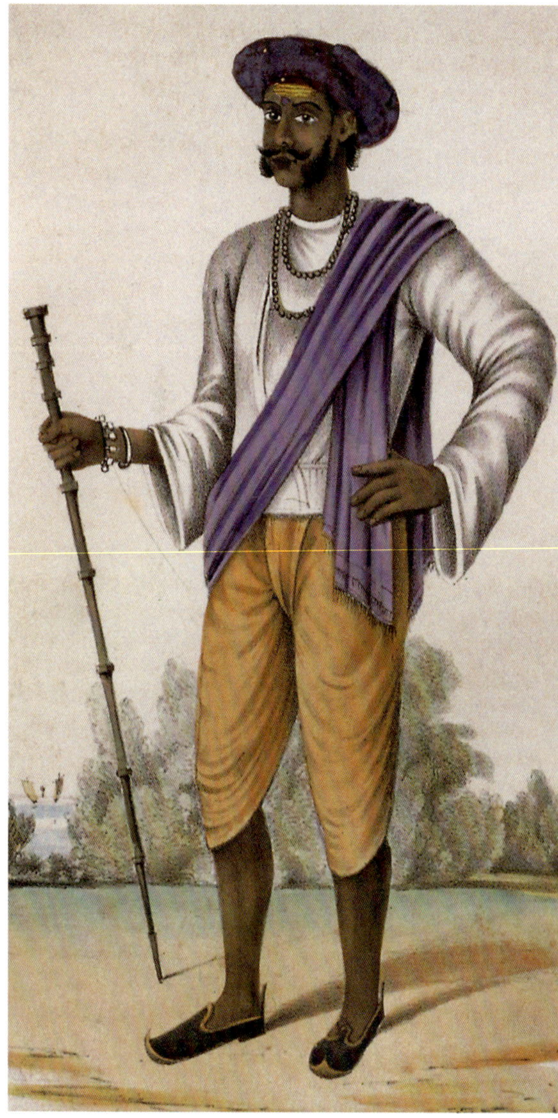

Durwan.
Coloured lithograph after a drawing by Fanny Parks, 1850.

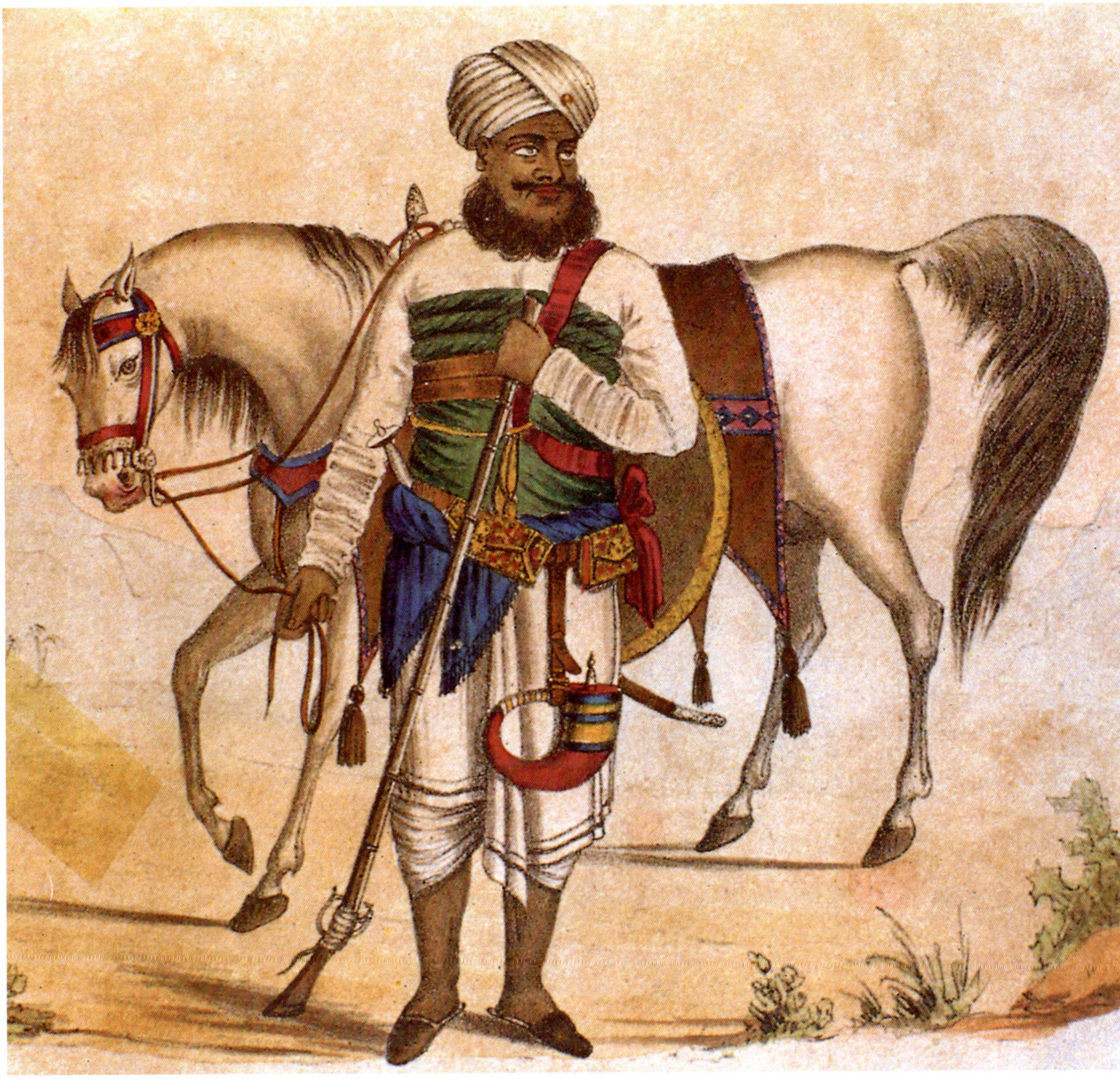

A Mercenary Soldier in Cutch.
Lithograph after a drawing by
Marianne Postans, 1839.

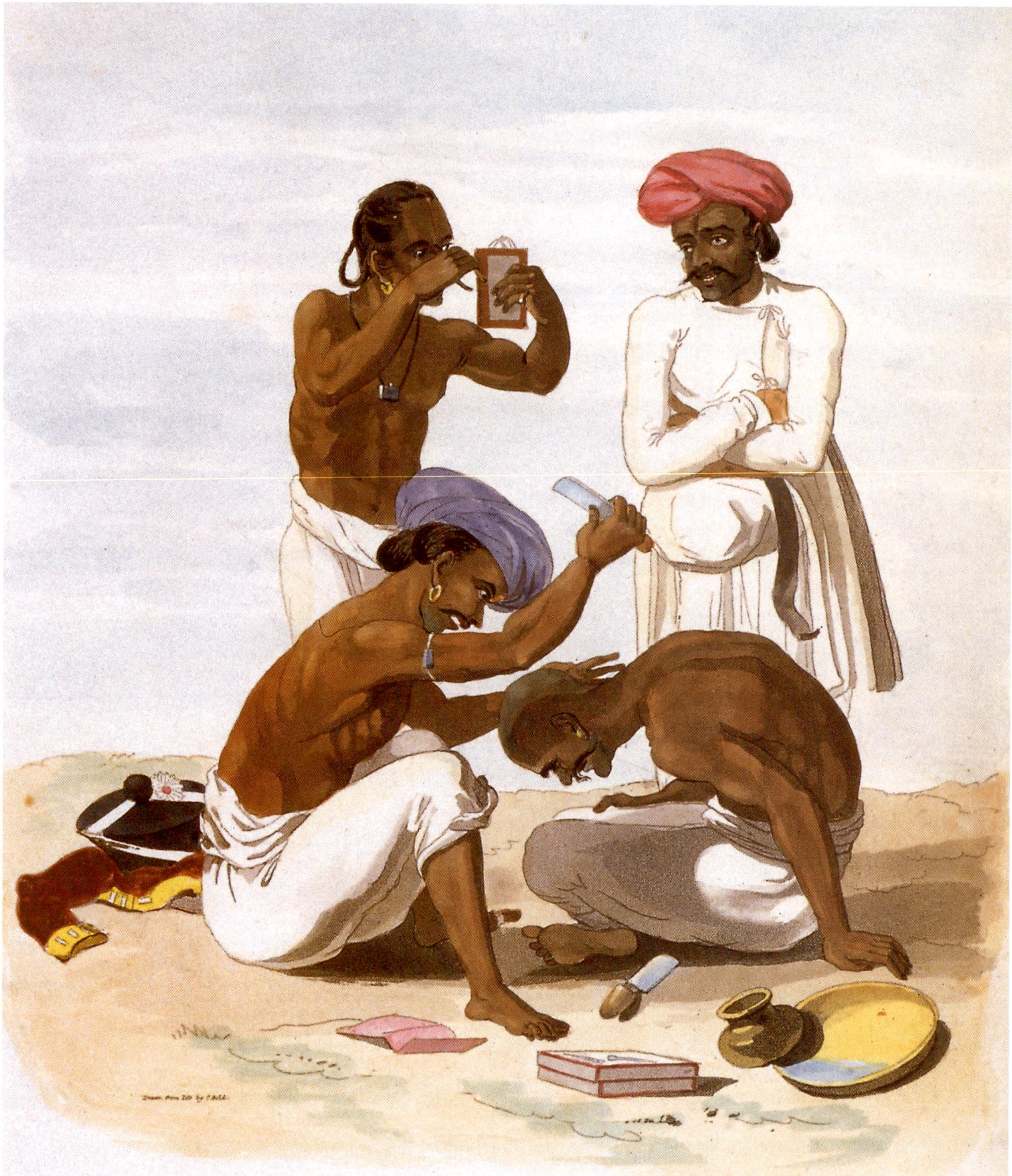

Barbers.
Hand-coloured aquatint engraving after a drawing by Captain Charles Gold, 1806.

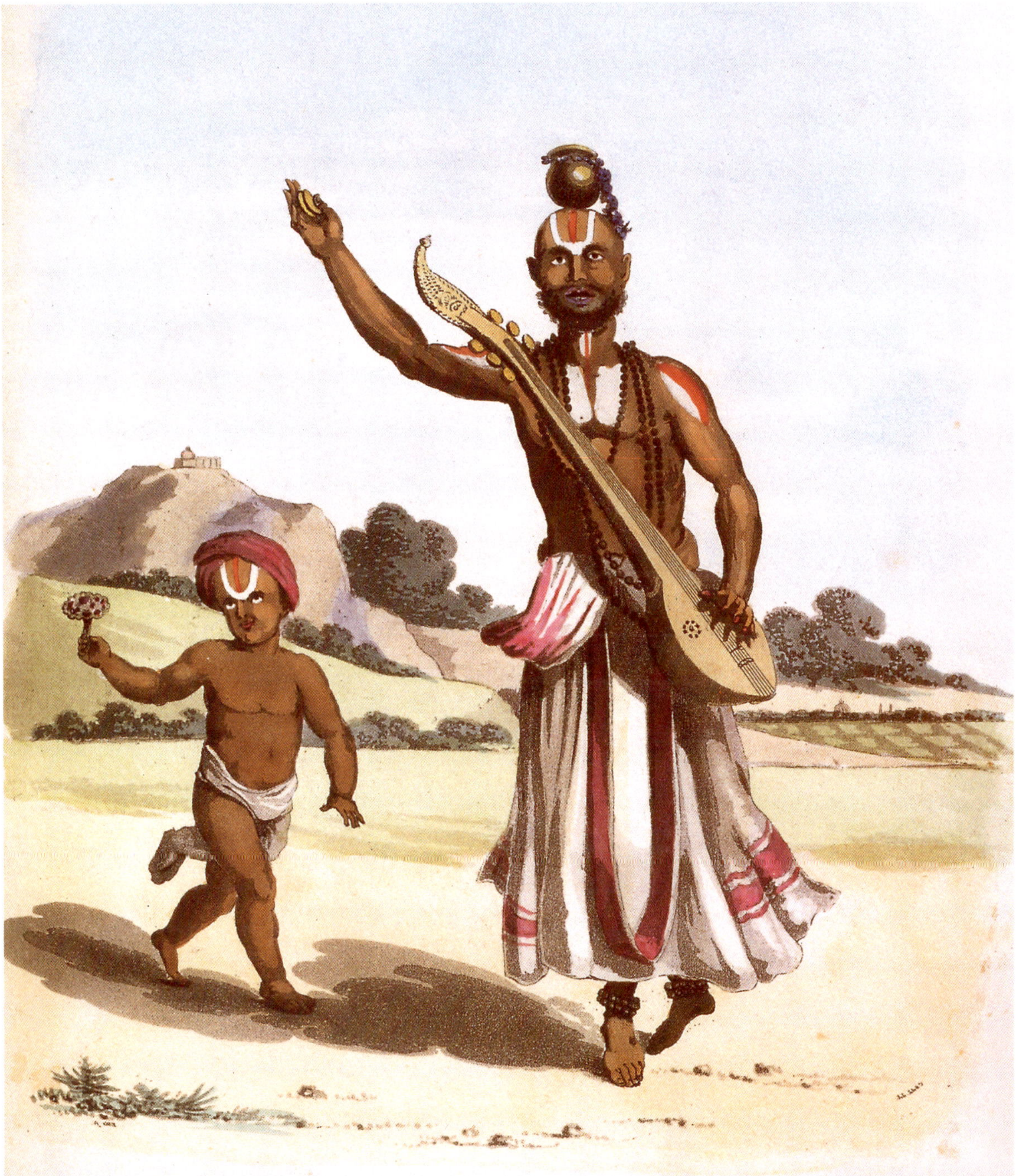

A Satadevan accompanied by his son dancing.
Hand-coloured aquatint engraving after a drawing by Captain Charles Gold.

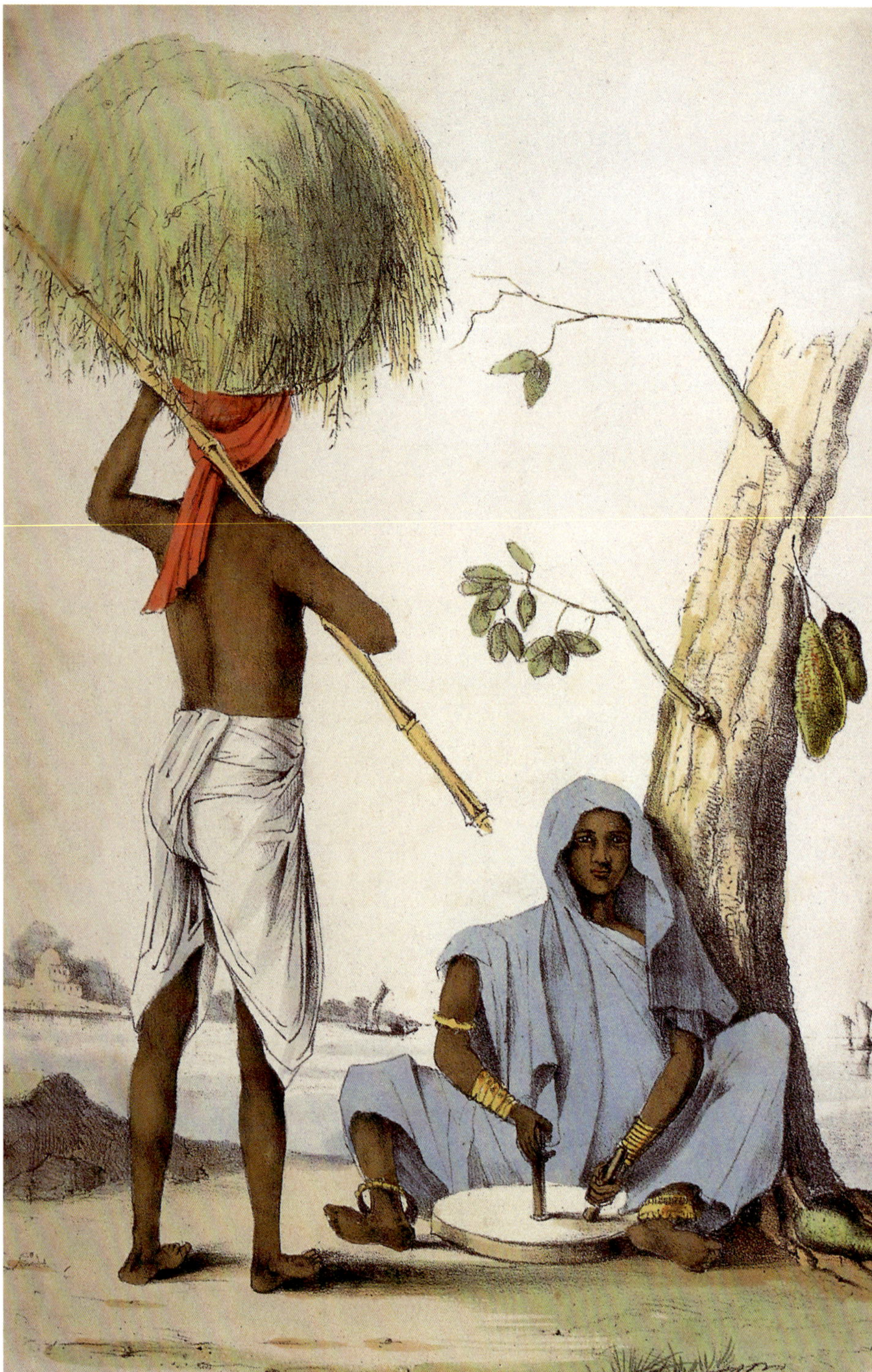

A Grasscutter.
Coloured lithograph after a drawing
by Fanny Parks, 1850.

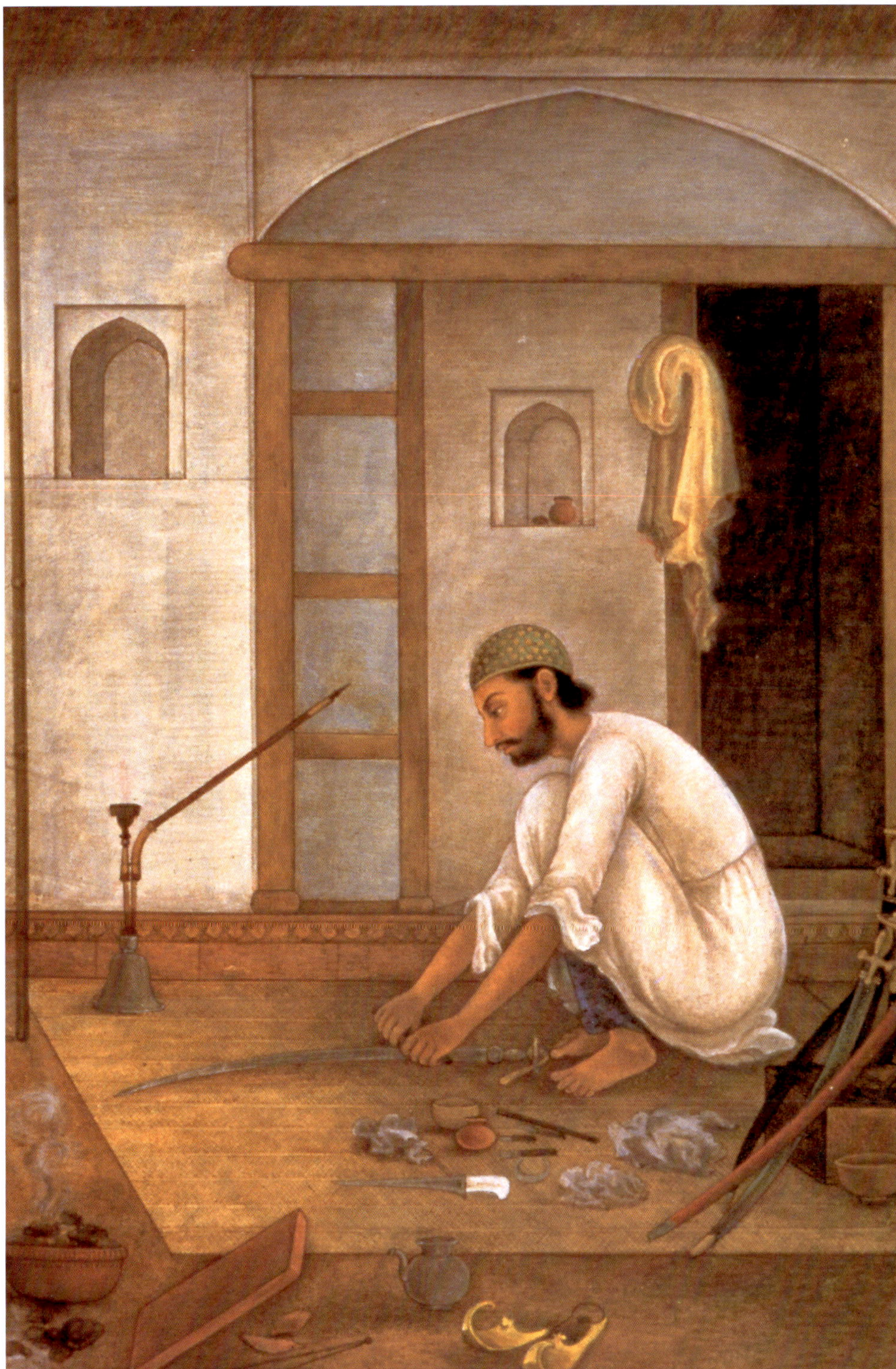

Sword maker.
Watercolour by a Delhi artist from the Skinner's Album, 'Tasrih-al-Aqwam,'1825.

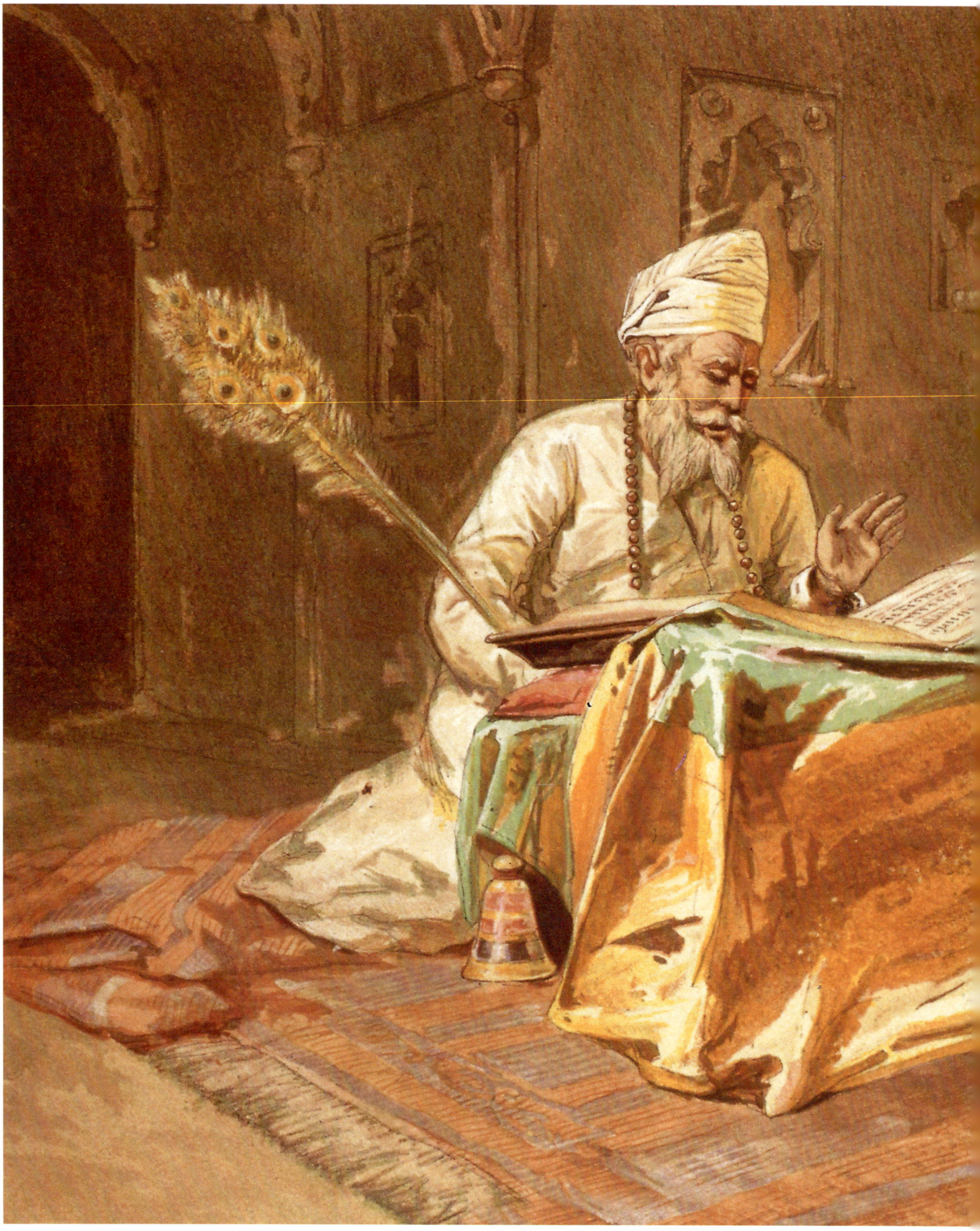

A Sikh Priest reading the Granth Sahib. Chromolithograph after a drawing by William Simpson, c. 1860.

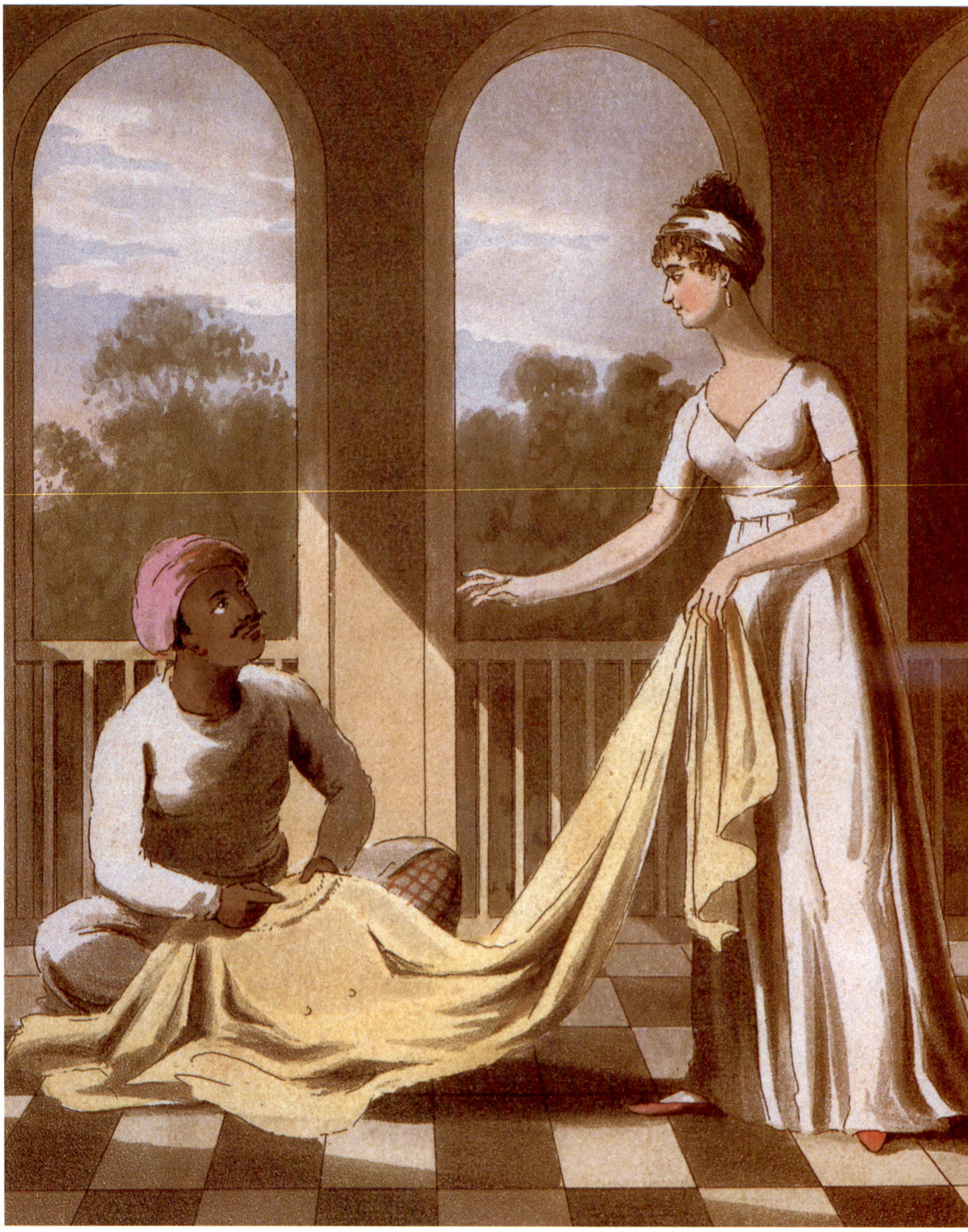

An European Lady giving Instructions to her Durzee, or Native Tailor.
Hand-coloured aquatint engraving after a drawing by Sir Charles Doyly, 1813.

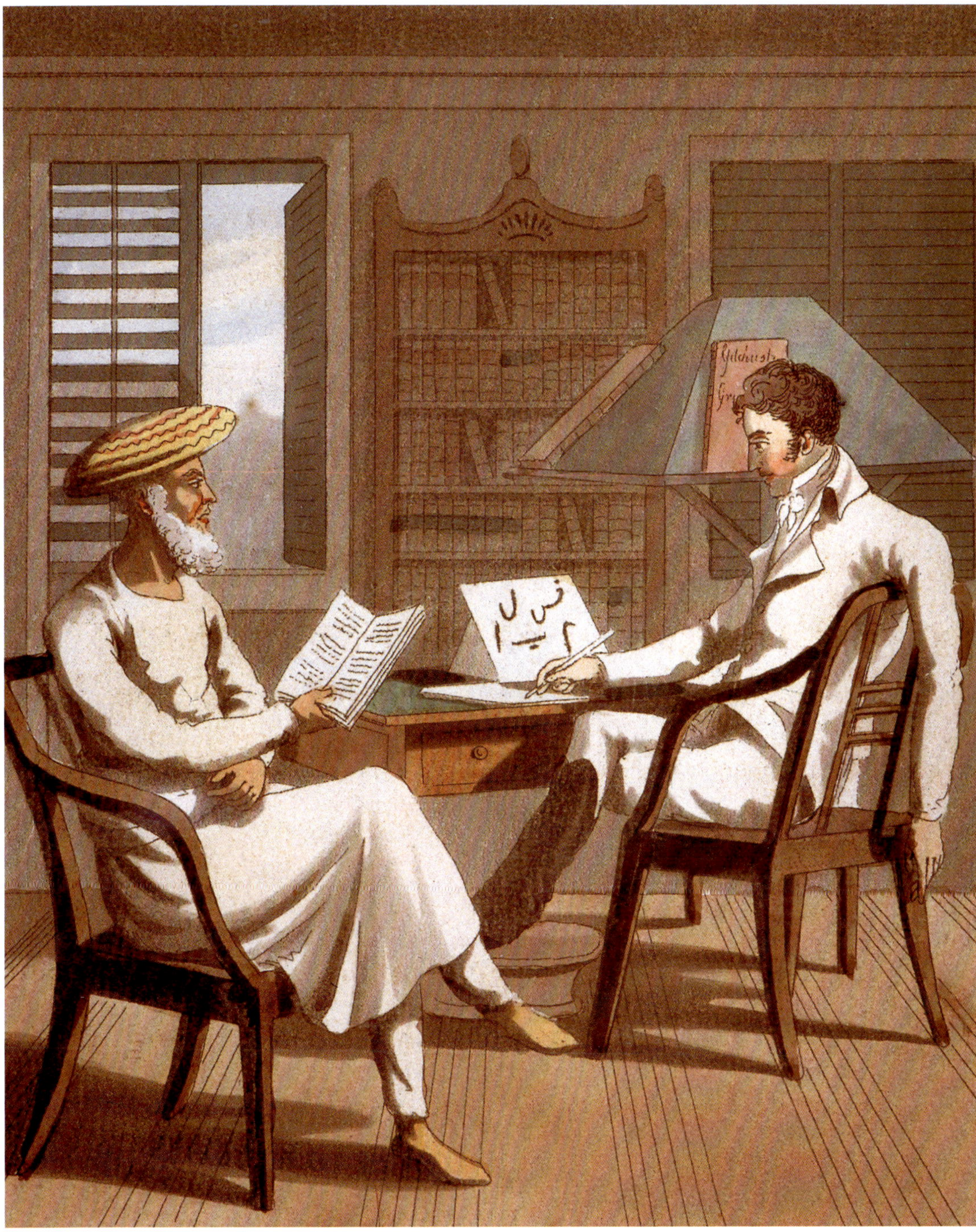

An European Gentleman with his Moonshee or Native professor of Languages.
Hand-coloured aquatint engraving after a drawing by Sir Charles Doyly, 1813.

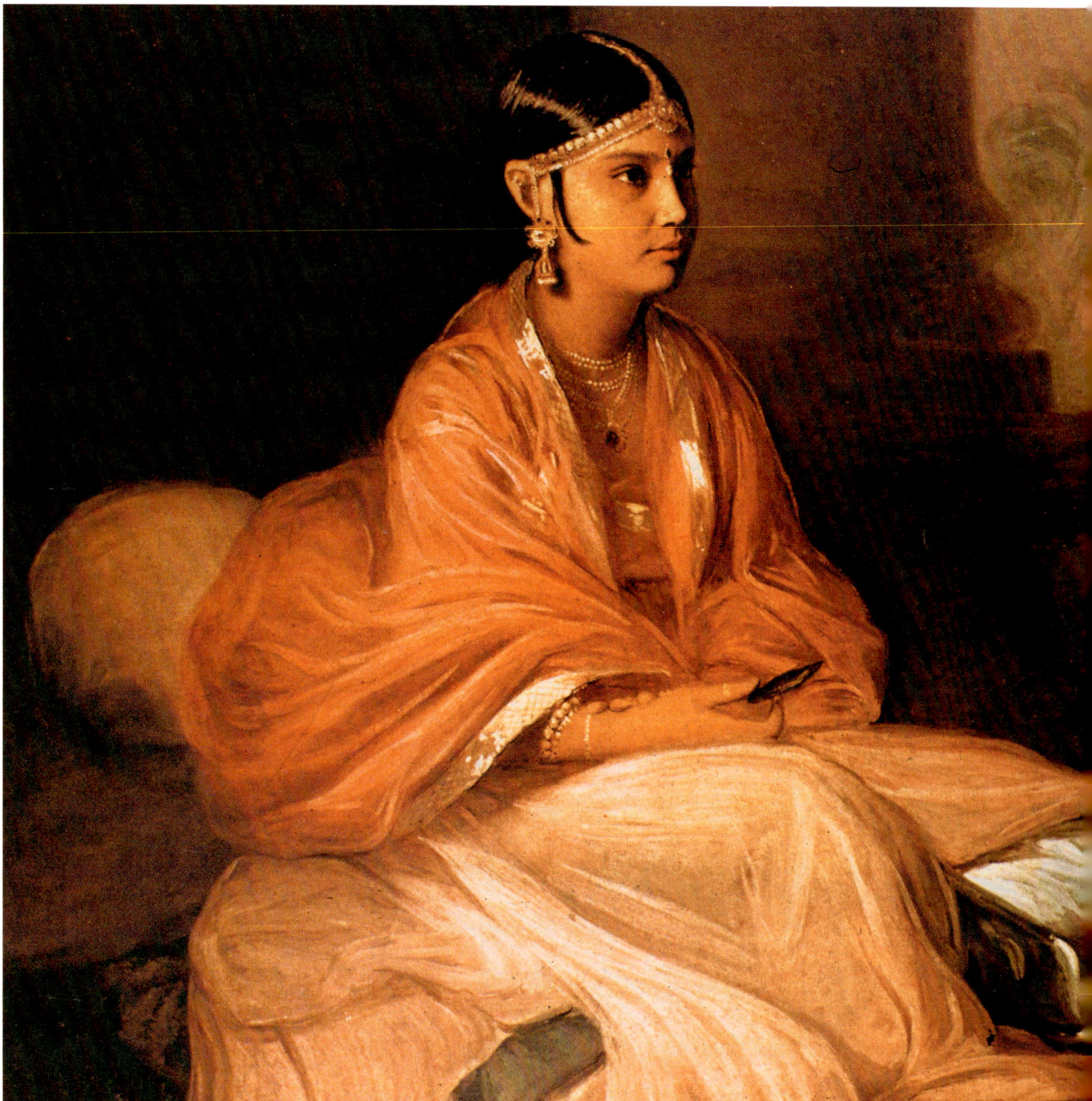

Portrayal of Indian Women

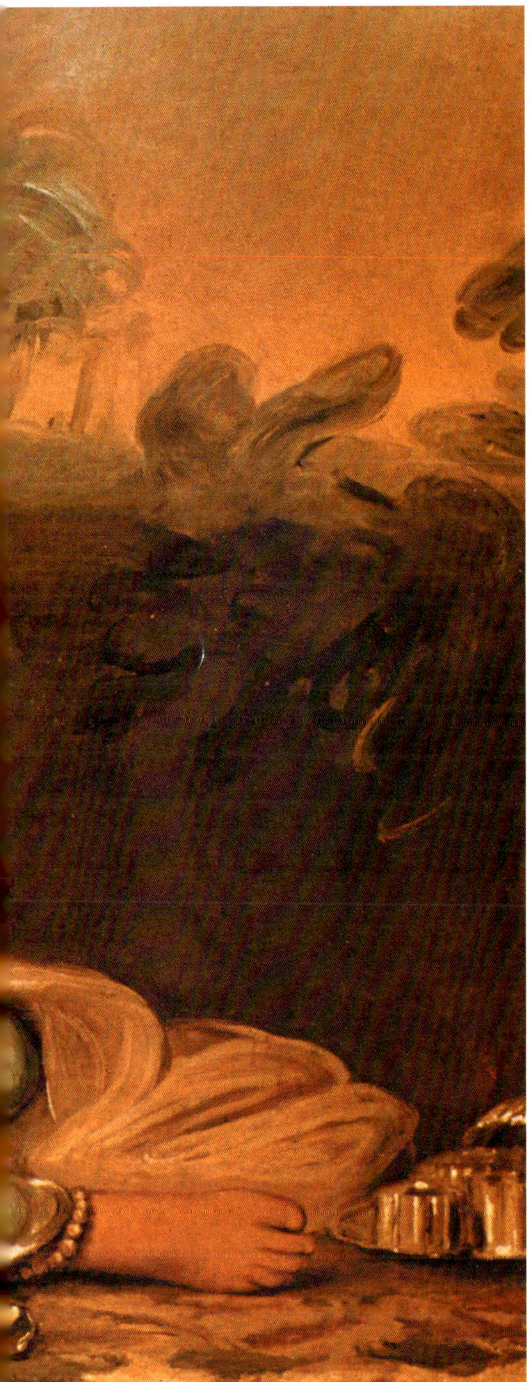

INDIAN WOMEN have always been considered among the most beautiful in the world and their charms have been celebrated by poets and artists throughout the ages. Until the middle of the 18th century there was no visual record of Indian people based on first-hand observations. British artists began arriving in India from the 1760s. Lured by the prospect of fame and fortune most of them concentrated on making portraits of the British elite and native princes, landscape paintings, or pictures of Imperial interest commissioned by the East India Company. However, there were some, both professional and amateur, who applied their talents to depicting the real India with its exotic people, especially the native women. Historian Robert Orme (1753) had already aroused their curiosity with his remarks that "nature seems to have showered beauty on the fairer sex throughout Indostan (sic) with a more lavish hand than in most other countries."

Ladies of the aristocracy in the cities, whether Hindu or Muslim, used to observe purdah. This practice was considered a mark of delicacy and refinement as well as an essential part of a respectable way of life. Hence, there was much curiosity about these ladies and their daily life. The zenana was perceived as a world of mystery and intrigue. The women who came into contact with the English sahibs were the bibis or unofficial wives of British officials, the nautch girls or the female servants. In the countryside, however, both in the plains and the hills, the Europeans saw women young and old out in the open as rural life was generally free from purdah.

Just as landscape painting was influenced by the British concept of 'picturesque,' the Western concept of beauty had its impact in the portrayal of Indian women. William Hodges, the first British professional artist to visit India in 1780, acknowledged that his portrayal of Indian women was based on ideas of classical beauty. He was in raptures after seeing village women at the ghats. He watched them bathing, observing that the younger women in particular delayed and lingered, "sporting and playing like Naiads or Syrens." He remarked that, "To painter's mind, the fine antique figures never fail to present themselves when he observes a beautiful female form ascending these

Indian lady, perhaps *'Jemdanee,'* bibi of William Hickey.
Oil on canvas by Thomas Hickey, Calcutta, 1787.

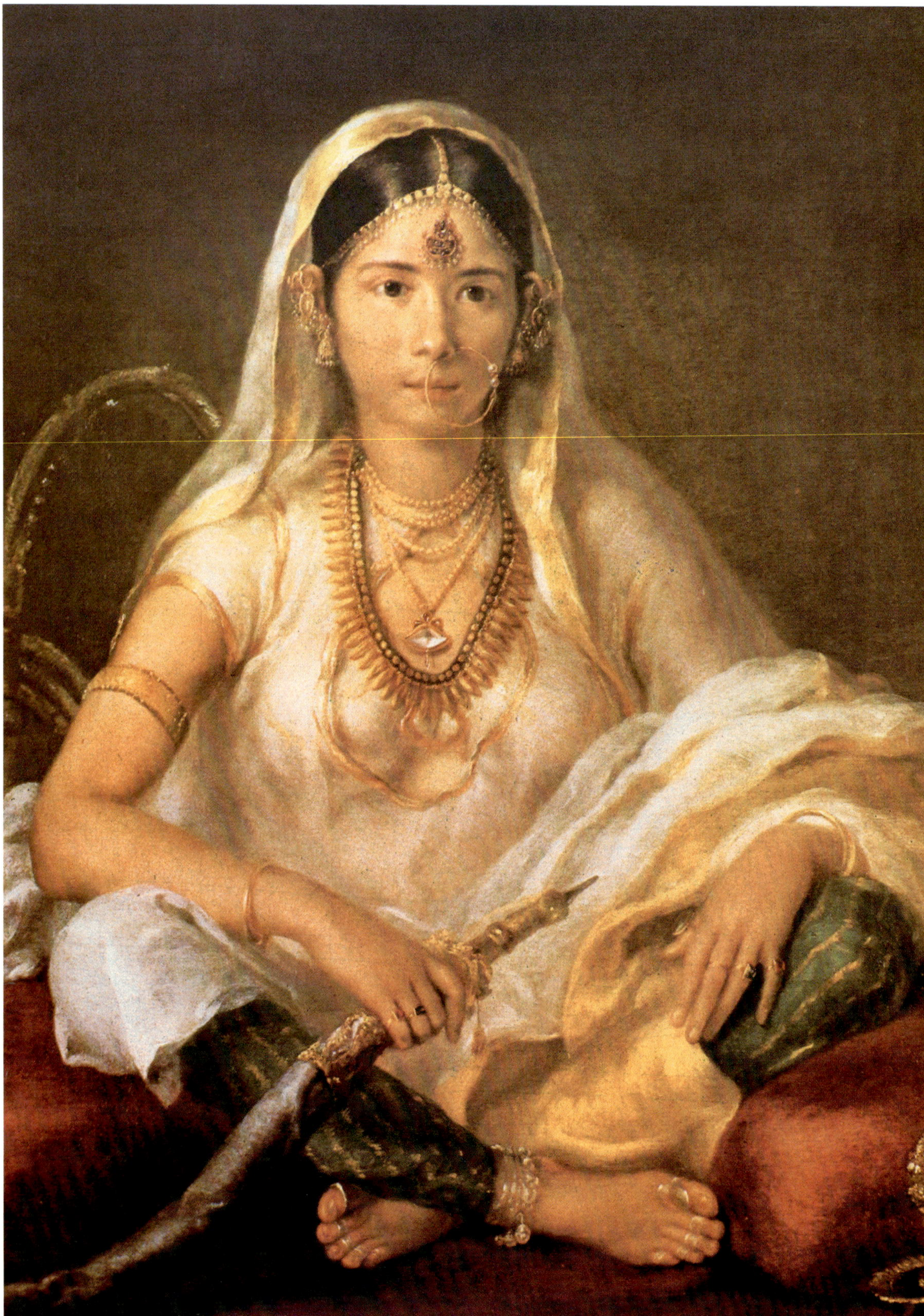

steps from the river in wet drapery, which perfectly displays the whole person, and with vases on their heads, carrying water to the temples."

The delightful sight of women at the river ghats inspired many a Company official and soldier to record his impressions in diaries and journals. Lieutenant Thomas Bacon was captivated by the grace and charm of women at the ghats of the Ganges and noted that they would make any Englishwoman envious. Bishop Reginald Heber of Calcutta (1823–26) was not immune to feminine charms and has made many references to pretty young women in his journal *Narrative of a Journey*. Heber was also greatly attracted by their skin colour and pointed out that "the deep bronze tint was more naturally agreeable to the human eyes than the fair skins of Europe."

There are a few perceptive portraits of Sahibs' bibis by some eminent British professional artists of the period like George Beechy, Tilly Kettle, Francesco Renaldi, Charles Smith and Thomas Hickey. An outstanding painting of an Indian lady of royalty was made by George Beechy who was the court painter of the Nawab of Oudh. It was said to be a likeness of one of the begums of Oudh but is captioned as 'Hinda,' a common Indian name. It was believed that the Nawab had permitted the artist access to his zenana for the purpose of painting the portrait of a royal favourite.

It is observed that British reactions to the physical appearance of native women were influenced by their general attitude to feminine beauty and also by their association with a particular region of the country. Kashmiri women figure in quite a few accounts and are extolled for their charm and beauty. James Forbes, a noted Company official (1965–84) in his *Oriental Memoirs* describes a noble lady he met at Surat as "one of the greatest beauties he ever beheld." Richard Burton, the famous scholar pays high compliments in colourful language to Sindhi women while Marianne Postans, wife of a Company official, eloquently describes the remarkable beauty of Kutch ladies. About Bengali women, Margaret M. Urquhart (1927) in her book *Women of Bengal* stated that "in figure she stands comparison with the finest races of the world." Nagar women of Gujarat are praised for their grace and charm and particularly their dark eyes "in whose depth glows a spark of passion around which humours and laughter play." Maratha ladies, especially of the aristocracy, are portrayed as singularly charming and credited with intelligence and refined manners.

Punjabi women have always been considered among the most beautiful in the country. Their romantic image has been captured by some artists who admired their grace, charm, and fair complexion with rosy checks. It was observed that they were particularly fond of jewellery. An Austrian artist Rudoff Swaboda (1859–1914) commissioned by Queen Victoria to make portraits of her Indian subjects showed a young girl of sweeper caste wearing jewellery. The maidens of the Punjab hills were extolled for their attractive, graceful figures and for their sense of humour. No wonder some sahibs took these 'daughters of nature' as their partners and chose to settle down with them in the beautiful environment of the Punjab hills.

Muslim lady seated with a hookah.
Oil on canvas by Francesco Renaldi, Calcutta, 1787.

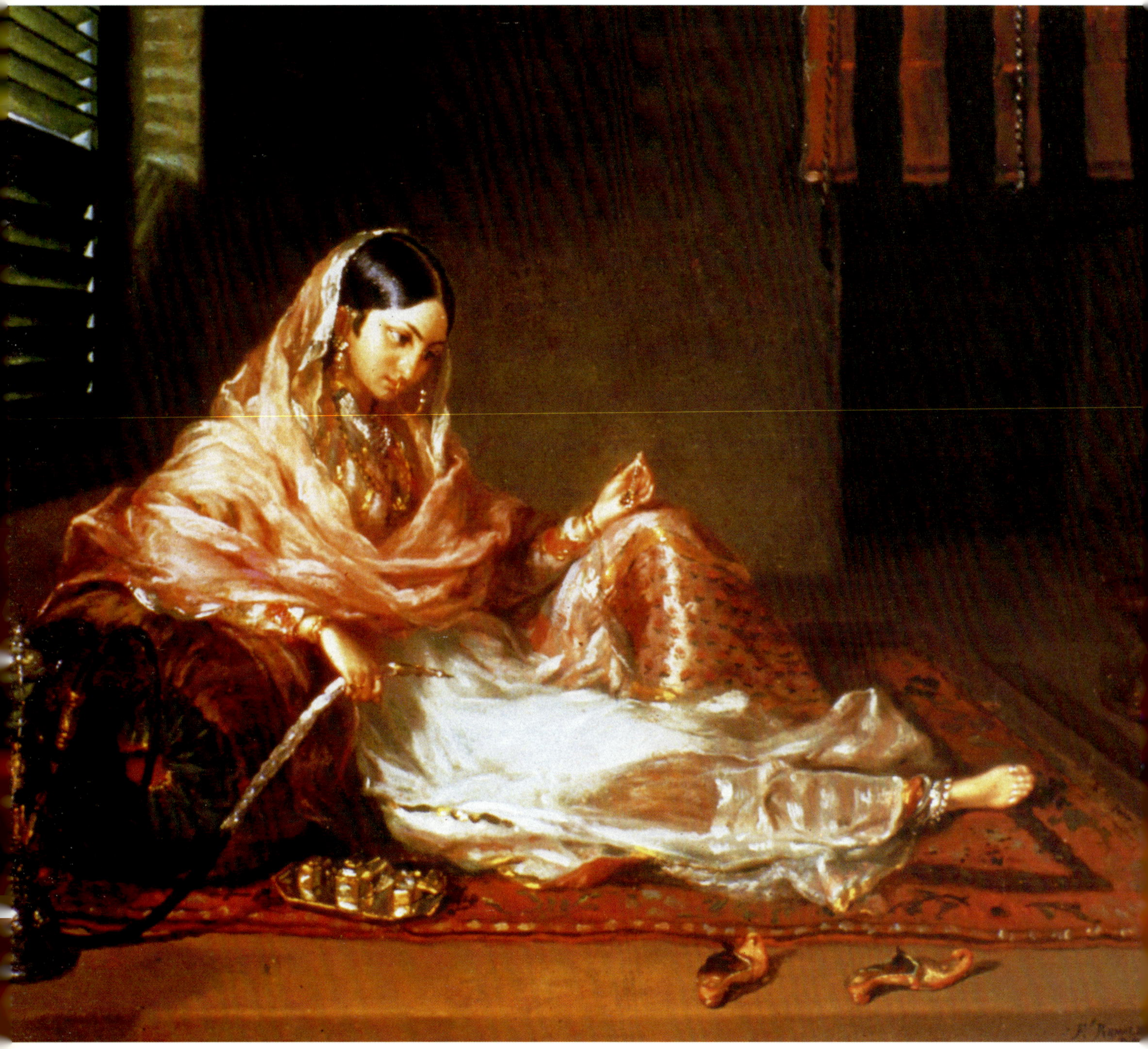

An Indian lady reclining on a rug and a cushion, presumably the bibi of an Englishman living in Dacca. Oil on canvas by Francesco Renaldi, Dacca, 1789.

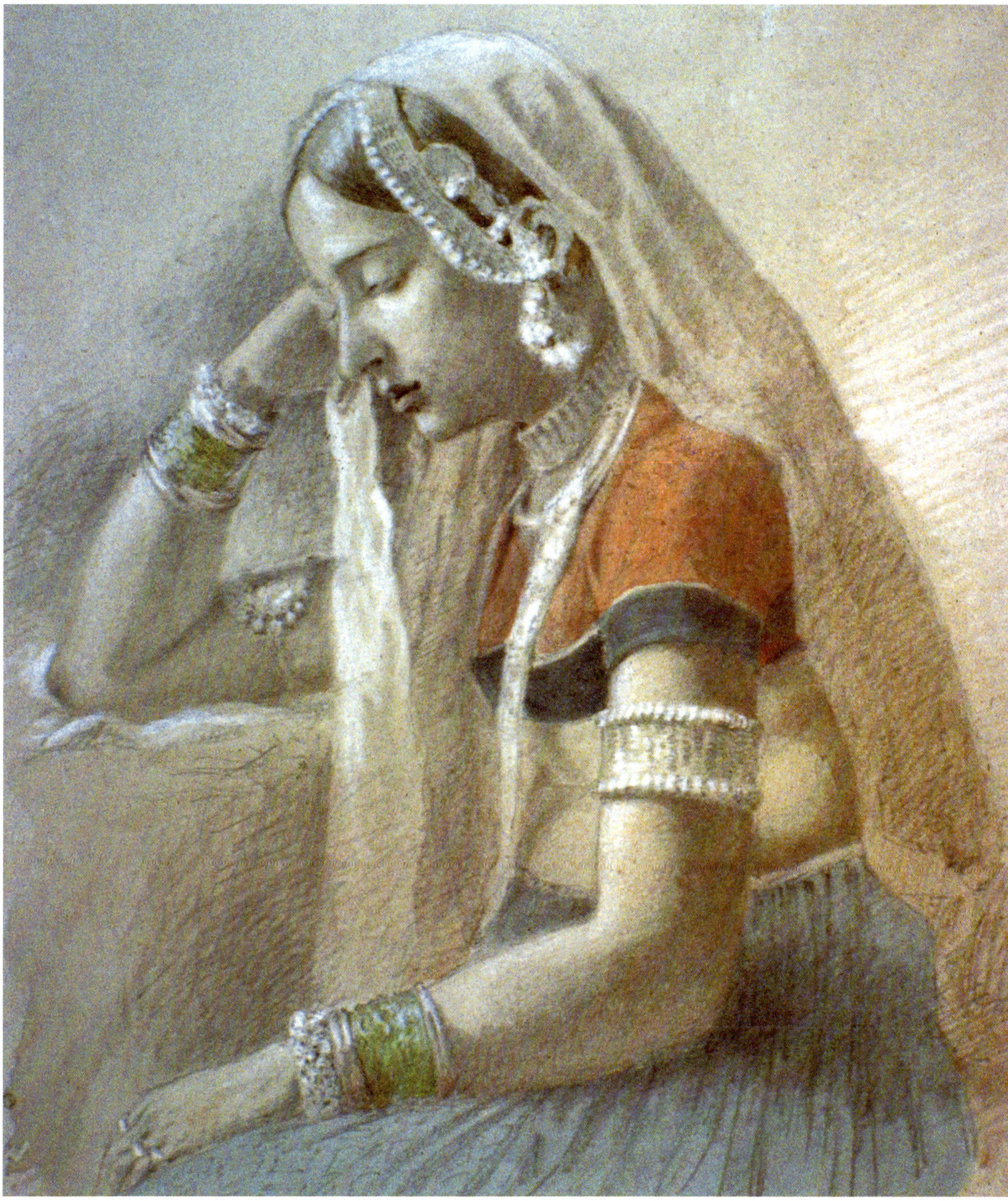

A Bengali lady wearing characteristic jewellery, watercolour by Fredrick W. A. De Fabeck, c.1860.

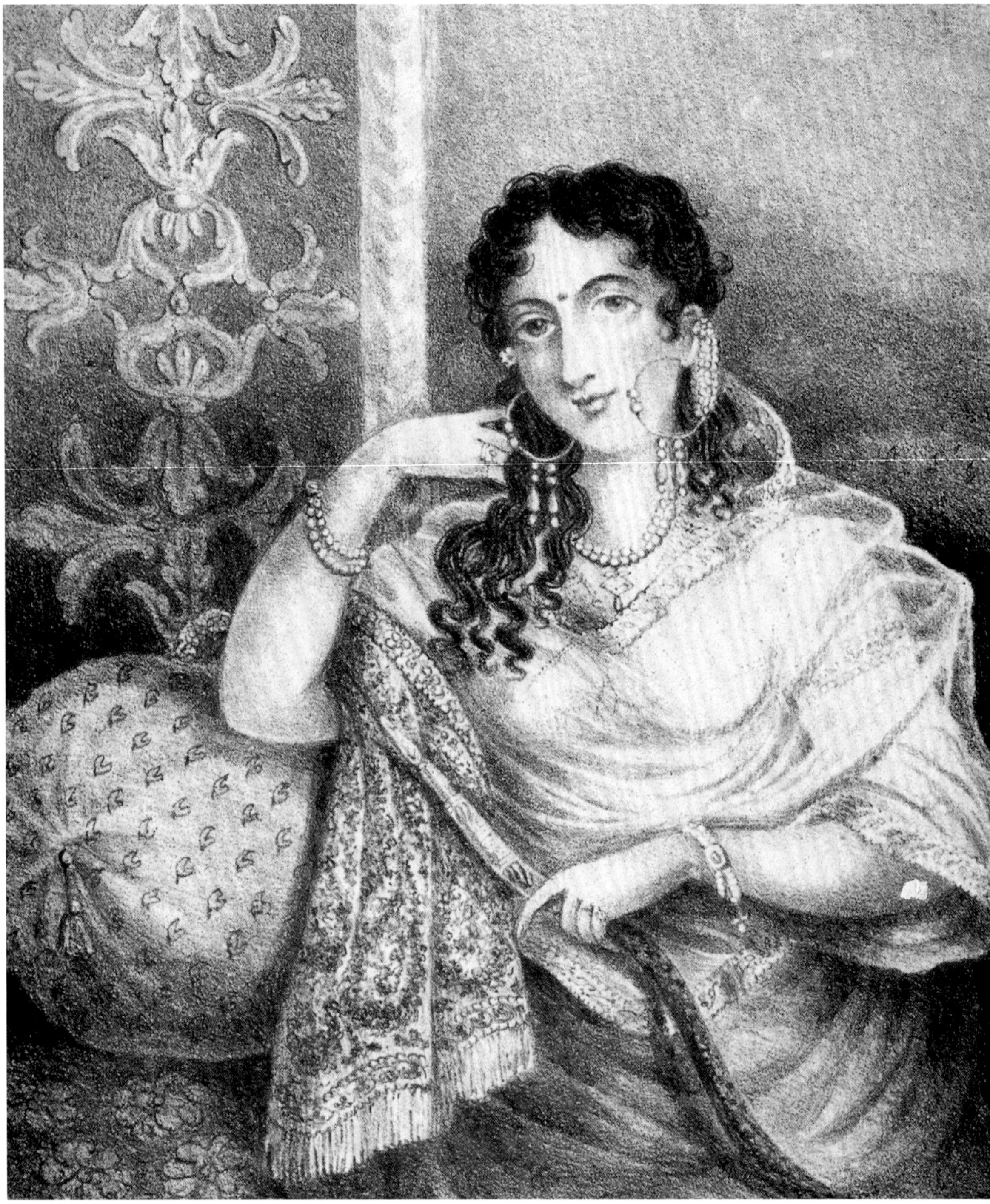

A Hindostany Lady of Rank.
Lithograph after a drawing by
Sir Charles Doyly, c. 1820.

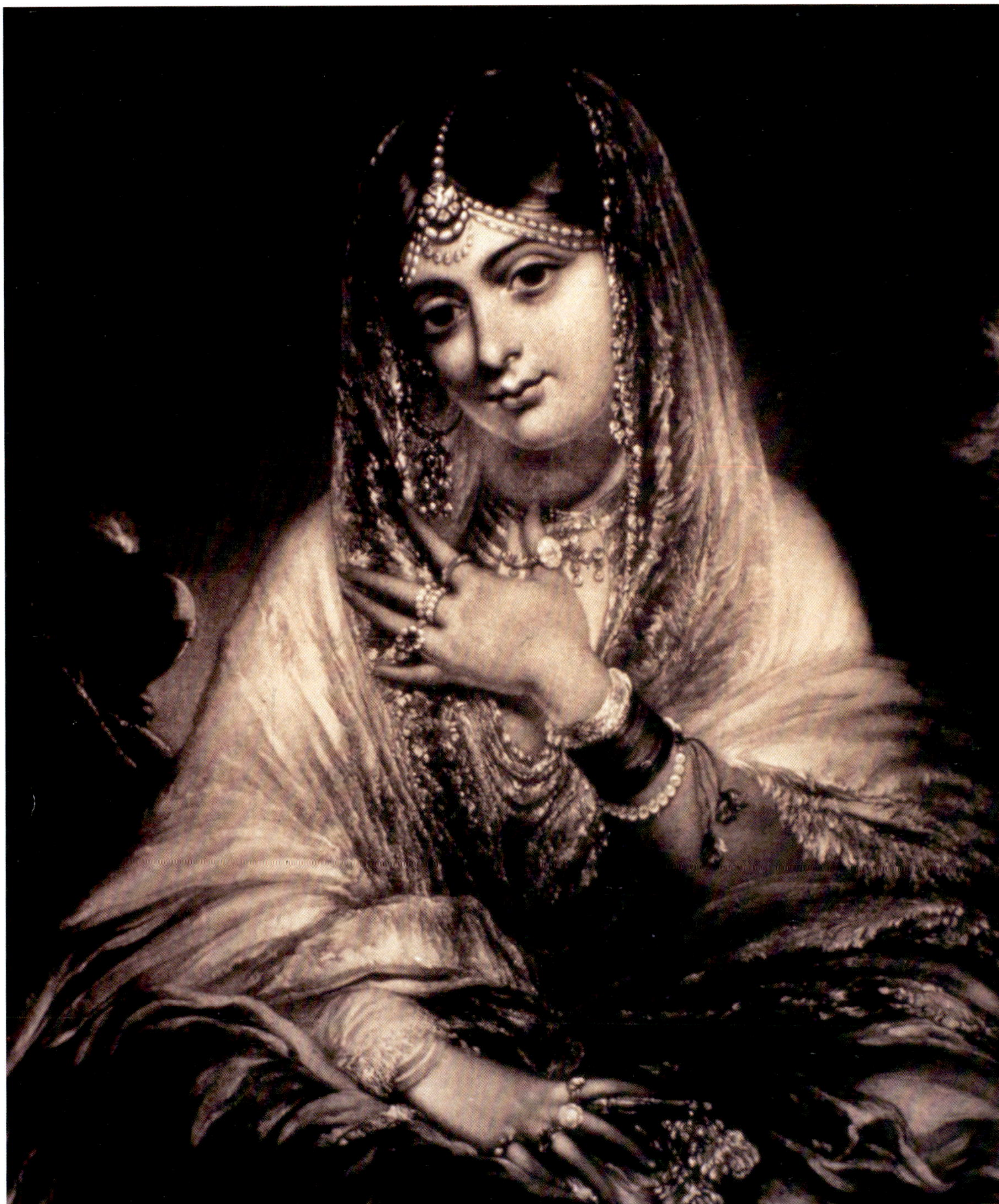

Hinda, a generalised name for an Indian woman, presumably, the favourite wife of the king of Oudh. Reproduction print after an oil painting by George Beechey, c. 1832.

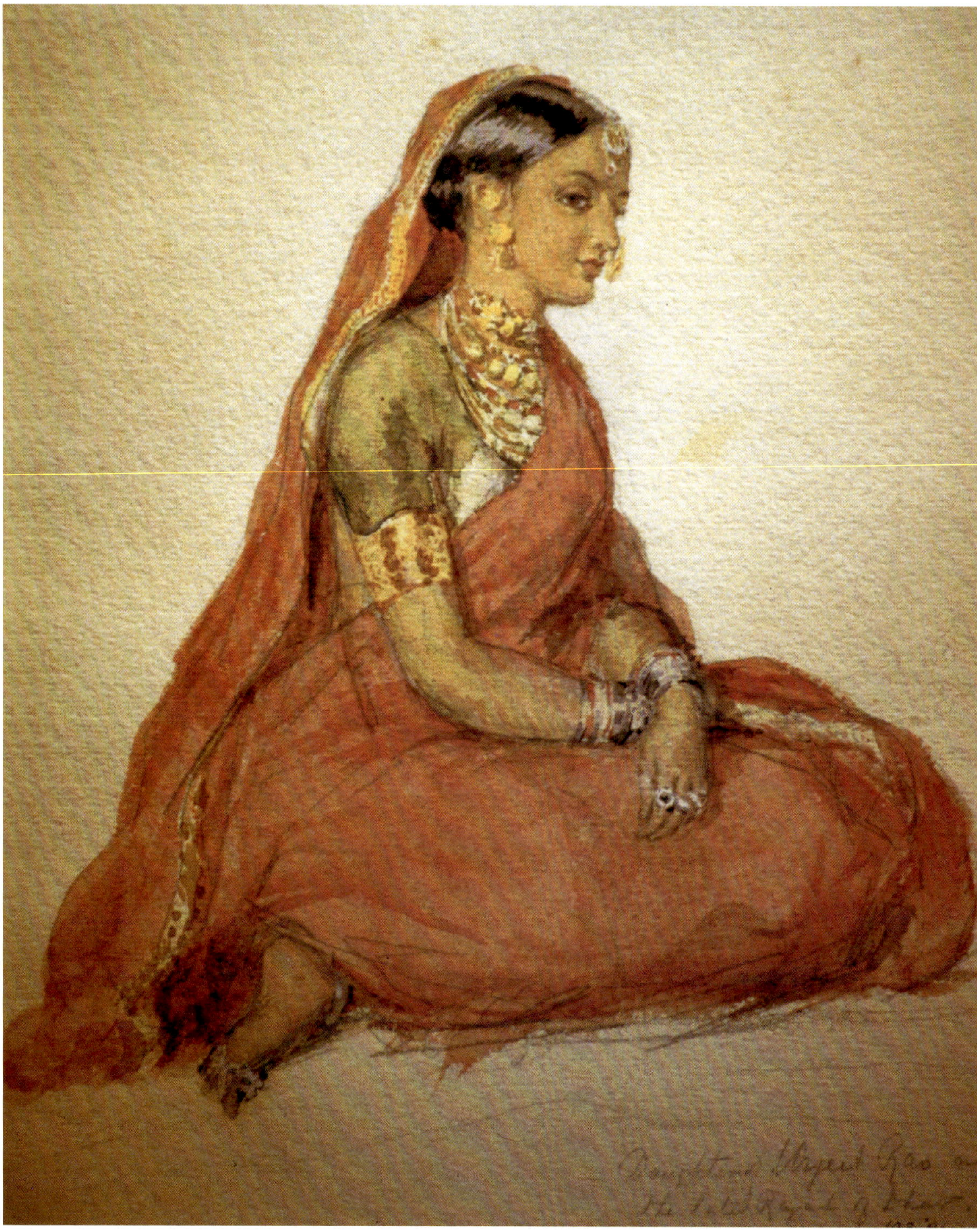

Daughter of Urjit Rao, natural son of Raja of Dhar.
Watercolour by William Carpenter, c. 1850.

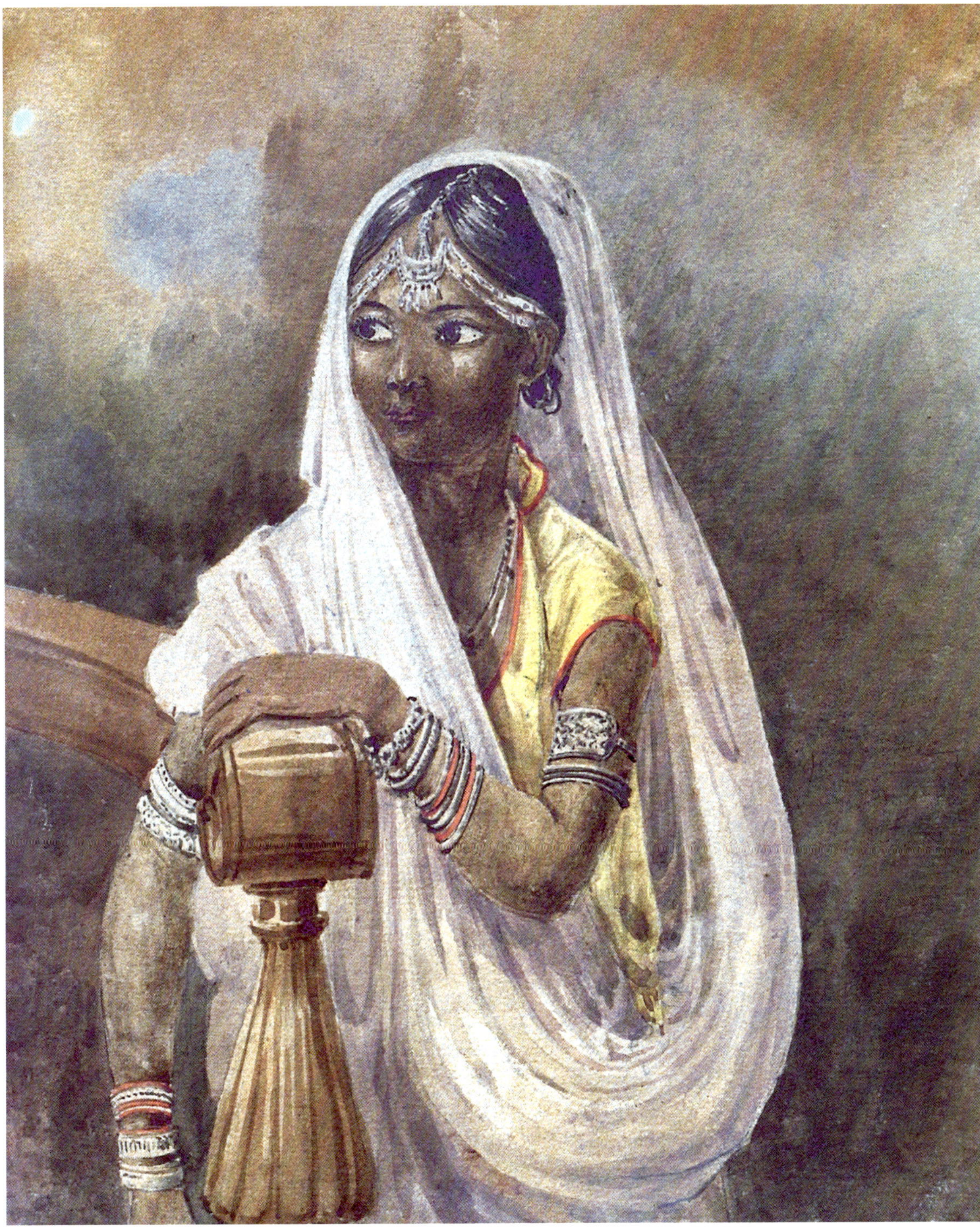

A Native Woman dressed for a Fete.
Watercolour by Emily Eden, c.1840.

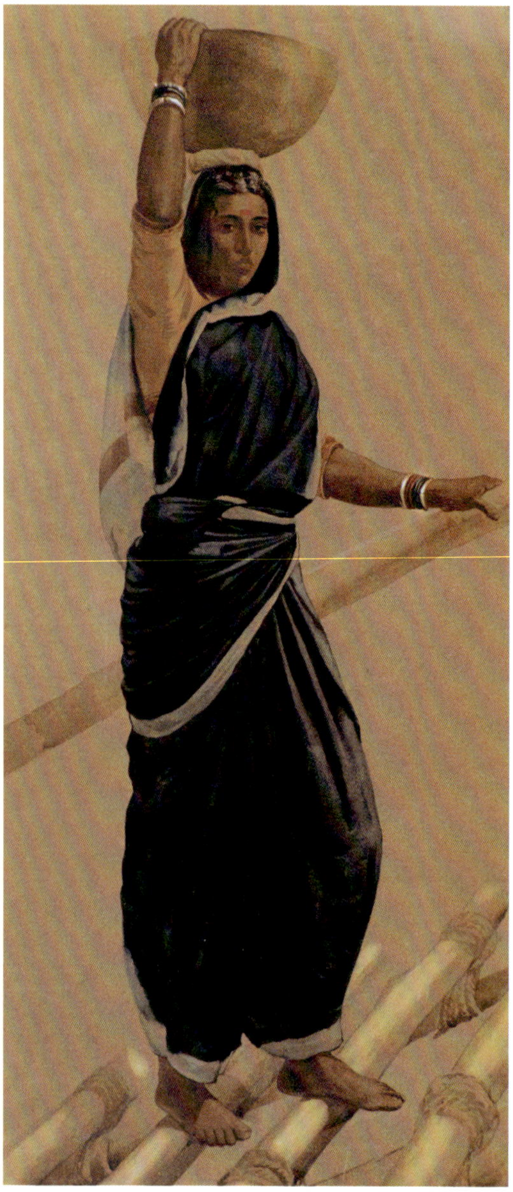

A woman labourer.
Watercolour by John Griffiths,
Bombay, c.1870.

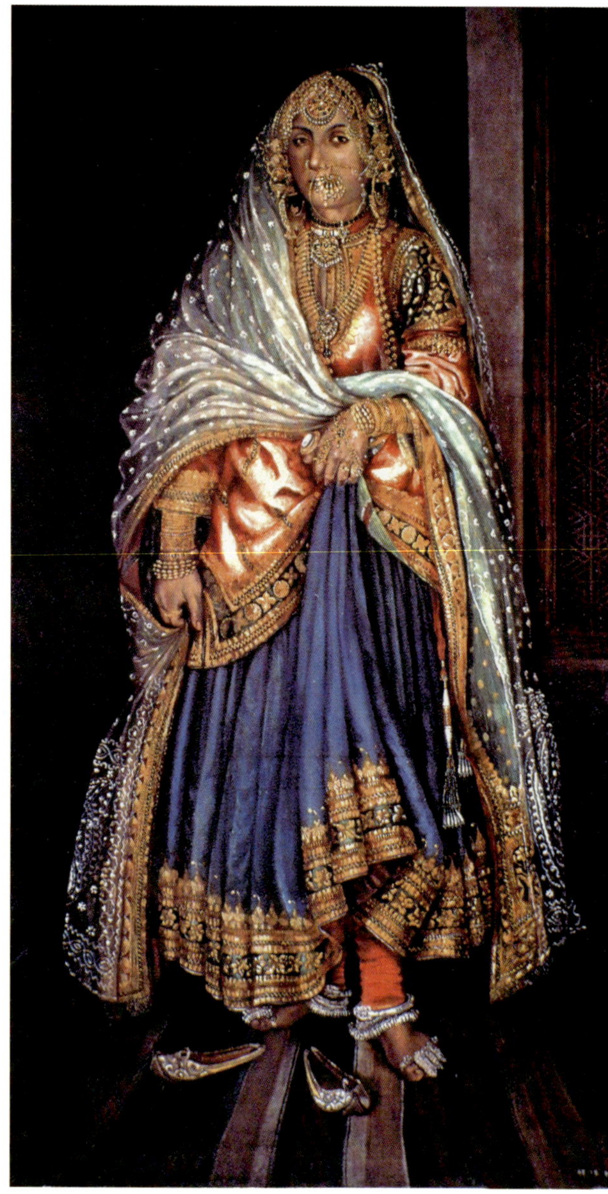

Native lady of Umritsar wearing a full set of Jewellery from head to toe and gold embroidered costume.
Oil on canvas by Van Smith, c.1880.

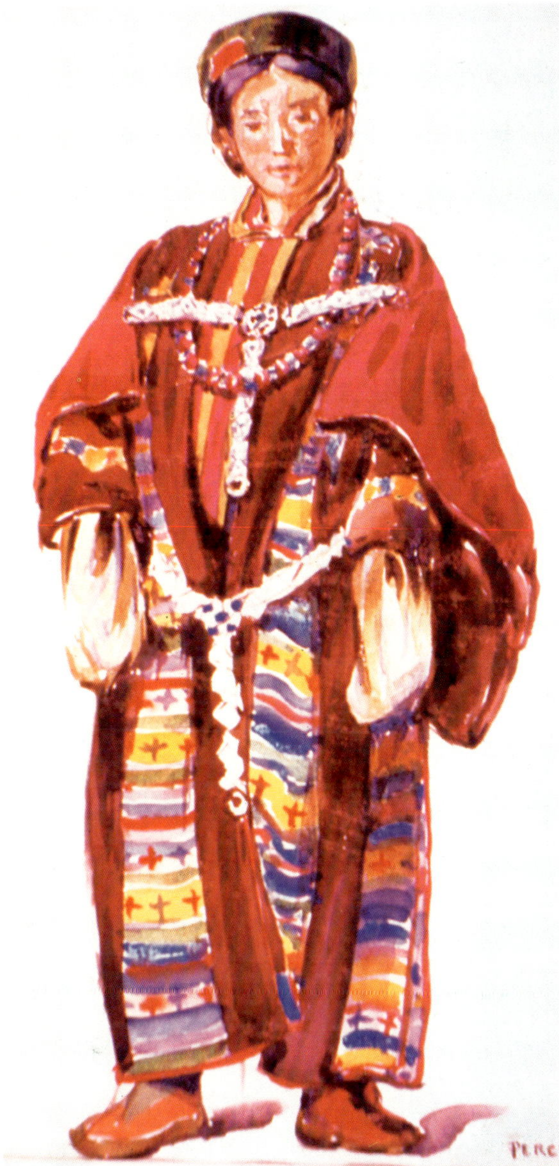

A woman of Chamba in the local costume.
Watercolour by Percy Brown, c.1920

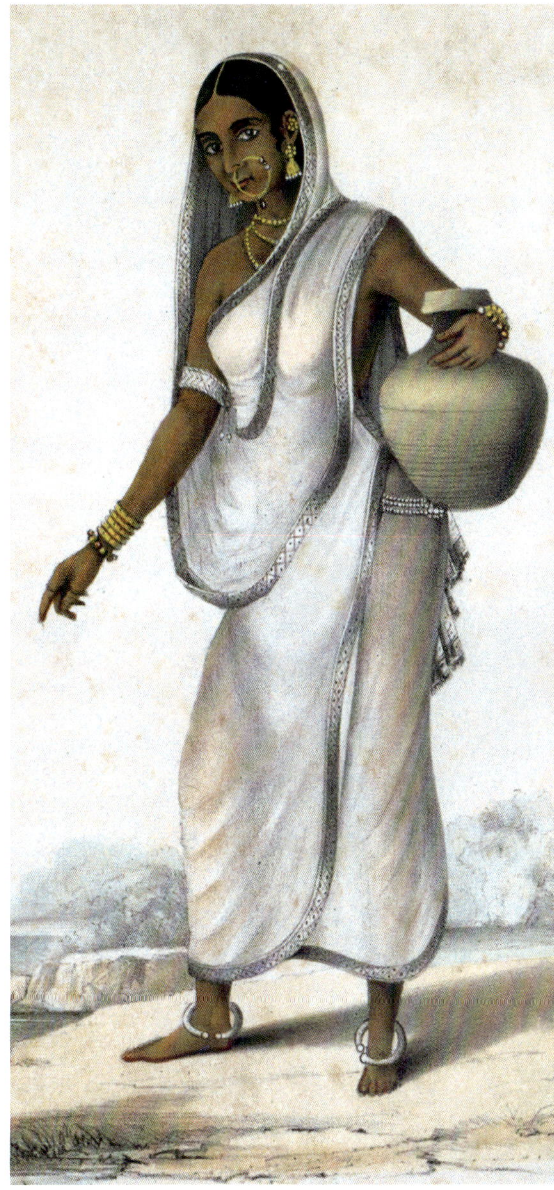

A Bengali woman.
Coloured lithograph after a
drawing by Fanny Parks, c.1850.

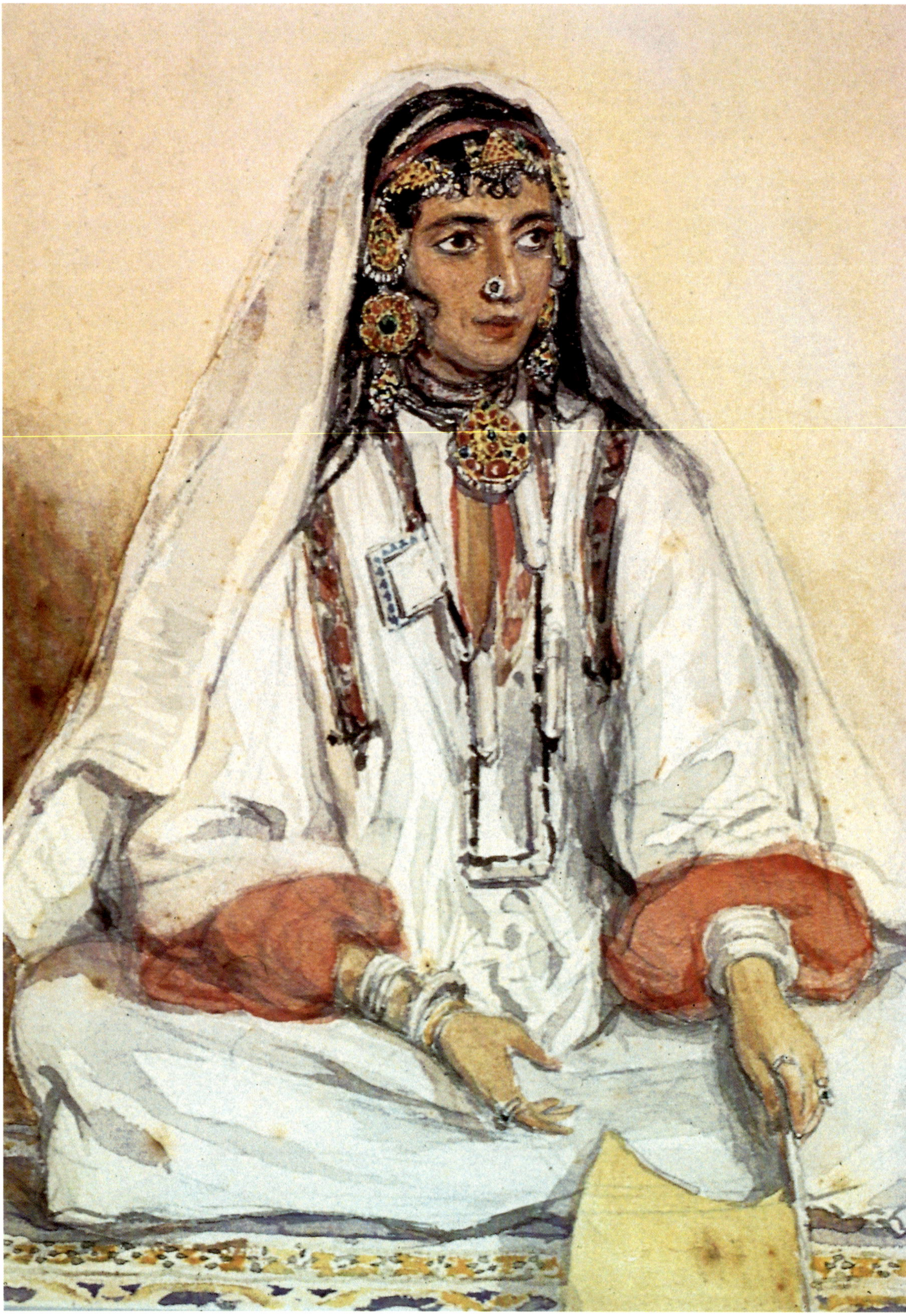

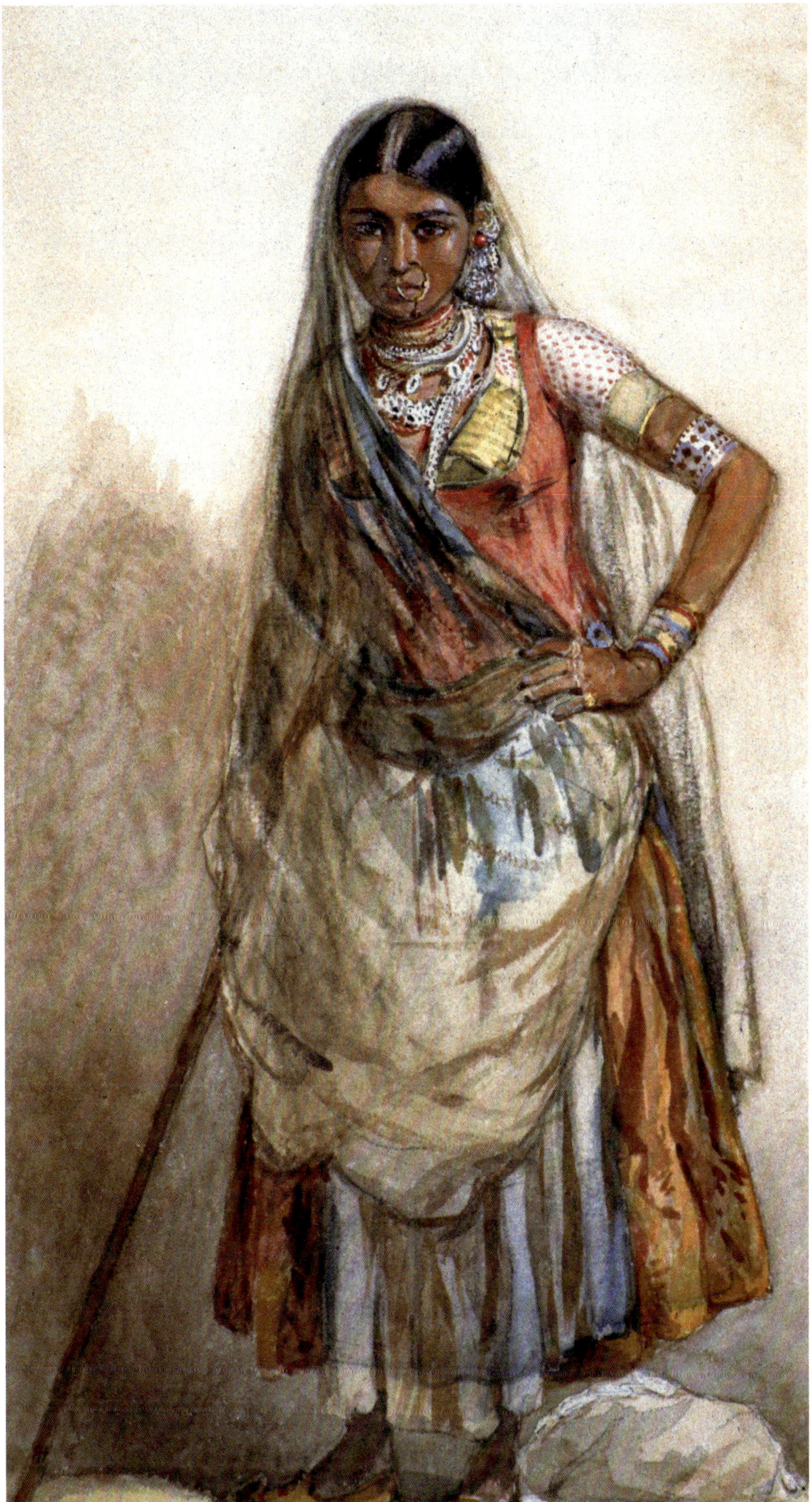

Left: *A Banjaran or Gypsy woman.*
Watercolour by William Carpenter, c. 1850

Facing page: *A Kashmiri Woman wearing gorgeous Jewellery and costume.* Watercolour by William Carpenter, Srinagar, c.1855.

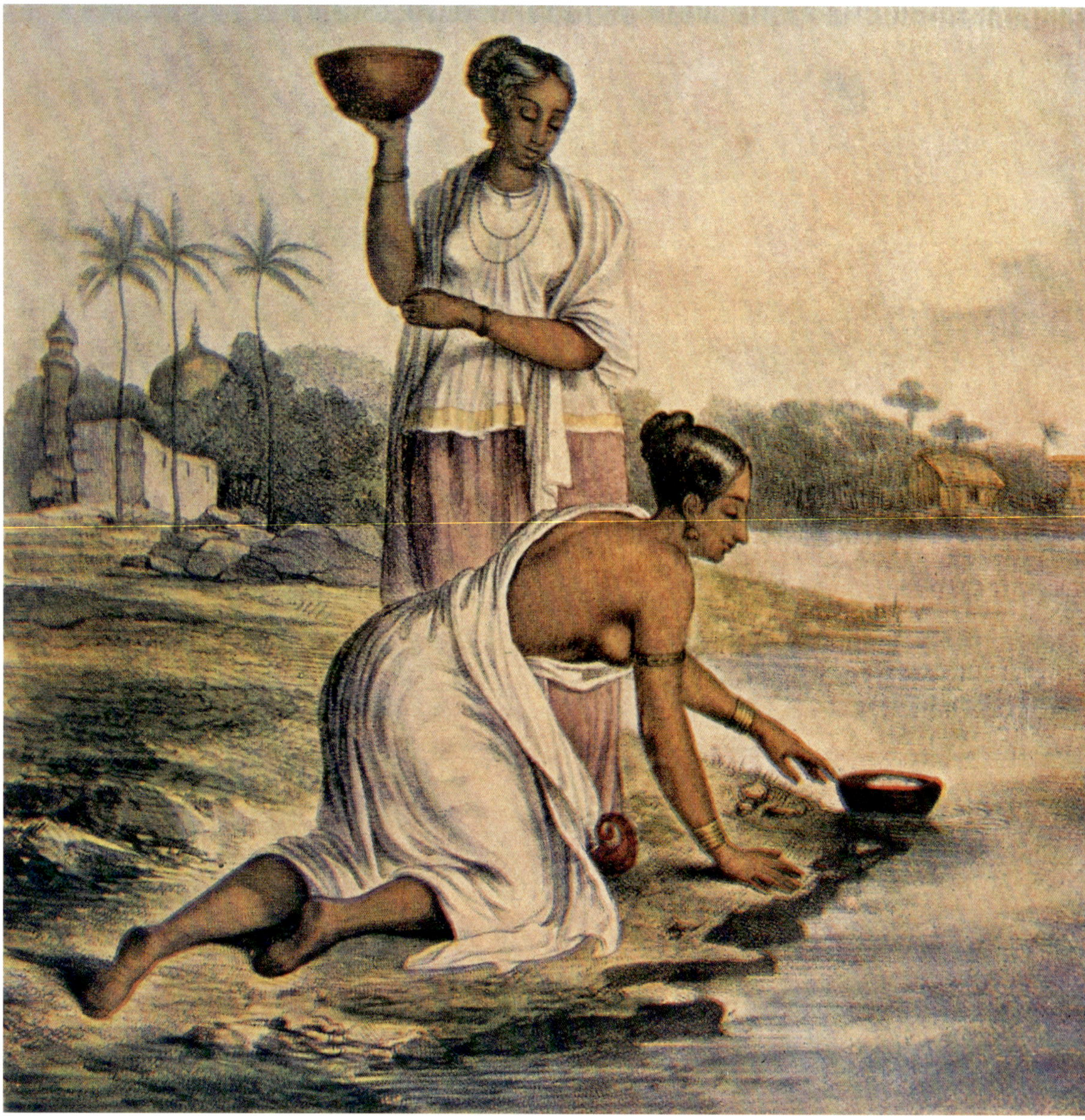

The *Fateeha* or offering to the Ganges. The two women are placing the earthen pan containing rice, ghee, etc., in the river to float in the current.
Coloured lithograph after a drawing by S.C. Belnos, c. 1820.

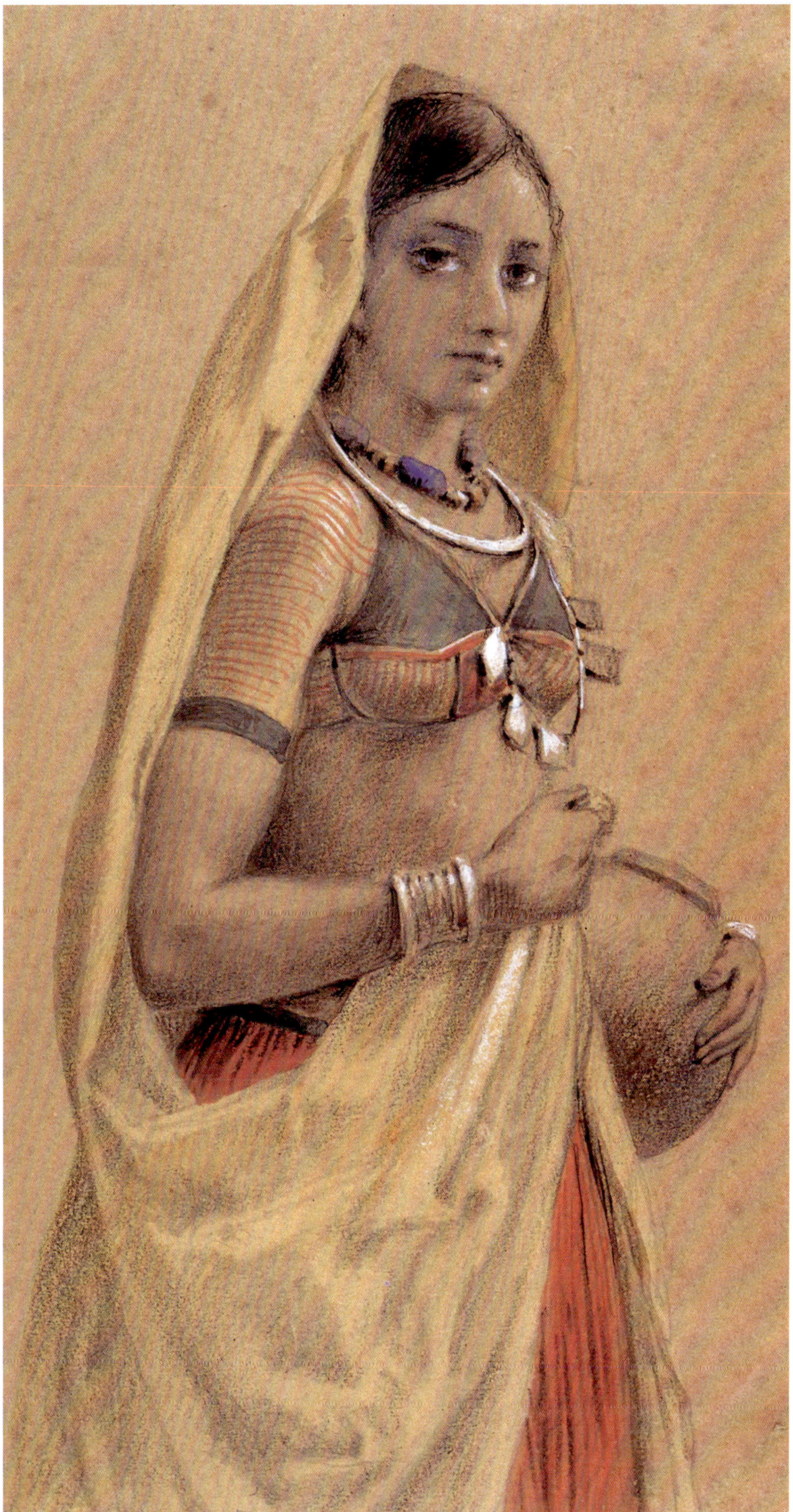

Bengali woman holding a pitcher.
Watercolour by Fredrick W. A De Fabeck, c. 1860

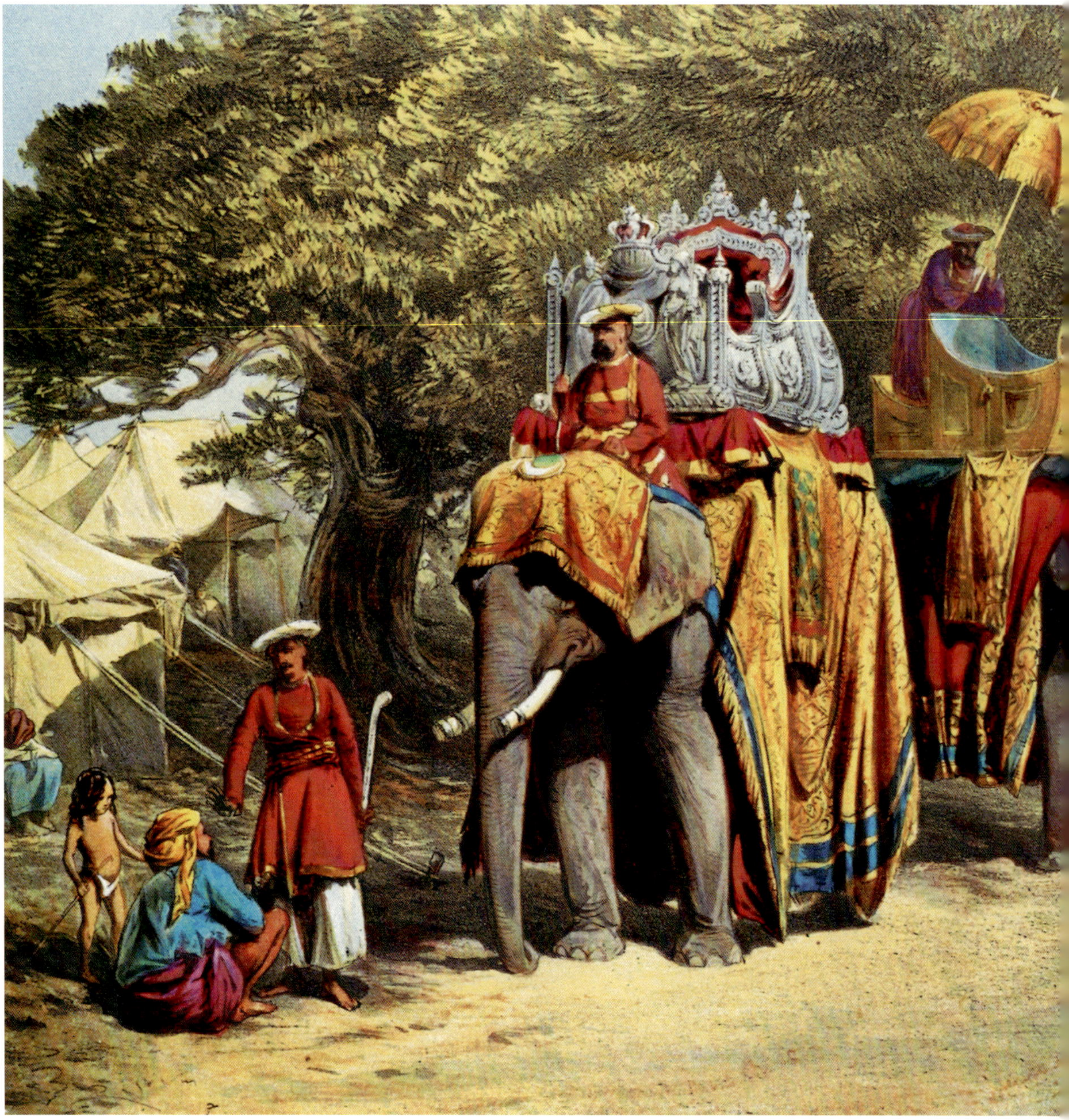

The Governor-General's state Howdah.
Chromolithograph after a drawing
by William Simpson, c.1860.

Modes of Travel

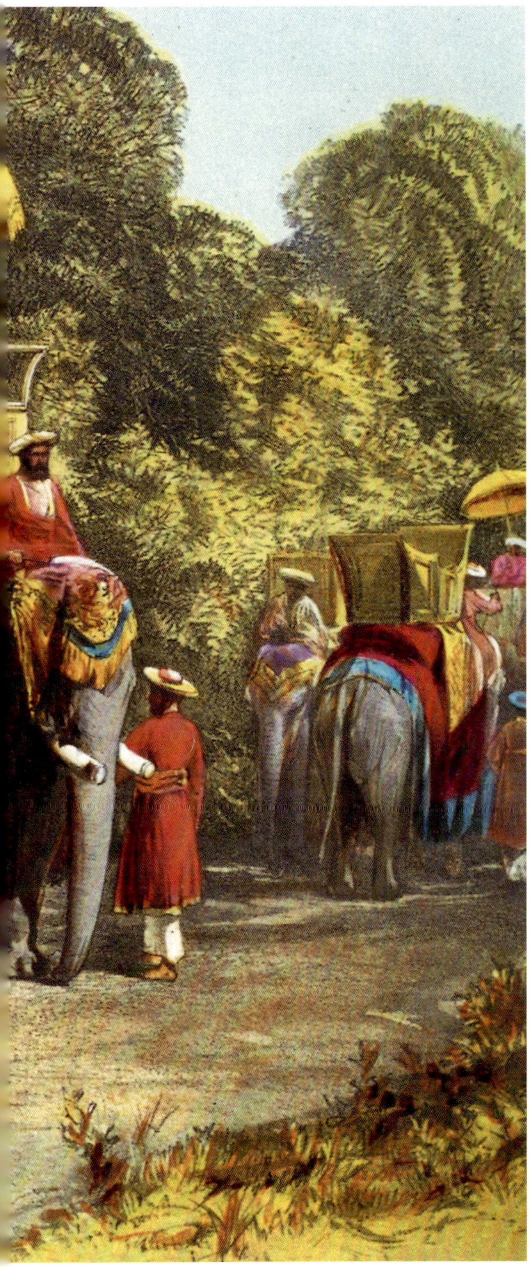

RIDING ON an elephant was a sign of dignity and grandeur. The British governors and residents in princely states followed the old Mughal style like native nawabs or rajahs, and moved about seated on elephants in their grand ornamented howdahs. General Sir David Ochterlony, the British Resident in Delhi who lived in a royal style maintained a stable of thirteen elephants for his thirteen Indian wives. We even come across paintings of the Governor-General's elephant with its splendid gilded howdah. The ordinary natives travelled in bullock, camel and horse-driven carriages of various types. The artist F.B.Solvyns gives an illustrated description of several such types of conveyances. But the Sahibs preferred to ride saddled horses or drive around for pleasure in horse-driven carriages in the streets of Calcutta, Bombay and Madras.

Until 1850's the palanquin or the palkee was the most popular mode of conveyance for going about in cities and towns. Palanquins were hired even for long distance travel such as from Calcutta to Agra and Delhi. A palkee was a carriage without wheels for one person, conveyed on the shoulders of men by means of a pole proceeding from each extremity which they supported. Four or more bearers carried the palanquin and the occupant reclined at full length on an elastic mattress with back and side cushions to match. In some cases the bottom was caned like a chair, and cushions were covered with morocco leather. The palanquins available for hire in the towns were called Ticca Palkees. According to a report of 1840, the charges for a day's hire in Calcutta were one rupee four annas, of which the bearers paid four annas for the use of the palanquin which was hired by them from a stand of palanquins belonging to another individual. Many sahibs, however, chose to have their own private palanquins and maintained a set of bearers on monthly wages of four to five rupees. Private bearers usually carried their master to his office in the morning and home in the evening but were at his and the family's service all day.

The carrying of a palanquin required the bearers to take great care in regulating their paces, in order to avoid jolting or tossing the occupant who in turn had to maintain the balance of the carriage by keeping himself as much as possible in the centre of the seat. Whenever the balance was disturbed, the bearers would remonstrate and bestir the traveller from his delightful reverie or snooze. The sahib's peon or messenger usually walked along by the side of the door and at night, torchbearers or mushalchis led the way. As long distance travel from one town to another was also undertaken in palanquins, the East India

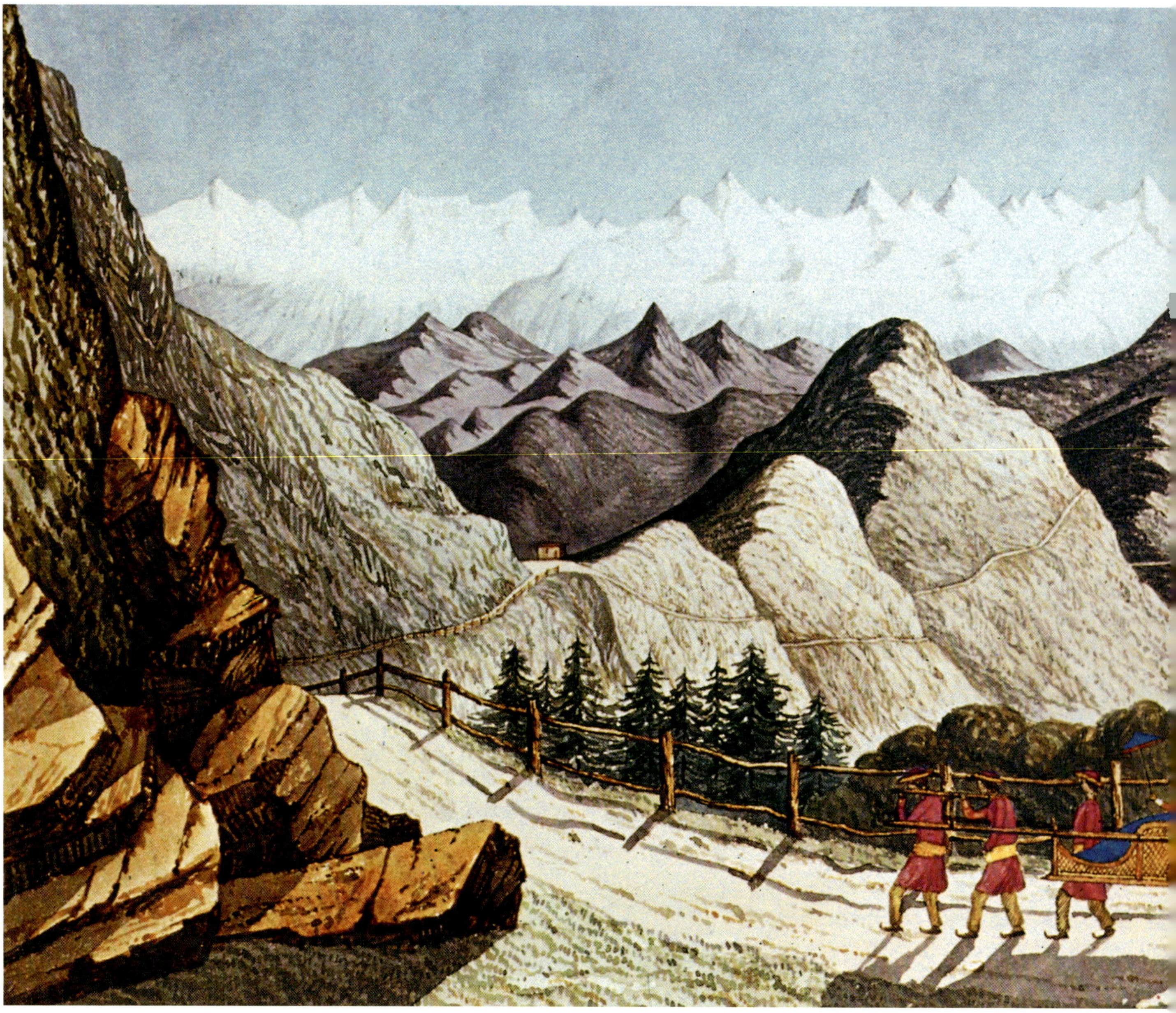

A Lady being Carried in a Jampan, a kind of Sedan Chair.
Watercolour by H. A. Oldfield c.1848.

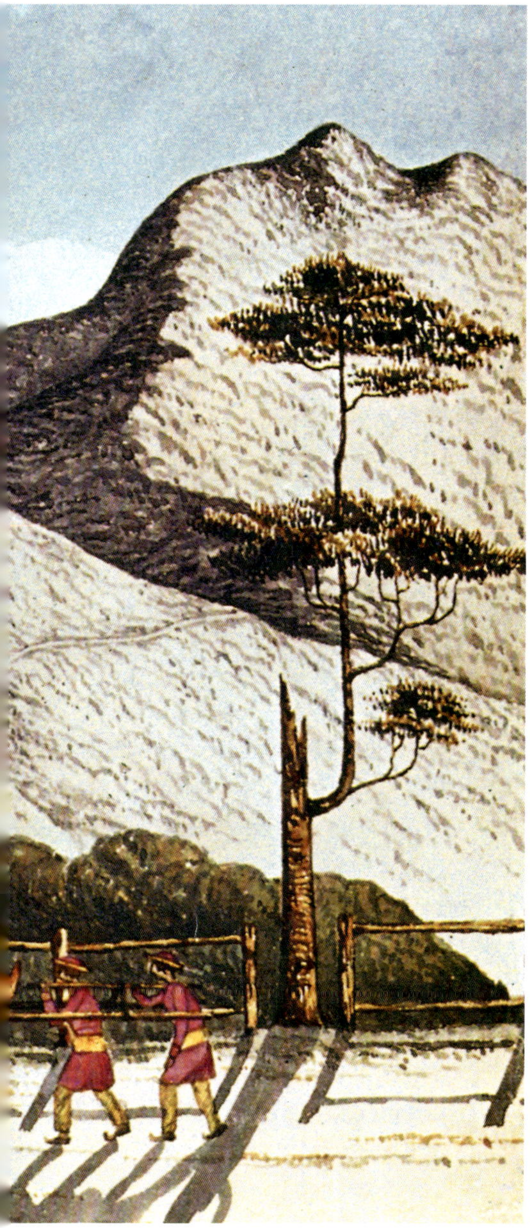

Company organized the system of 'Dawk Palkee' which provided for the day and night travel with fresh sets of bearers being posted at certain fixed points on the road. The average speed came to about four to five miles an hour. People preferred to travel in the cooler hours of the night and they were protected from the approach of wild beasts by the blaze of torches carried by men walking alongside.

Albert Hervey in his 1850 account of travel to Vellore by palanquin wrote: "These poor fellows run for upwards for thirty miles, with scarcely any rest, at the rate of four miles an hour taking little or no sustenance all the time. When they arrive at the end of their stage, they put down their load and walk off." It was possible to cover a distance of up to a hundred miles a day. The 'Dawk Palkee' was fitted with such conveniences as extra drawers and pockets, lamps, hat slings, glass and bottle racks, and fire-arm receptacles. One memsahib in her account (1838) wrote cheerfully: "I can sleep a good part of the night and being able to sit up or lie down at pleasure, with plenty of room, I find it far less fatiguing than being cramped up all day on a carriage."

At Simla and other hill stations, the popular mode of transport for the ladies was the Jampan, a kind of sedan chair slung on poles carried by four porters. Rickshaws were introduced in the late nineteenth century. This was a two wheeled carriage with an adjustable hood as a protection against rain hauled by four men who ran downhill ringing the bell and pulled it uphill with loud groans. The high ranking sahibs maintained their private rickshaws with liveried porters.

Until the advent of railways in the 1850's another popular mode of travel from Calcutta to upper India towns of Allahabad, Benaras, Cawnpore and beyond was by river boats on the Ganges. A number of British travellers including professional artists have left graphic accounts of their journeys including a visual record of the river ghats and historic monuments along the river. F.B. Solvyns sketched more than thirty types of boats. The boats used for travelling on the Ganges and its tributaries by Europeans and affluent Indians were called 'budgerows' which could sail with the wind and also be rowed. They varied in sizes with a crew of twelve to twenty boatmen. They were fairly commodious and gave the appearance of a floating house and could be hired for three to five rupees a day. The introduction of steamboats in the 1830s gradually replaced the 'budgerows,' followed by a regular steam service between Calcutta and Allahabad. Emma Roberts in her journal gives a fascinating account of her steamboat voyage on the Ganges.

The arrival of the railways ended the era of the leisurely river voyage. Travelling became much faster and also far more comfortable. Louis Rousselt, famous for his voluminous journal on his extensive travels in India during his six-year stay (1863–69), has left an interesting account of his rail journey from Kanpur to Calcutta in one of the sleeping carriages newly introduced by the East India Railways.

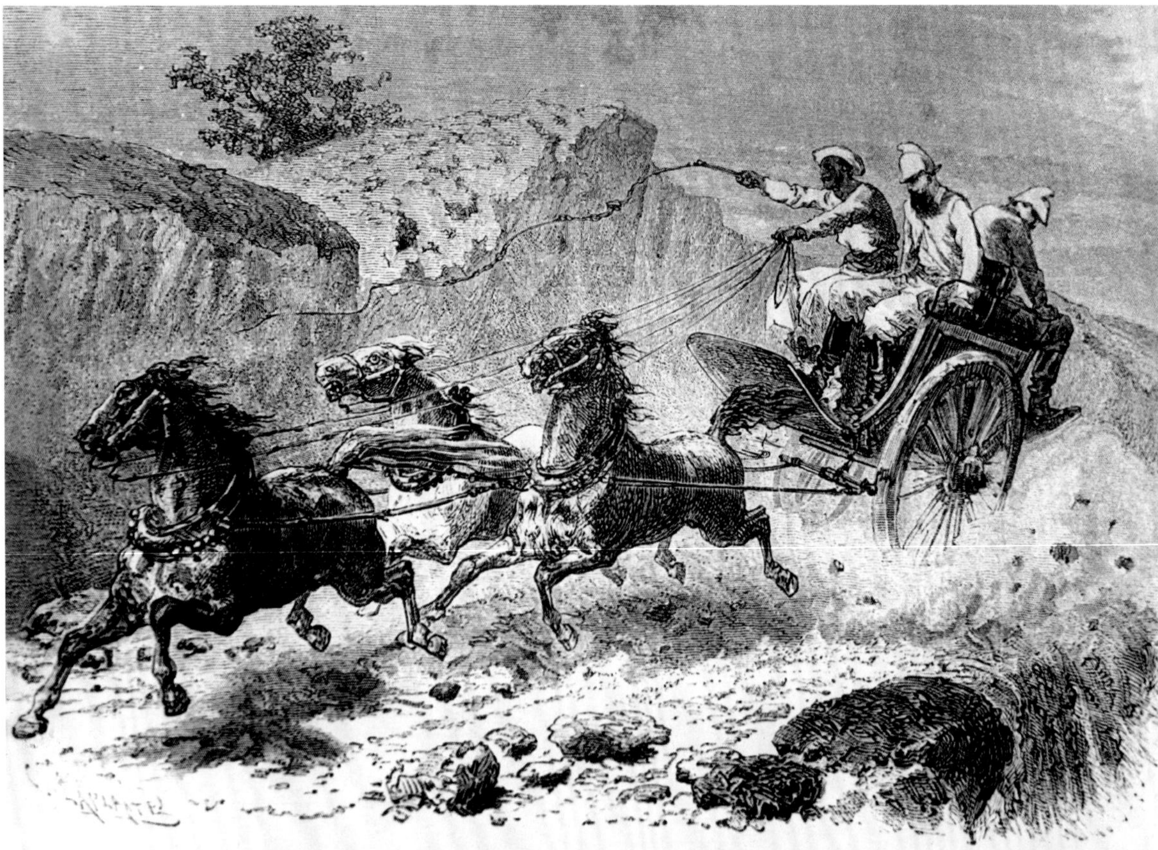

Above: *The Mail Cart.* Engraving from 'India and its Native Princes' by L. Rousselet, London, 1875.

Right: *Chopaya, A carriage driven by four bullocks.* Engraving from 'India and its Native Princes' by L.Rousellet, London, 1875.

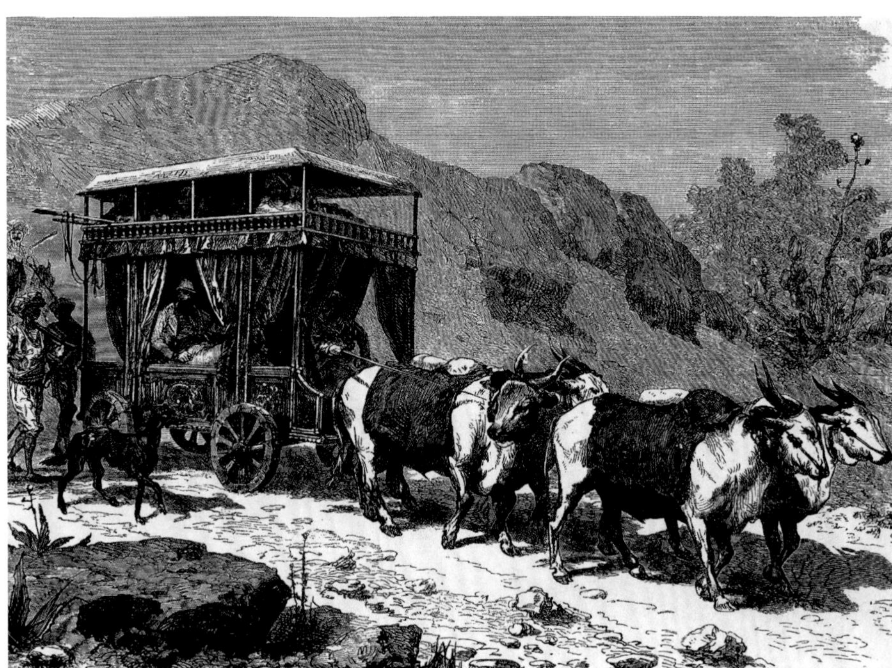

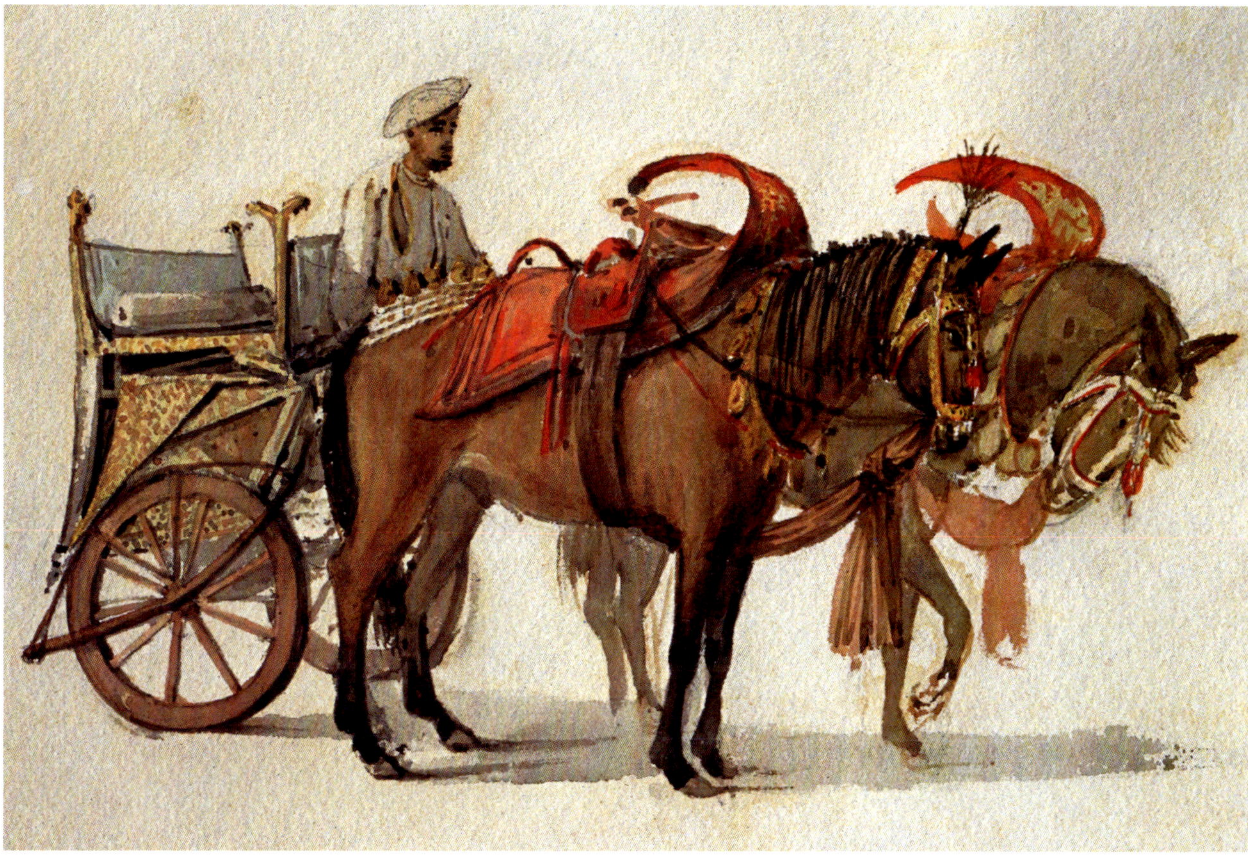

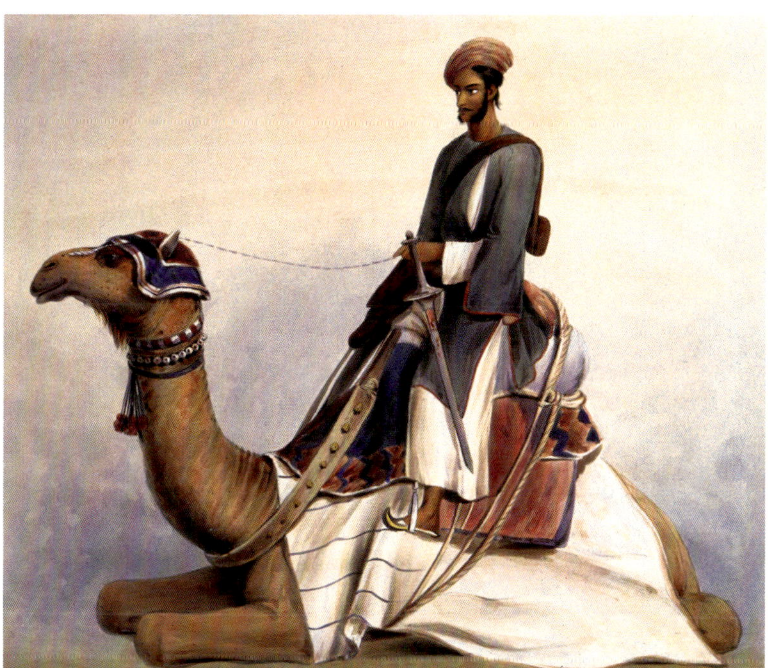

Above: *A horse Carriage belonging to the Raja of Bharatpur.*
Coloured lithograph after a painting by Emily Eden, c.1840

Left: *A shooter-suwar or swift-camel Rider.*
Coloured lithograph after a painting by Emily Eden, c.1840.

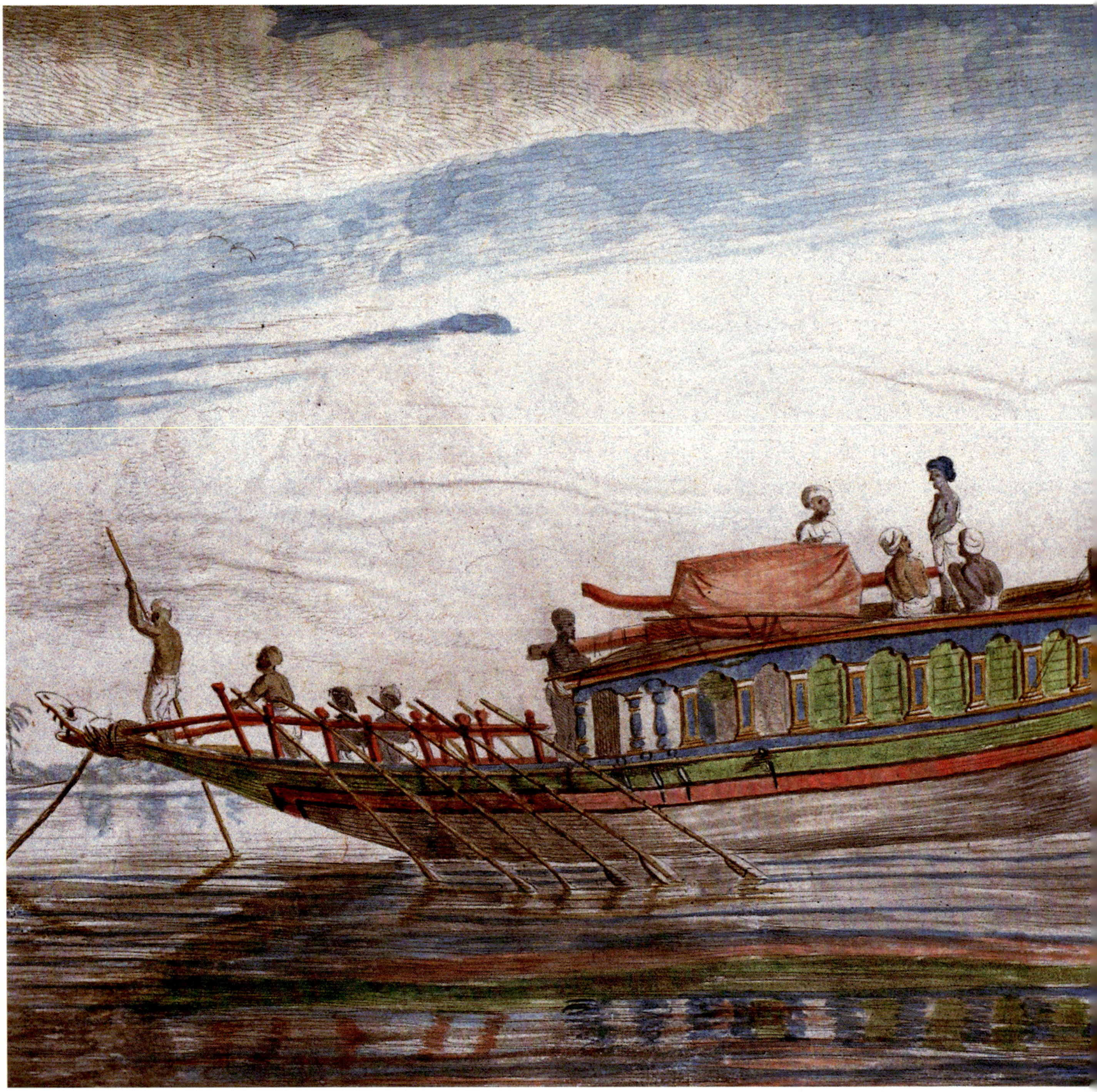

Budgerow or Bengalee Barge.
Hand-coloured etching by F. B. Solvyns, c. 1795.

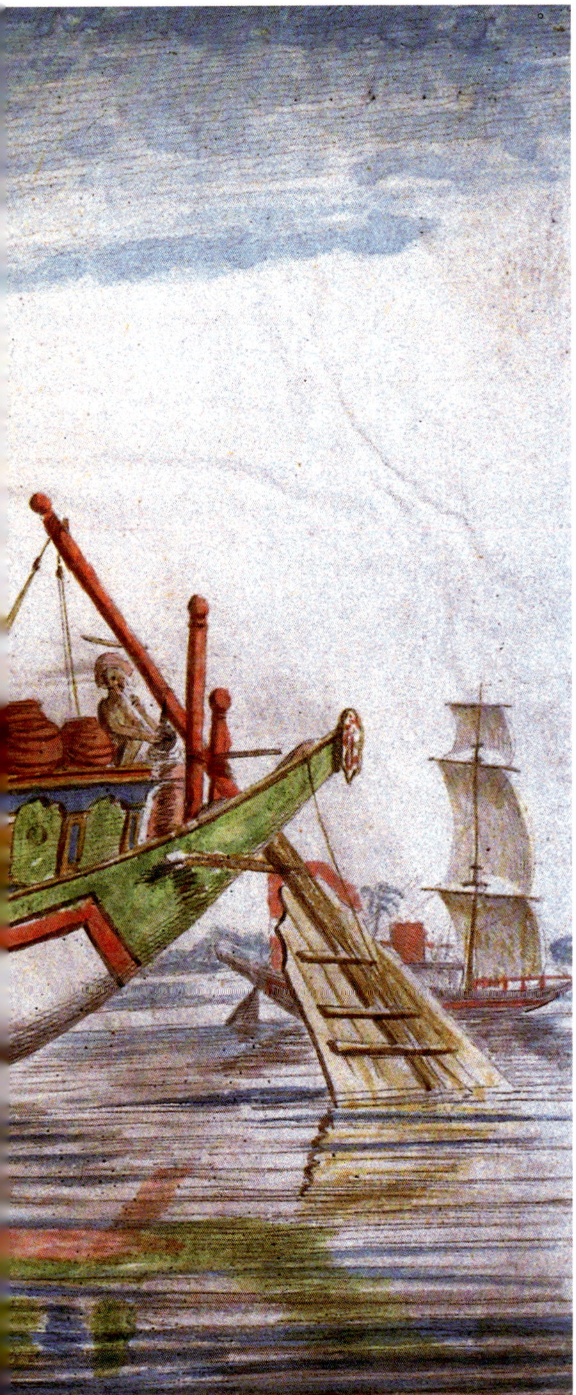

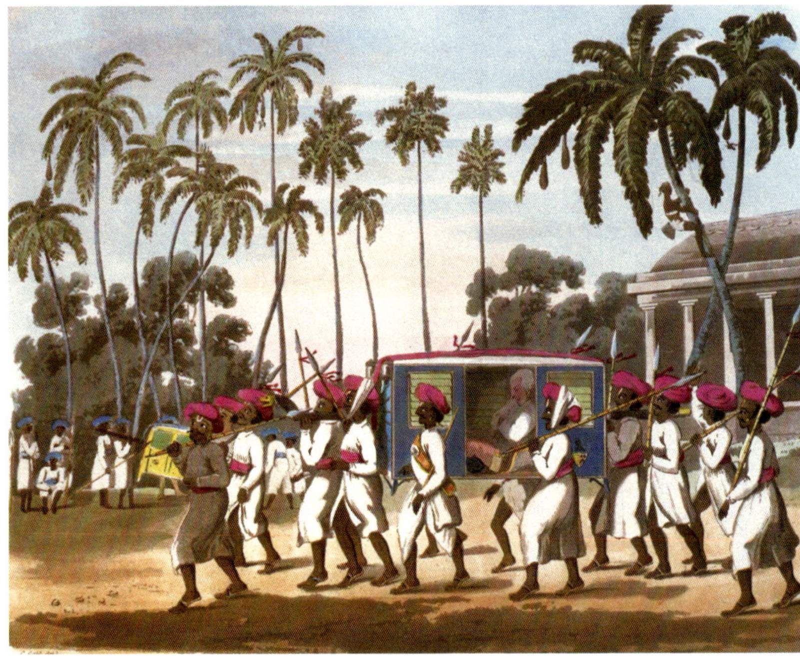

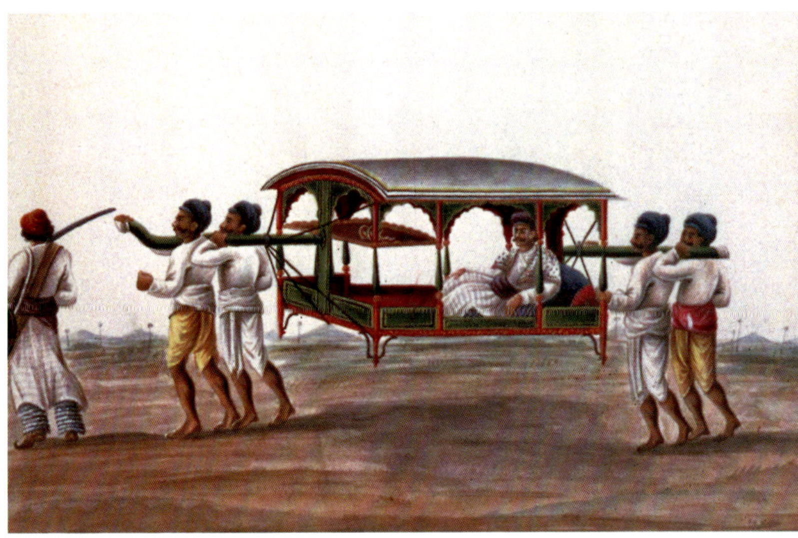

Top: *Palquin aur Bhehera Loag.* Palanquin bearers, a Patna artist, c.1826.

Above: *Palankeen passing through a tope of cocoanut, palmyra and arica trees.* Hand-coloured aquatint engraving after a drawing by Captain Charles Gold, 1806.

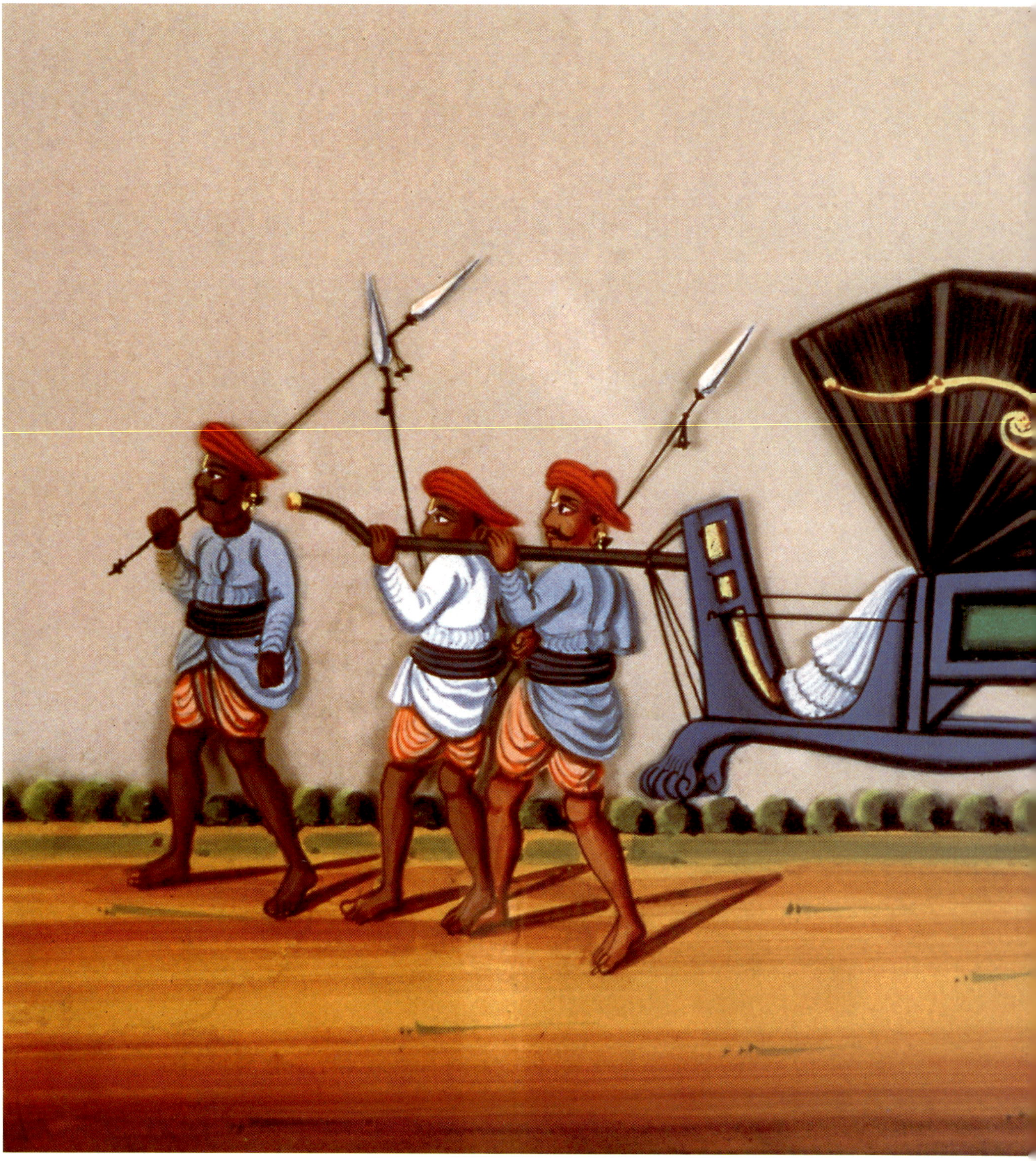

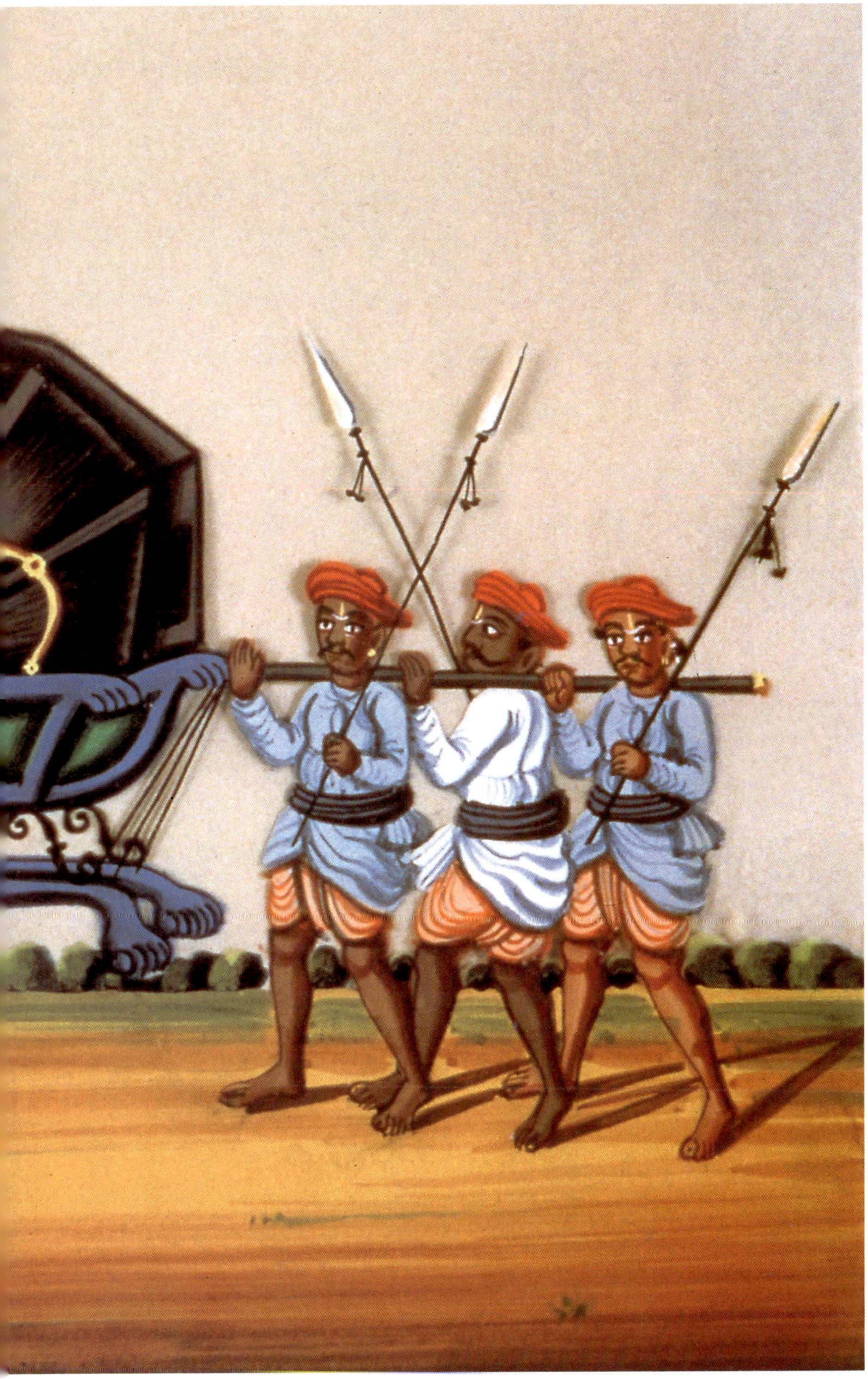

A European lady being carried in a palanquin.
Mica painting by a local artist, Trichinopoly, c.1850.

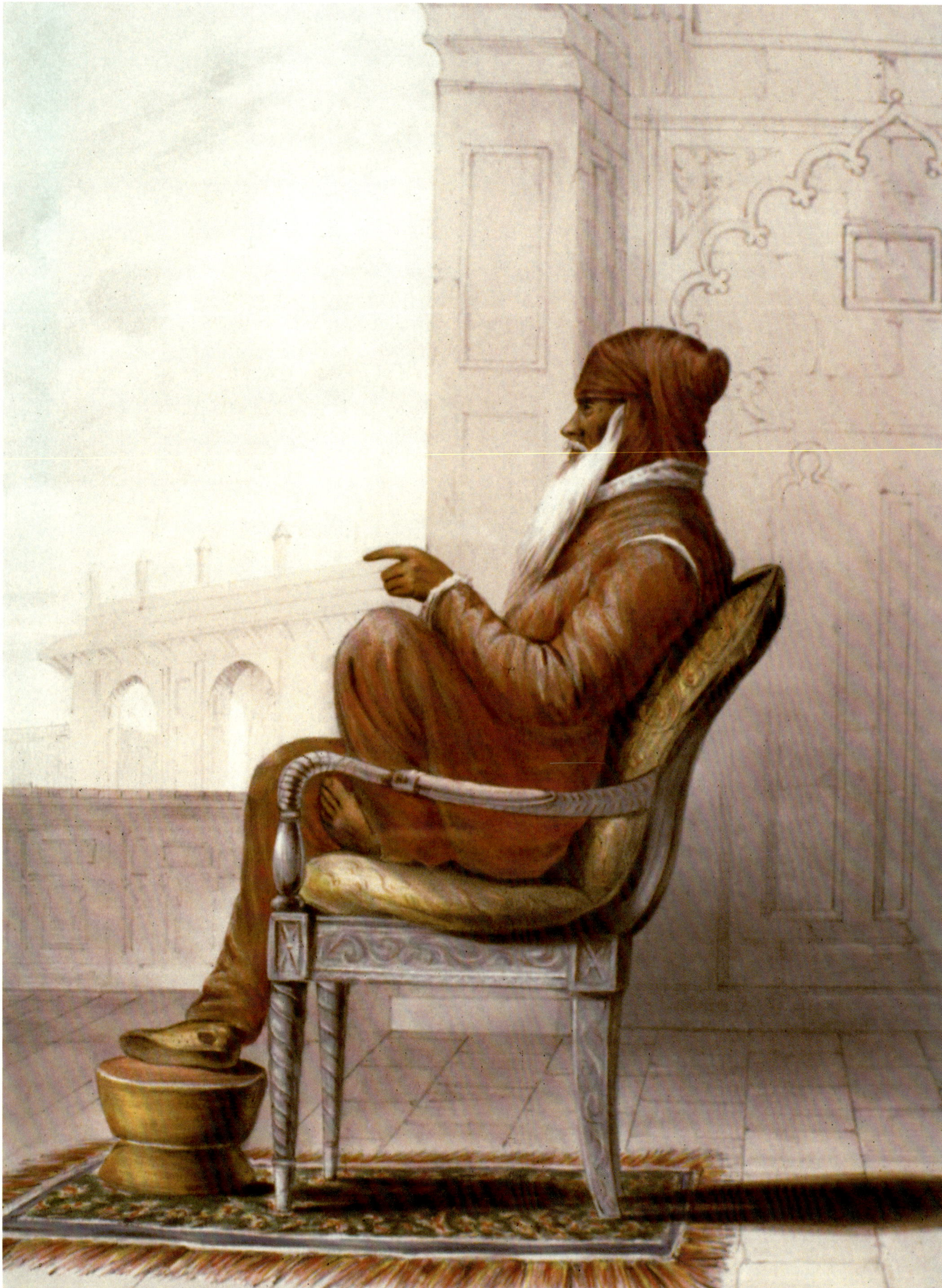

About the Artists

THE LAST quarter of the eighteenth century witnessed a remarkable flowering of British interest in Indian history, literature, antiquities and the customs and manners of its people. Lured by the prospects of fame and fortune, a number of British professional artists began arriving in India. Until then, there had practically been no true to life visual record of the Indian scene. British artists working in India devoted themselves to landscape painting, which had a ready market or to painting portraits of the British elite and the Indian nawabs and princes. There were also amateur artists both men and women who had received training in drawing and their works were of a high standard. They applied their wonderful talents to depicting Indian people and their way of life.

William Hodges (1744-1797)

WILLIAM HODGES was the first professional artist to sketch the scenic splendours of India and portray the common people based on keen personal observation. Sensitive to the sights, smells and colour of his habitat, Hodges depicted his subjects with utmost fidelity and amazing detail.

Born in London in 1744, Hodges came from a very humble background. While working as an errand boy, he was taken as a pupil by the famous British artist, Richard Wilson, who was impressed by the boy's artistic talent. Hodges came to India in 1780 and spent over three years in the country and made numerous sketches during his travels. Warren Hastings extended his generous patronage to him and many a time Hodges joined the Governor-General's entourage as it journeyed across the land. He was particularly struck by the light and atmosphere around the country. He noted in his journal:

> *"...the clear blue cloudless sky, the polished white buildings, the bright sandy beach, and the dark green sea, present a combination totally new to the eye of an Englishman."*

Hodges was particularly charmed by the winsome manners and the polished behaviour of the Indian people which he considered as the hallmark of a most highly civilized state of society. Unassuming and endowed with great personal charm, he made himself at home in remote villages which had never been visited earlier by any European.

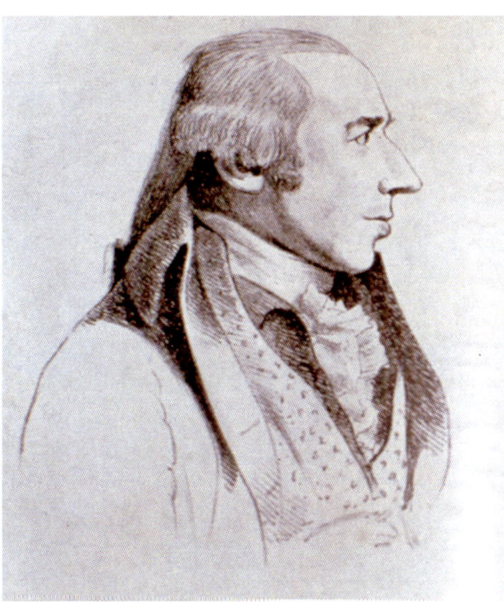

Above: *William Hodges*

Facing page: *Maharaja Ranjit Singh.* Watercolour by Emily Eden, 1838.

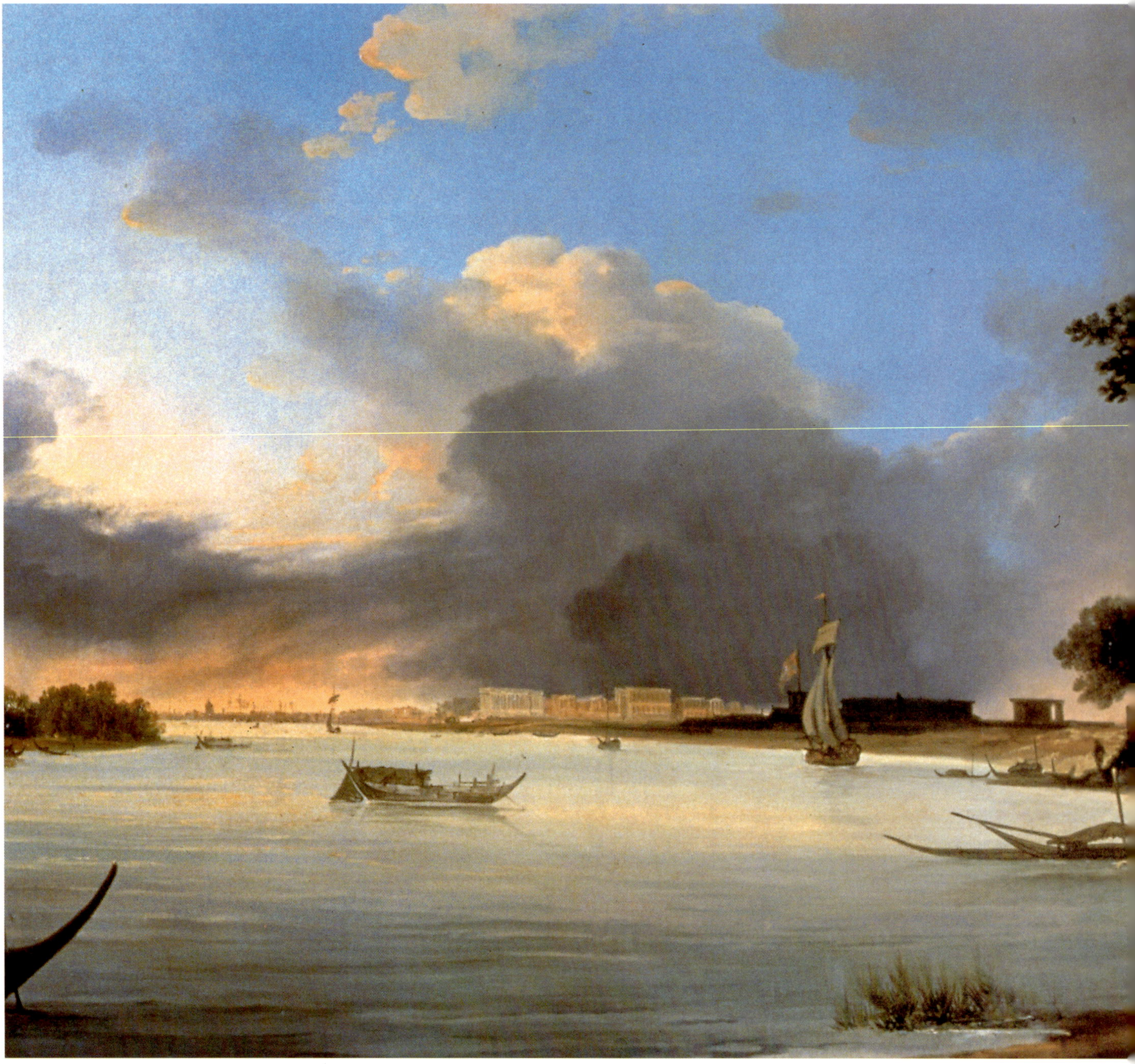

View of Esplanade from Garden Reach, Calcutta.
Oil on canvas, by William Hodges, c.1780.

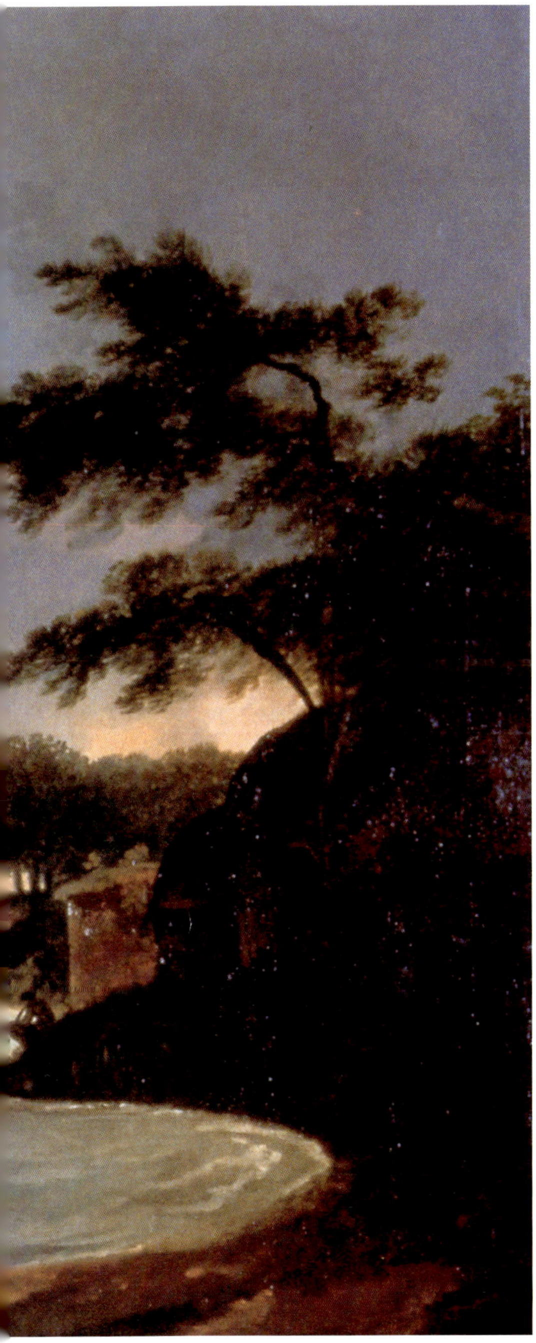

He admired the simple country-folk and mixed freely with them, enjoying their hospitality with curries and 'pillaw.'

Hodge's journal of travels in India (1780–83) was published in 1793. It is a remarkable historic document with some of his observations verging on the poetic and others highly illuminating, as well as amusing and romantic. While awestruck by the inspiring grandeur of the mighty Ganges he was equally captivated by the "simplicity and primitive appearance of the people." Admiring the river, he said:

> *"the meandering of the river Ganges through the flat country, and glittering through the immense plain highly cultivated, as far as the extent of the horizon where the eye is almost at a loss to discriminate the termination of the sky and land."*

Just as the British concept of picturesque influenced their landscape painting, the western concept of beauty had its impact on their portrayal of the native people. Hodges openly admitted that his portraits of Indians, particularly of women, were based on ideas of classical beauty.

Hodges enjoyed travelling by palanquin instead of taking the river route. He could afford that since he received a substantial salary from the East India Company through Hastings. He gives a vivid description of the facilities for travellers including wells and shady banyan trees, and makes a special mention of Sher Shah Suri for his "most humane attention to the comforts and accommodations of his people."

After spending over three years in India, Hodges returned to England and began work on his *Select Views of India*, a series of 48 acquatints which were published during 1785–88. It was an unprecedented work, for people in the west had never before seen such a vivid array of Indian monuments and scenery from sketches made on the spot. However, it was a financial failure. He also failed to get recognition from his peers despite having exhibited a number of times at the Royal Academy. Faced with his failing health and mounting debt he committed suicide in 1797. A subsequent re-appraisal of his light-filled artworks by some art historians reveals him as an artist who was ahead of his times.

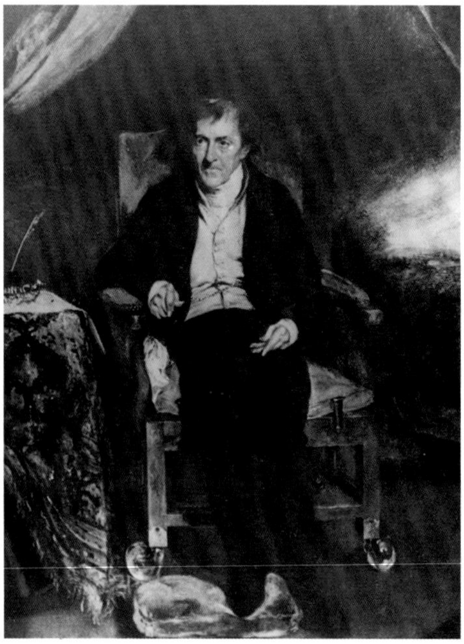

Thomas Daniell

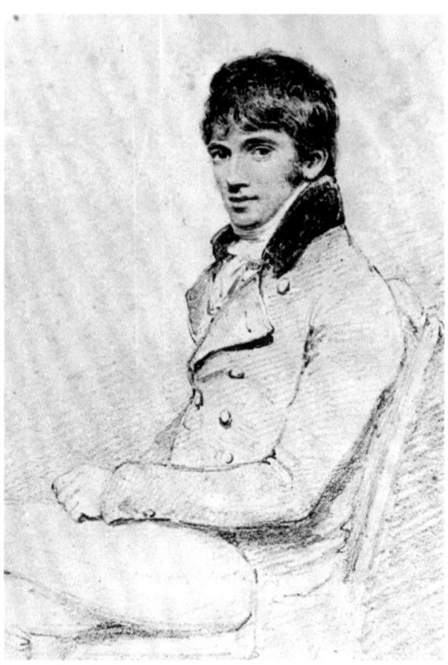

William Daniell

Facing page: *The Rajpootanee Bride.* Oil on board by William Daniell, 1826.

Thomas Daniell (1749-1840)
William Daniell (1769-1837)

WE OWE it to Thomas and William Daniell's uncle-nephew team for presenting us with a popular vision of India. Never before had India been explored for such pictorial subjects or recorded in such a superbly evocative manner. The duo landed at Calcutta in 1786. In a very short time they produced a series of twelve acquatints entitled *Views of Calcutta*, which fetched enough funds for them to proceed ahead with their grand tour of India.

During the years 1788 to 1791, they travelled from Calcutta to Cawnpore by a river boat stopping and sketching the monuments and other sights enroute at Patna, Benaras and Allahabad. They then travelled to Delhi and Agra and made a large number of drawings of historic Mughal monuments. From Delhi they went north right up to the foothills of the Himalayas. They were the first Europeans to visit Garhwal and draw its fine mountain scenery. In 1789 they set off on their return journey to Calcutta. They travelled by land and riverboat down the Ganges, stopping and painting every picturesque landscape and monument in Allahabad, Chunar, Benaras, Sasaram and Gaya. Sometimes using the camera obscura, William would make the preliminary sketch and Thomas would then complete the drawing.

They then journeyed south to Madras and visited many of the great hill forts, as well as the magnificent temples of Madurai. They went as far south as Cape Comorin. Finally, they travelled by sea to Bombay, exploring the Western Ghats and the famous cave temples of Elephanta and Salsette.

By 1794, they were back in England. Now the Daniells worked tirelessly on their large stock of drawings which depicted many places in India for the first time. Making acquatints was a formidable task as they wanted to produce a print that looked like a watercolour. Between 1795 and 1808 the Daniells brought out the famous *Oriental Scenery,* a vast publication of 144 acquaints issued in six parts, each containing 24 plates and costing £210 a set. The publication was a tremendous success that ensured fame and fortune for the Daniells. It also had its impact in Britain and Europe in different fields like architecture, scenic wall papers and ceramics. A contemporary review proclaimed *Oriental Scenery* to be a profound study for the architect or antiquary and a source of delight to a lover of the picturesque. Both artists were elected to the Royal Academy and are today acclaimed as masters of the aquatint technique.

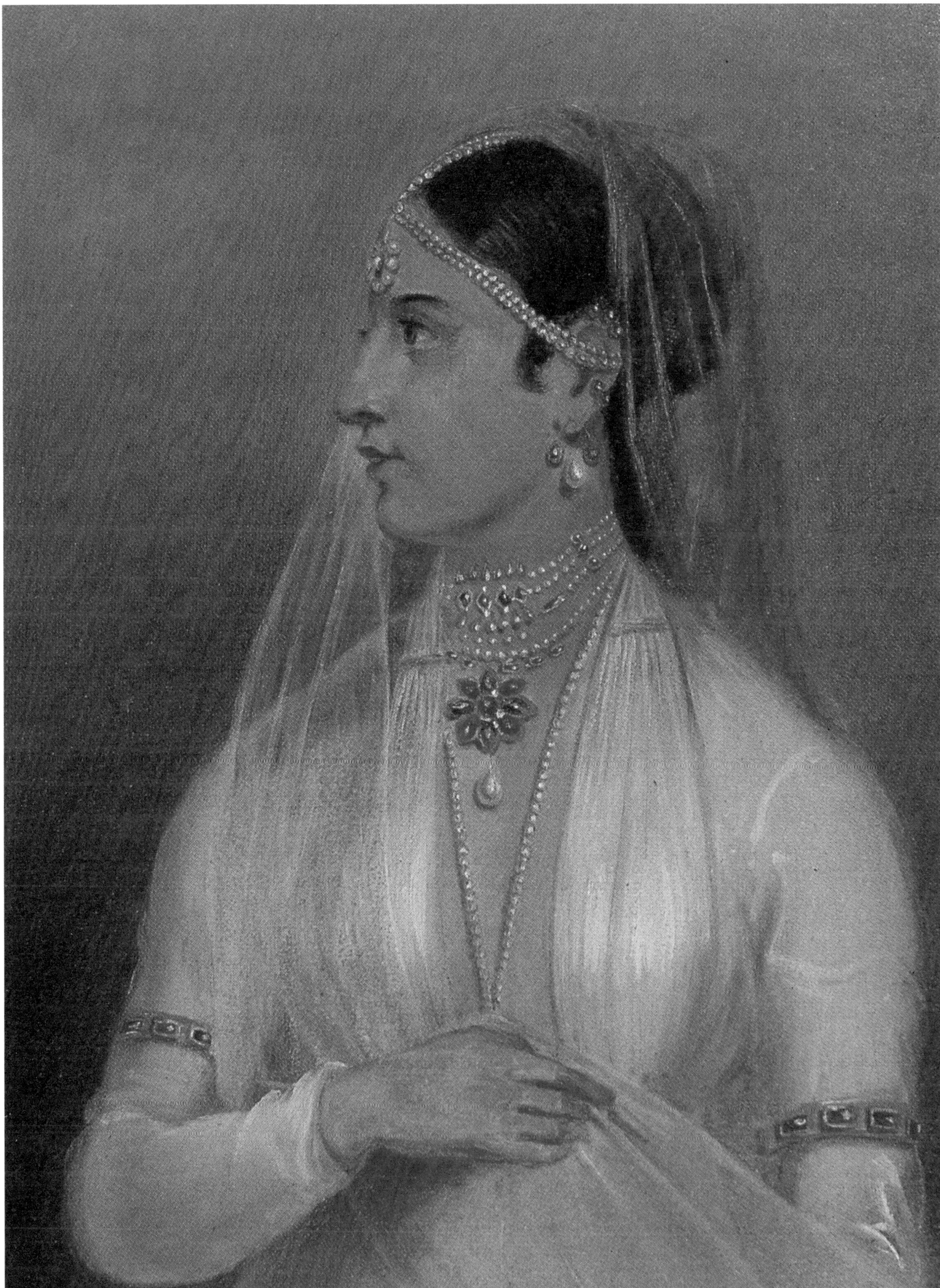

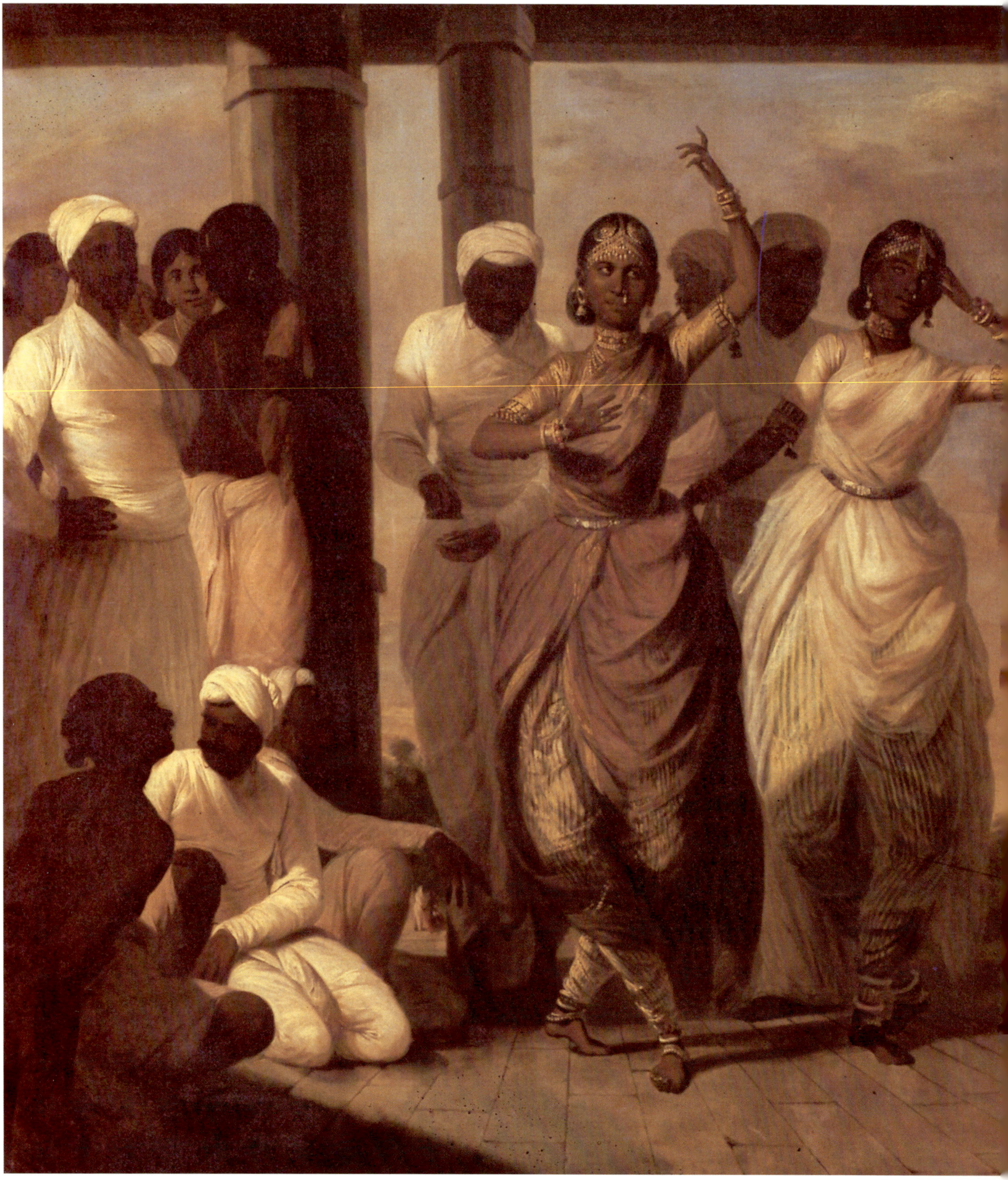

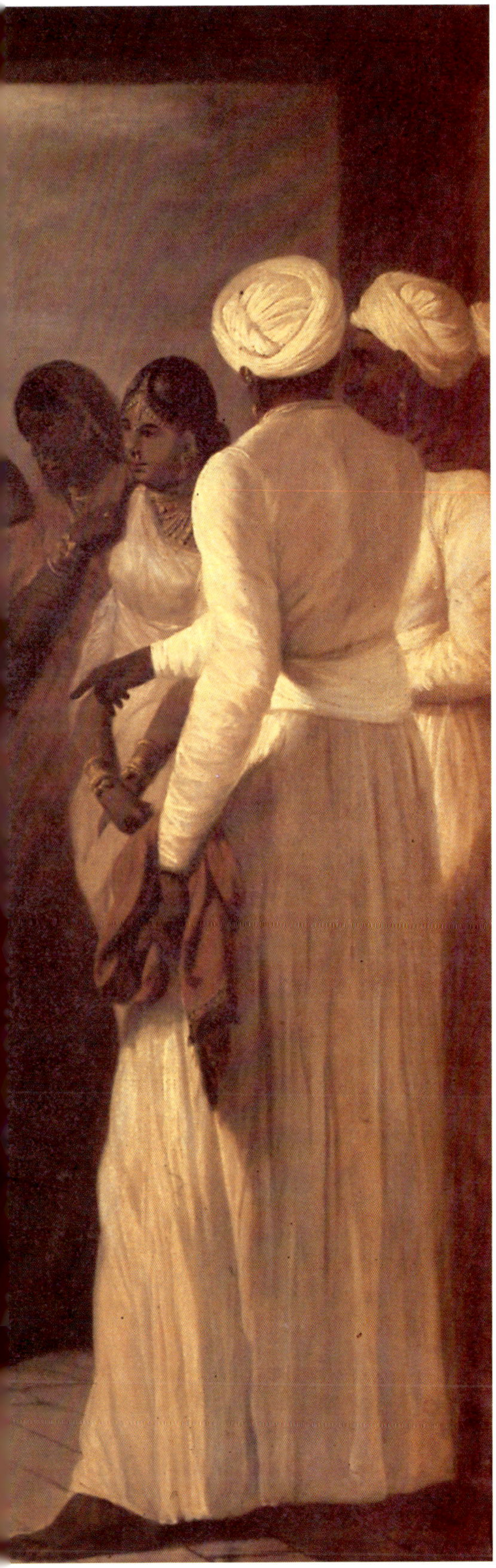

Tilly Kettle (1735-1786)

TILLY KETTLE was the first British portrait painter to go to India. Born in London in 1735, he received training from his father, a house painter, and also studied at the Art Academy. He became competent enough to produce dignified portraits in a style influenced by Reynolds, a leading painter of the time. He tried hard to exhibit his work between 1764 and 1768 and get some fashionable patronage but without success. After his omission from the list of forty original members of the newly formed Royal Academy, Kettle sought East India Company's permission to go to Bengal and try his luck setting up a career as a painter in India.

He sailed for India in December 1768 and landed in Madras in June 1769. He spent the next two years in Madras painting portraits of the British East India Company's officials and soldiers. The Nawab of Carnatic, Muhammad Ali, was anxious to adopt British manners. He came to know about Kettle and commissioned him to make his portrait with his five sons. Kettle also painted an equally majestic solo portrait of the Nawab in his royal robes. Kettle was attracted by the dusky beauties of the south especially the dancing girls (devadasis) and made pictures of them performing outside the temple.

Kettle left for Calcutta in 1771 and succeeded in getting commissions from high-ranking Company officials. Armed with an introductory letter to the Nawab of Oudh from the Governor of Fort William, he travelled to Faizabad, the capital of Oudh. He stayed there for a year making numerous portraits for the Nawab who considered ownership of oil paintings as a source of prestige. Kettle also obtained an Indian bibi by whom he was to have two daughters, Ann and Elizabeth. Like so many of the British, he was also attracted by the Indian nautch girls. One of the finest portraits was that of a dancing girl loaded with ornaments and standing on a carpet holding the stem of a hookah. Kettle was impressed by the glamour of the court of Oudh and its rich oriental atmosphere. A few of his Faizabad paintings were copied by Indian artists for their British patrons. His short stay in Oudh was the most productive and lucrative of his career. On his return to Calcutta, Kettle gained access to the top strata of Company's civil and military officials including the Governor-General Warren Hasting, of whom Kettle made three portraits. As a result of all these commissions Kettle amassed a respectable fortune and returned to London in 1776. However, back in the home country, he suffered many troubles and disappointments. He failed to win any popularity or distinction in his field. In 1786 he set out again for India but unfortunately did not survive the arduous overland journey.

Dancing-girls, Madras.
Oil on canvas by Tilly Kettle, c. 1770.

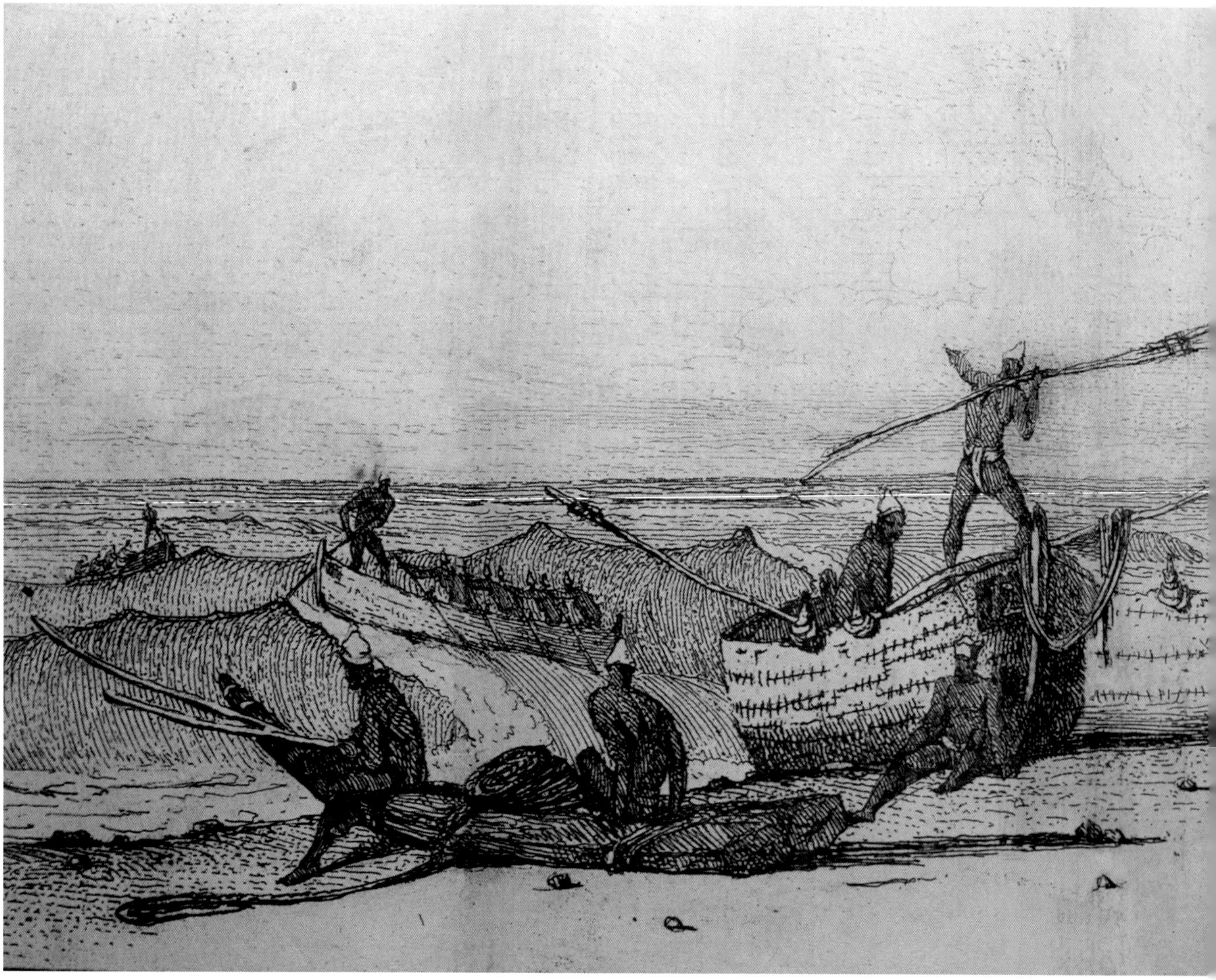

Massoolah Boals, Madras.
Etching after a drawing by
George Chinnery, 1807.

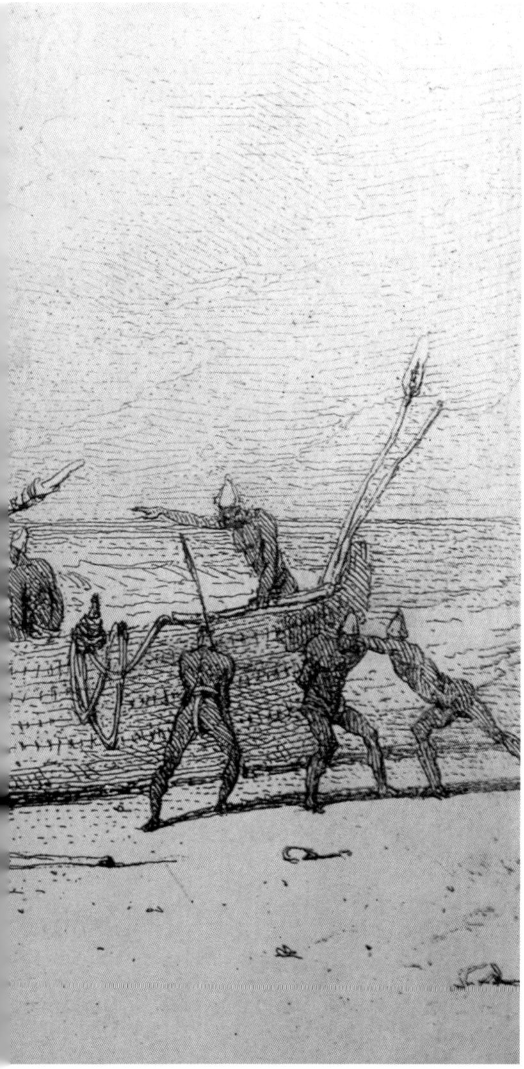

George Chinnery (1774-1854)

GEORGE CHINNERY studied art at the Royal Academy in London. After establishing his calibre as a portrait painter he came to Madras in December 1802 and then moved to Bengal in 1807. Working in watercolour, oils and miniatures, he soon emerged as the foremost portrait artist in Calcutta and became a favourite amongst all classes. It became so that every dignitary wished to have his portrait painted by Chinnery. Though wayward and eccentric, he was a likeable man and endowed with the gifts of a genius as revealed in his marvellous portraits.

While portraiture was the source of his living and fame, his true interest lay in landscape painting. He had a zest for depicting local scenes and Indian people. In Madras he was inspired by local sights and made sketches of batmen dragging their masula boats to the beach.

Chinnery also enjoyed teaching and gave art lessons in Calcutta. Sir Charles Doyly also took lessons from him, and when posted to Dacca, Doyly persuaded Chinnery to accompany him. Chinnery stayed in Dacca until 1811 painting portraits for the Nawab and other company officials. He explored the Bengal countryside and made several sketches of village scenes, great rivers and boats.

On his return to Calcutta, he was again immersed with many portrait commissions and a hectic social life. He frequently went out to the nearby countryside and made numerous sketches depicting villagers with their daily chores, cows, bullock carts, and thatched huts. Chinnery was especially delighted to capture life around him, a task that gave him a pleasing diversion and peace of mind. These numerous sketches were often bound into albums and some of these designed with title pages were presented to his friends and pupils. These sketches and their style of execution had a great influence on a whole generation of amateur artists in forming their perception of the Indian scene.

Chinnery lived beyond his means indulging in lavish entertainments. Burdened with debts, he left Calcutta in 1825 and went to Macao and he remained there until his death in May 1852. According to Sir Charles Doyly, though not having gained the reputation he deserved, Chinnery stands out as one of the finest portrait painters who worked in India.

F.B. Solvyns (1760-1824)

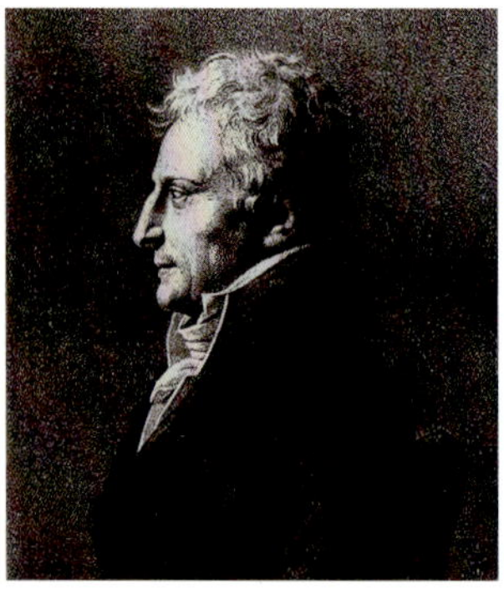

FRANCOIS BALTAZARD Solvyns came to India in 1791 after having received training as a painter, sketcher and engraver. He took up odd jobs from the East India Company for ceremonial decorations and the cleaning and restoration of paintings, and also made a living as a drawing master. His one steady source of income was the ornamentation of coaches and palanquins.

Solvyns was the first professional artist to undertake a study of the Indian communities, costumes and customs. Noticing the keen British interest in this field, he launched a grandiose project to produce 250 coloured etchings descriptive of the manners, customs, character, dress and religious costumes of the 'Hindoos.' He was supported in this gigantic task by Sir William Jones, the renowned Orientalist and founder of the Royal Asiatic Society at Calcutta, which brought in sufficient subscriptions that enabled Solvyns to move ahead with his project.

He began drawing his subjects from life which included men and women of every possible caste or calling from high caste Brahmins to milk women and sweepers. After completing these drawings, Solvyns made etchings that he coloured by hand. He completed his project in 1796 but continued to work for eight more years on further sets ordered by his subscribers. His work was published in Calcutta in 1799. Of these drawings, 249 are held in the collections of the Victoria and Albert Museum in London. However, the venture was a financial failure. His engravings were not much appreciated by the British public who were by now used to aquatints of excellent quality. That Solvyn's project was a well-conceived, pioneering work of its own kind was proved by the success of a pirated edition of 60 prints of redrawn Solvyns subjects brought out by a London publisher Edward Orme. But Solvyns gained nothing out of it and was able to continue with his work thanks to the financial support of his English wife who had private means of income.

Solvyns left India for France in 1804. He resumed his work in Paris and produced a French folio edition of 288 plates, entitled *Les Hindous*, published in Paris between 1808 and 1812 in four large volumes. The accompanying descriptive text with each plate gives detailed information about the subject depicted. *In his Introduction of Les Hindous* Solvyns describes 'Hindoostan' (sic) as a paradise, with fertile soil, agreeable climate and abundance of all necessary for a pleasurable life. He refers to the 'Hindoos'(sic) as:

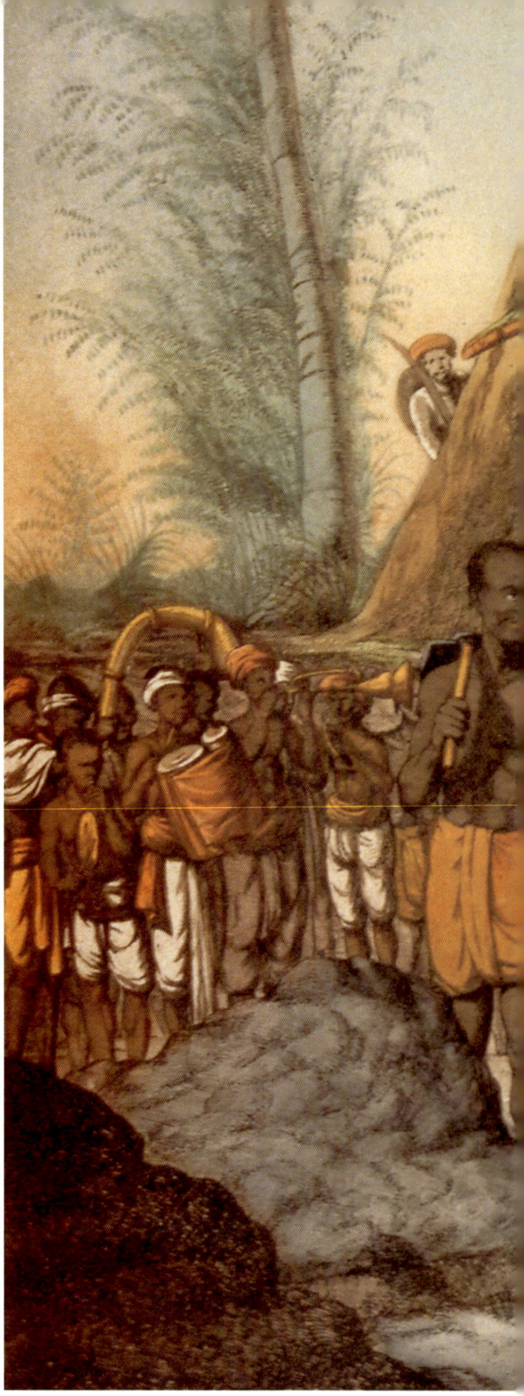

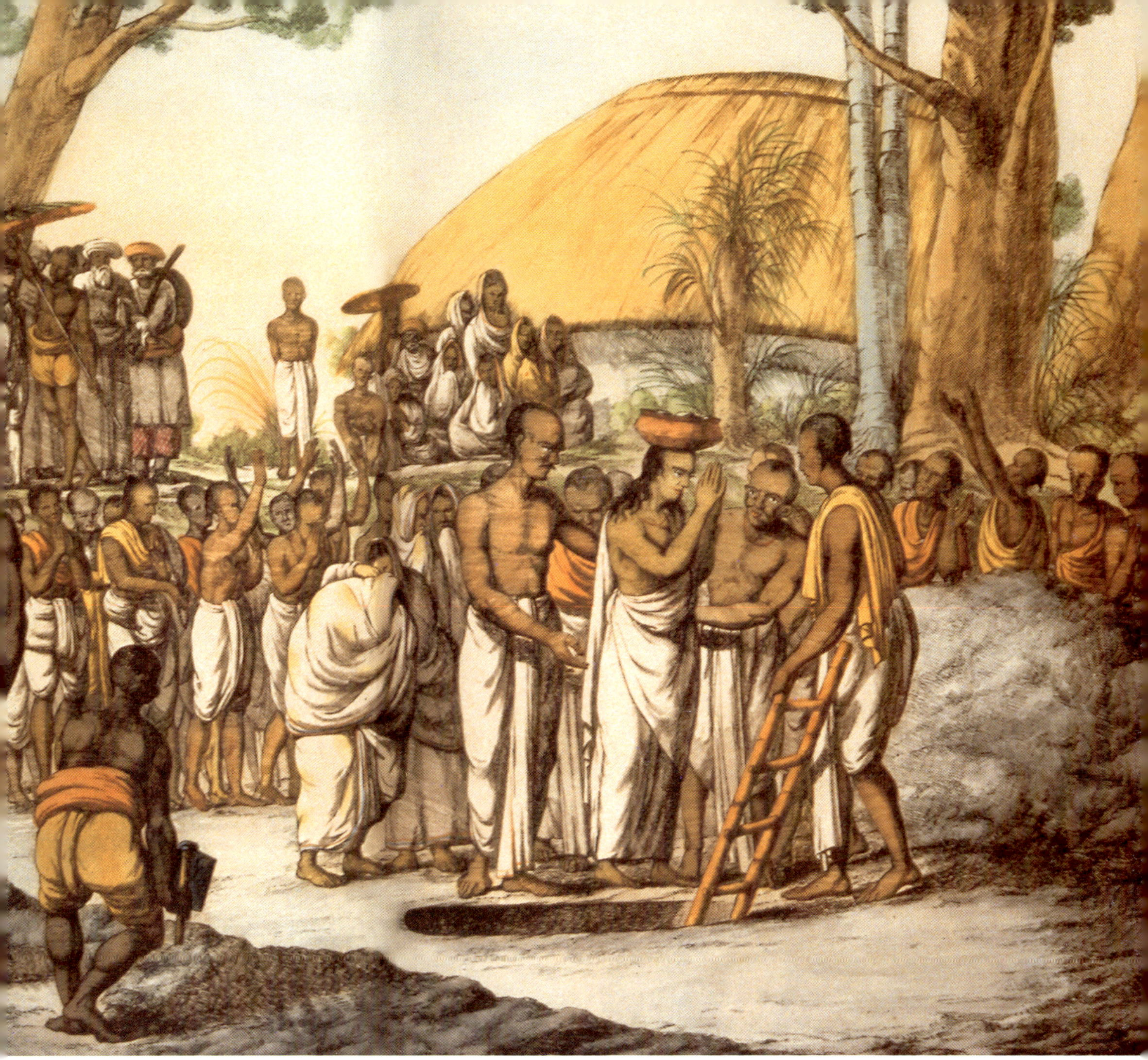

Sahagamna, the wife of the Joggee buried alive with the Corpse of her husband. The Joggee, and the race of Facquirs, called Vaisnavas are the only classes of the Hindoos, whose Bodies are buried. Coloured etching by F.B. Solvyns, c. 1790.

"a portion of mankind exempt from ambition, from vanity, from curiosity, satisfied in the enjoyment of what nature bestowed, and possessing in their mild and calm disposition that happiness which they themselves had pursued so long in vain, through the mazes of philosophy and science."

The French edition of his work was also a financial failure. Later, he did not even succeed in organizing a lottery of his works. On his death in 1824, the obituary carried by the Calcutta Gazette ascribed the artist's failure to certain shortcomings in his engravings. All the same, his work is of great historic value as it is a unique survey of the Indian people. He had a tremendous influence on the fortunes of Indian painters seeking the patronage of the British, as they found Solvyns sketches as the best guide about subjects that would appeal to their British clients.

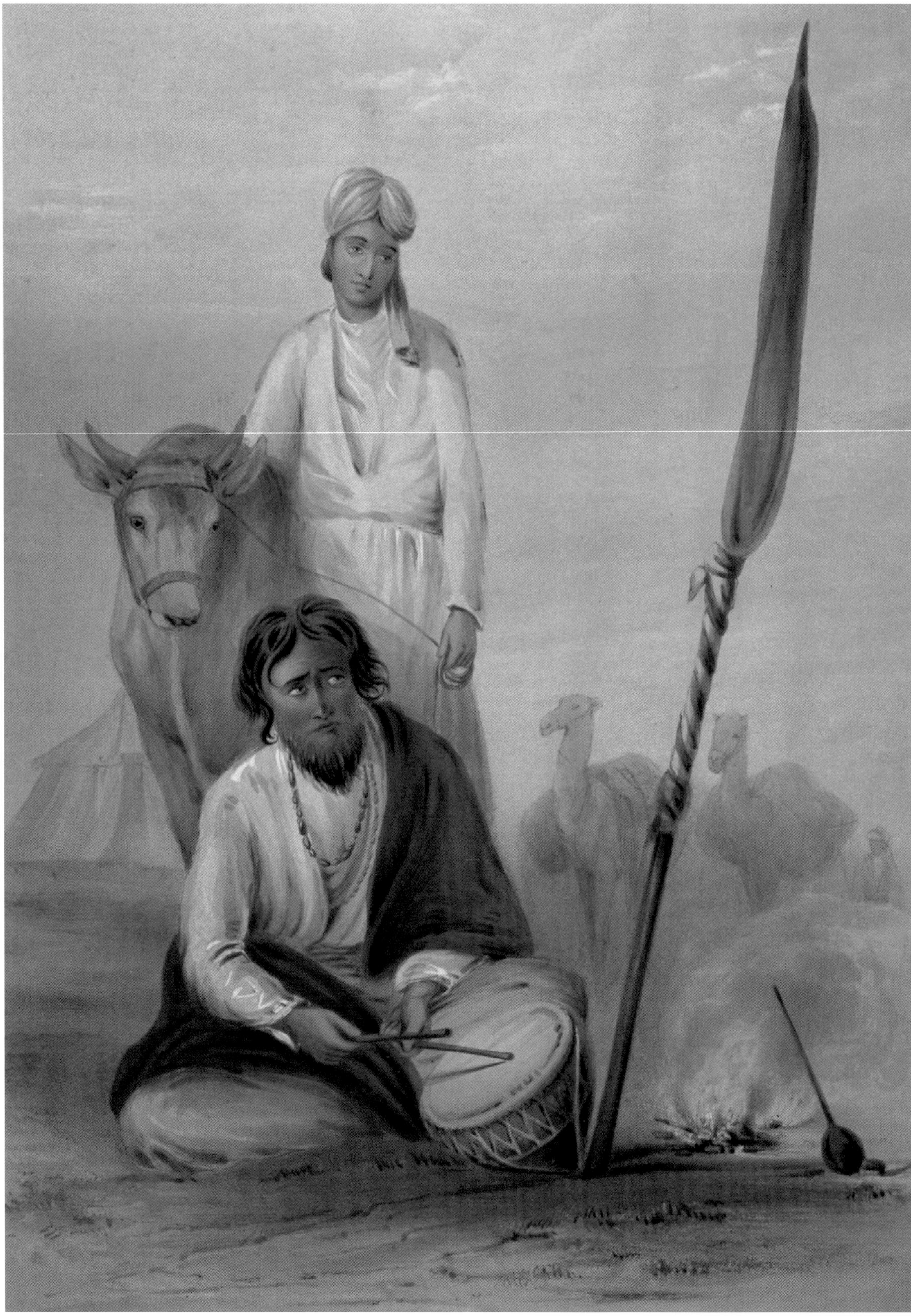

Emily Eden

EMILY EDEN along with her sister Fanny accompanied their brother, Lord Auckland, who look over as Governor-General of India in 1836. She spent six years in India and went along with her brother on a grand tour of the Upper provinces in 1837, going upto Simla. She also visited Lahore when Lord Auckland called on Maharaja Ranjit Singh. She was skilled at watercolour and throughout her stay in India she made a large number of paintings, depicting the country with its landscape and monuments, the people in their varied costumes and the bejeweled princes in their colourful, rich attire.

Emily did not feel at home in India and always missed her friends at home since she could not find accomplished European women in Calcutta. She gave vent to her depression in her letters to her relatives and friends as she wrote about her experiences in India. These letters were published in 1866 as *Up the Country,* which turned into a classic reference for students of the Indo-British connection.

Emily was drawn to whatever caught her fancy and had a friendly attitude to Indians and showed considerable compassion towards her servants. She enjoyed making their sketches. It was at a review of Maharaja Ranjit Singh's troops that Emily went to a quiet corner to make a sketch of the Sikh ruler. This was to be the last portrait of the Maharaja as he died six months later.

After her return to England, Emily began working on hundreds of drawings that she had made in India. Eventually a selection of her artistic study comprising 24 plates was published in 1844 under the title *Portraits of the Princes and People of India.* Later, she started selecting from the vast store of her drawings and set apart 193 sketches.These represent the most colourful visual record of Indian people made by any foreign artist. Bound in three volumes these were sold by the family at Christie's in 1907 and were later acquired in 1911 by the Victoria Memorial in Hall, Calcutta, where they are still preserved.

Fakeer attached to the Suite of the Governor-General in camp. Coloured lithograph after a drawing by Emily Eden c. 1838.

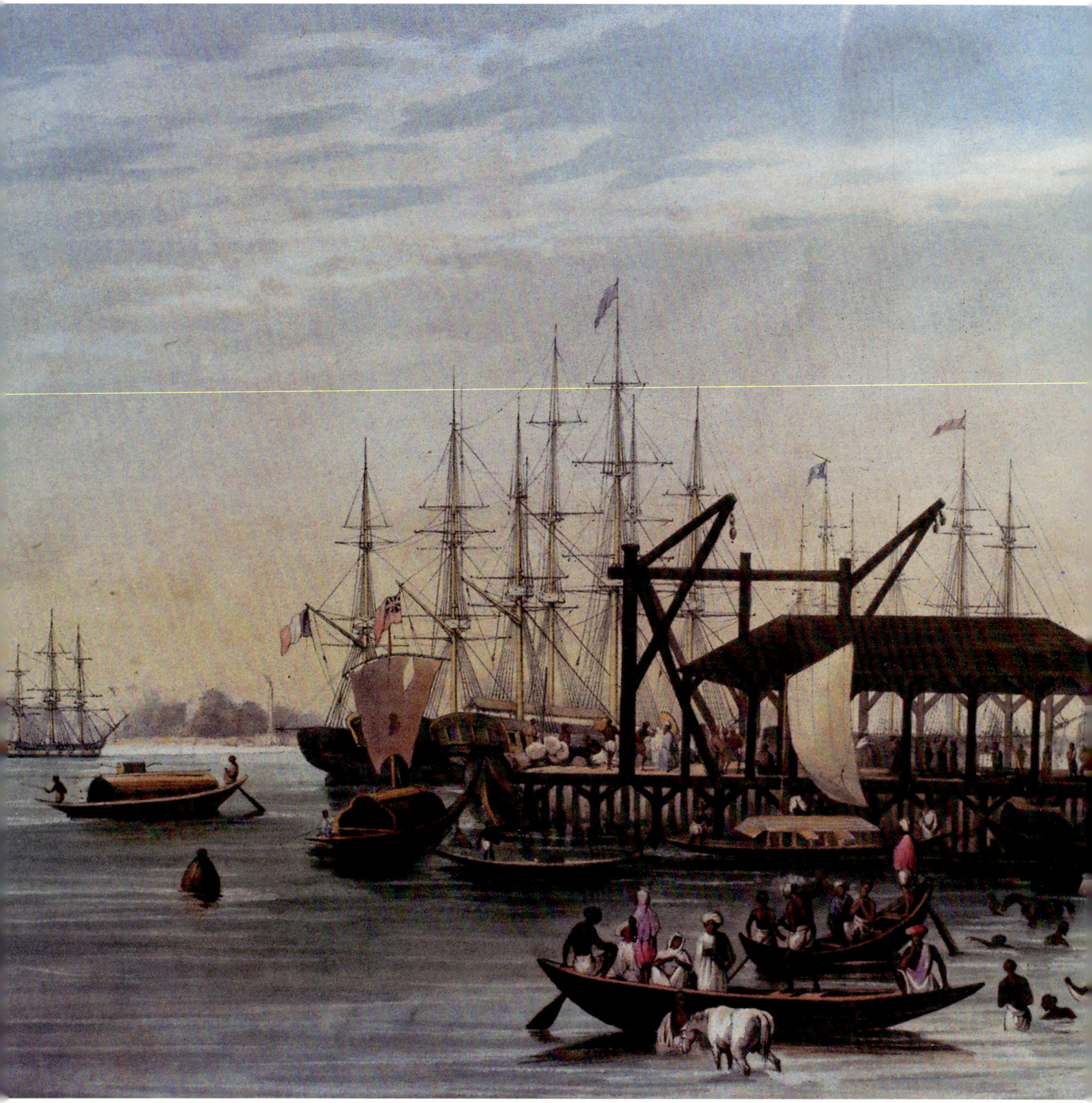

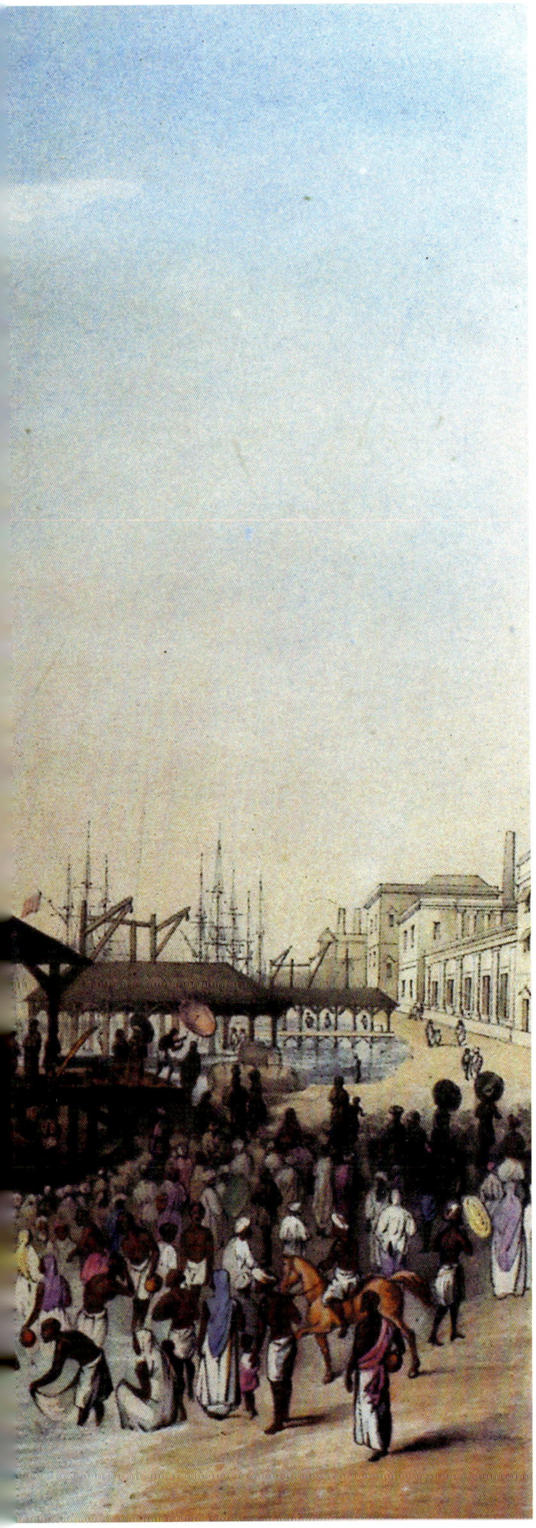

The Custom House Wharf and River Hoogly, Calcutta.
Coloured lithograph after a drawing by Sir Charles Doyly, 1848.

Sir Charles Doyly (1781-1845)

SIR CHARLES Doyly was the most famous amateur artist in India in the first half of the 19th century. Son of a well-known East India Company 'nabob', he was born in Calcutta in 1781. After receiving his education in England, he returned in 1798 to join the Company's service. He took lessons from George Chinnery, a famous artist of that time in Calcutta. Doyly was extremely perceptive and responsive to the sights, smells, colours and shapes of the environment around him. He had great powers of observation and boundless curiosity. He devoted himself to recording intimate scenes and making on-the-spot sketches in watercolour and ink.

One of the most striking elements of Doyly's voluminous work is his portrayal of Indian women, which he has done with extraordinary competence. He had studied Chinnery's portrait techniques with great care and this is evident in his drawings. Doyly stayed in Patna for twelve years (1821–33) and this was the most productive period of his painting career. It was in Patna that he achieved fame as an artist and came to be admired by the British community.

Doyly was a very generous and popular host. When the river-boats moored for the night at Patna, many Europeans enjoyed his hospitality and viewed his drawings. In his journal, Bishop Heber describes his visit to Doyly's house in 1824 :

> *"I found great amusement and interest in looking over Sir Charles' drawing books. He is the best gentleman artist I ever met with. He says India is a picturesque country if people would stir but a little away from the Ganges and his own drawings and paintings make good his assertion."*

Doyly's work inspired British amateur artists and also influenced many Indian artists, notably Sevak Ram and Jai Ram Dass, who worked with him in Patna and adapted their artistic skills to suit the taste of British patrons. He also imported a lithographic press from England in 1824 which he ran in Patna with the help of local Indian artists. He encouraged his friends to make sketches which he published in the periodical *Behar Amateur Lithographic Scrap Book.* A large collection of Patna paintings dealing with castes and occupations is attributed to Doyly and his Indian associates. Most of the scrap books published by Doyly in Patna can be found in the British Library, London. He published several books; most of these are collections of sketches. His claim to literary fame is based on *Tom Raw, the Griffin: A Burlesque Poem.* This describes the adventures of a cadet in the Company's Bengal Army. It is illustrated by Doyly in colours. It was published anonymously in 1828 and has since become a classic.

Captain Charles Gold (d.1842)

CHARLES GOLD belonged to that group of amateur artists who were skilled enough to produce drawings comparable to those of the professionals. He joined the East India Company army as a captain in 1776 and was curious about the country and its people. He was indeed the first to make a pictorial study of the local people of different castes and classes in South India. Just as Solvyns took his subjects from Bengal, Gold presented a composite picture of South India. Scenery, costumes, occupations and customs are blended into his sketches with utmost skill.

Gold made drawings of various local people he met while he was traveling with a detachment of Royal Artillery between 1791 and 1798. fifty of these drawings were reproduced as aquatints in *Oriental Drawings* published in London in 1806. Most of Gold's drawings are remarkable for their spontaneity, directness of observation, a kindly feeling for Indians, and at times for their lively humour. Being an army officer, not a professional artist, he tells us that "not being enabled from his professional duties to go in search of the extraordinary subjects with which it (India) so eminently abounds," he was "necessitated to take them as they occurred." Gold adds that he "allowed none to pass his quarter, without an invitation to walk in, which they always accepted, and most readily permitted him to draw their portraits." He assured that the "dresses are minutely attended to and the characters strictly preserved." The drawings range from a dramatic duststorm to a marriage procession, to a wandering minstrel, villagers going about their work, women pounding rice, barbers and even a pious Brahmin making offerings in a temple in Madras. Such scenes and subjects were so unfamiliar to the English that Gold gave a comprehensive descriptive account explaining the sketches. These accounts displayed Gold's knowledge and his extensive study of Indian texts. With regard to his sketch of Hanuman, he noted:

> *"On visiting the Pagoda (temple) we were permitted to view some of these curiosities... I had only time to sketch the one nearest the door, which was in the best light and from his countenance he appeared to be Hanuman, immortalized for the services he performed under the God Rama at the conquest of Ceylon."*

Hindu festivals and religious ceremonies aroused great interest among the British and Gold provided illuminating comments and observations on these topics with vivid paintings. His discerning eye was able to identify the Vaishnavites from the Shaivites and he painted many religious and festive scenes portraying them. He left behind interesting accounts of Indian snakes and reptiles and also wrote about

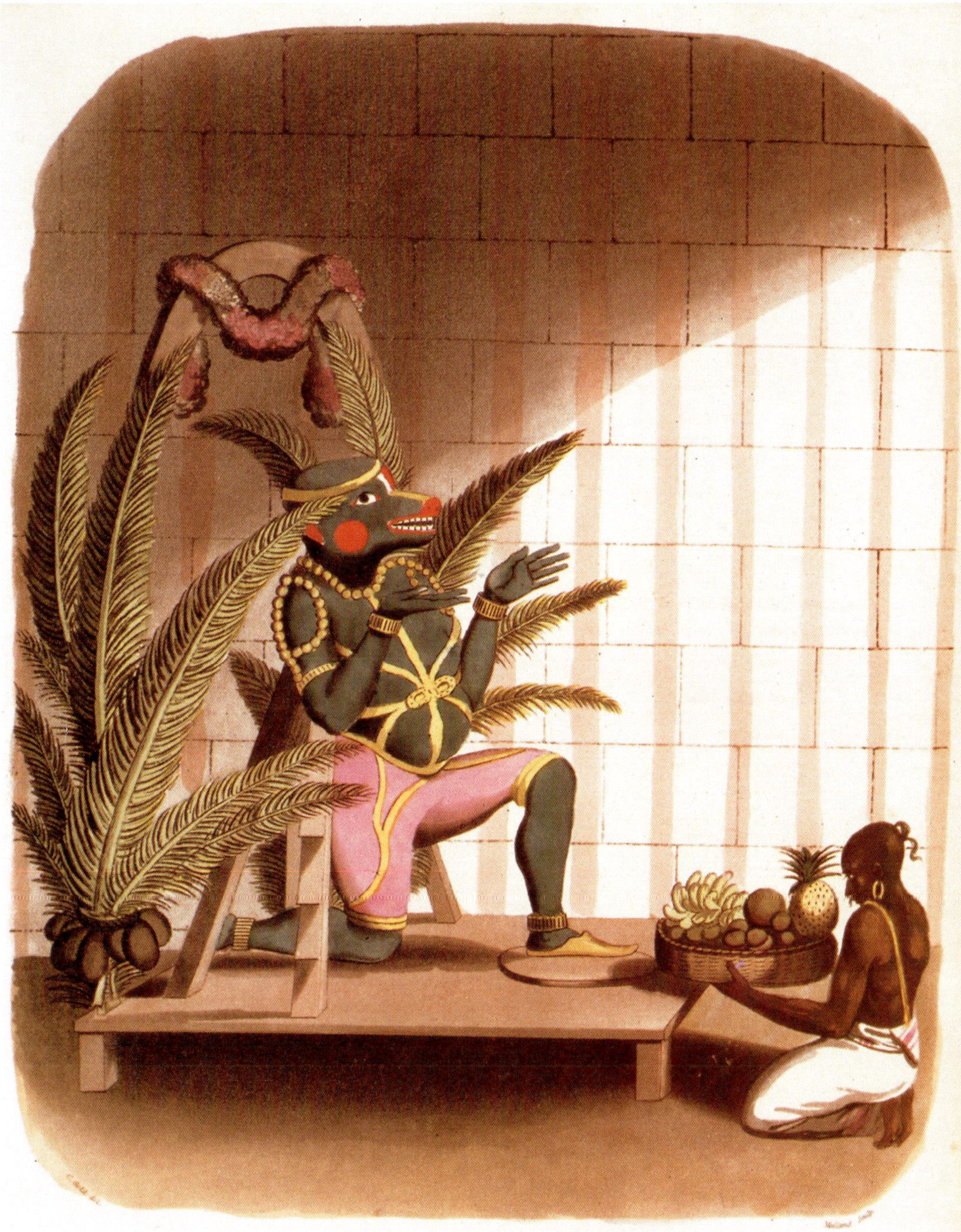

Hanuman, King of Apes, an Indian Deity.
Hand coloured aquatint engraving after a drawing by Captain Charles Gold, 1806.

the origin and practice of serpent worship in India. Impressed by the performance of snake charmers, Gold was led to believe in the force of music which he thought was responsible for luring snakes out of their lairs. Yet another subject that intrigued Gold was the wandering mendicant or fakir and he wrote and painted extensively on different types of fakirs, their religious habits, their backgrounds, rituals and practices. He was also inspired by the sets of pictures sold by Indian artists portraying men and women of various castes and occupations.

Fanny Parks (1794-1875)

ENAMOURED OF India with its picturesque landscape and natural beauty, its diverse people in exotic costumes, its festivals, rituals and rites, its music and dance and even its cuisine, Fanny Parks is one of the most appealing chroniclers of the Indian scene in the first half of the 19th century. Fond of a wandering life and adventure and unmindful of creature comforts, she traveled extensively during a twenty-four years stay in the country (1822–49). A talented amateur artist, she recorded her experiences in a monumental two volume journal entitled, *Wanderings of a Pilgrim in Search of the 'Picturesque.'* Illustrated with sketches and paintings drawn by herself which are both interesting and competent, the journal is replete with lively eyewitness accounts of her encounters in India. Full of information on practically every aspect of Indian society and culture, her journal is a favourite document with historians of the Raj who recognize it as a classic chronicle of the times.

Born in England in 1794, daughter of Captain William Archer, Fanny married Charles Parks, an East India Company civilian and came with him to Calcutta in 1822. She was impressed by the grandeur of the 'City of Palaces' and the luxurious lifestyle of English civilians and soldiers. She wanted to discover the mysterious India and while traveling in the north from Allahabad where her husband was stationed, she was captivated by the holy cities of Benaras and Mathura and became an eager student of Hindu mythology and iconography.

A high-spirited Memsahib, Fanny Parks shunned drawing-room gossip, needle work or playing piano but rather preferred less lady-like and adventurous pursuits such as shikar, riding, stone-cutting, bird-stuffing and above all exploring. She made several trips up and down the Ganges and traveled up to the Himalayas. In 1838 she wrote,

> *'how much there is to delight the eye in this bright, this beautiful world, roaming about with a good tent and a good Arab, One might be happy forever in India. I have a pencil instead of a gun and believe it affords me satisfaction equal if not greater than the sportsman derives from his Manton'.*

Besides giving an absorbing account of the contemporary British official and social life, Parks' journal also contains over forty full-page illustrations from her own drawings and watercolours. The romanticized or idealized images of people and the views of Indian scene were vividly captured by her with remarkable detail. It is interesting to note that she inscribed her signature on the sketches in the Persian script. In one case she points out that her picture of 'Kaniyajee and the Gopees,' is based on an original Hindoo painting.

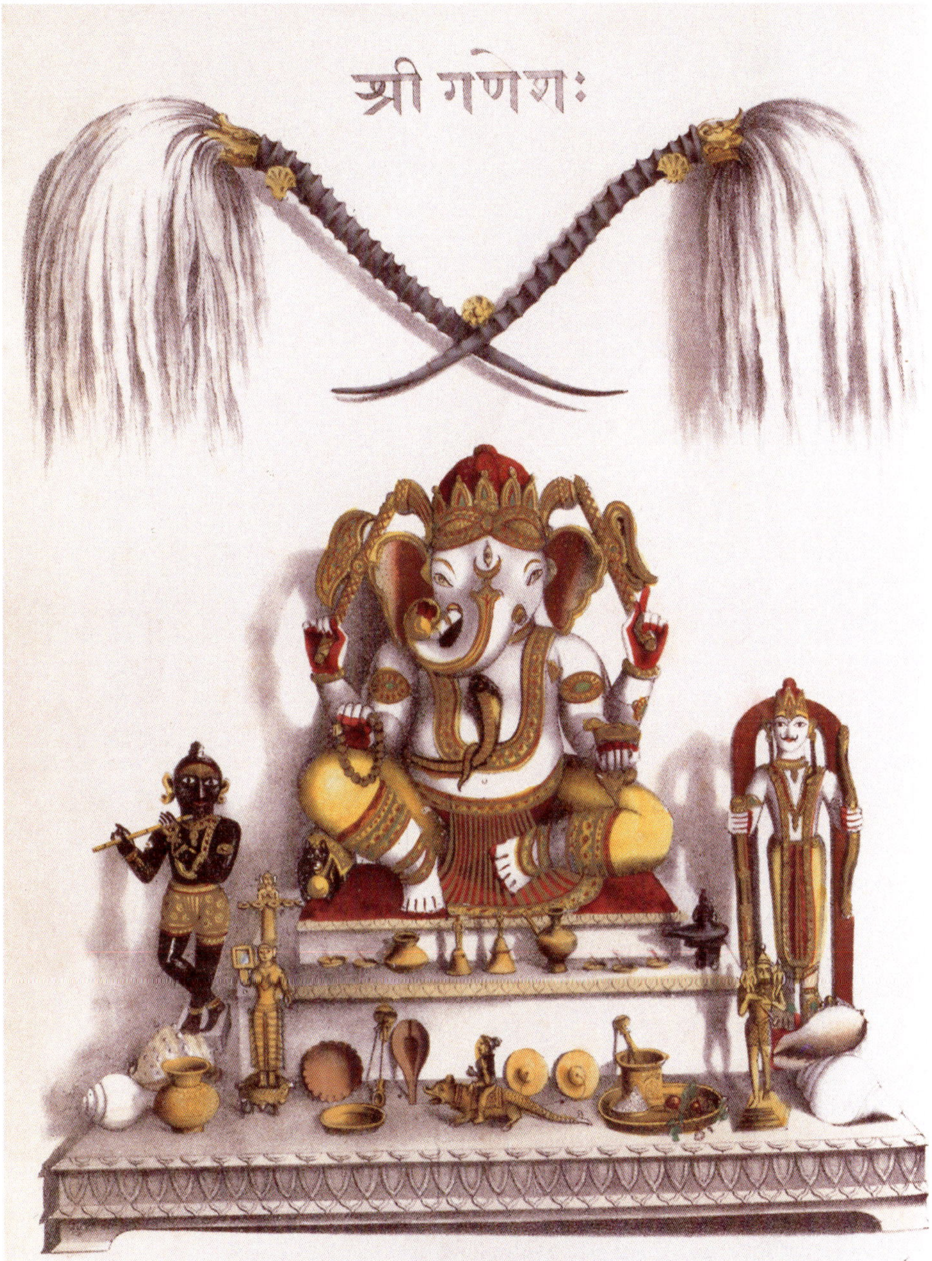

Ganesha. Coloured lithograph after a drawing by Fanny Parks, c. 1850.

It is indeed a superb replica of the original. Once, she was greatly amused by the story of an angry native wife telling her husband she wished she was married to a grass cutter, who were too poor to have more than one wife. Fanny then sketched her own grass cutter from a real model. Then, the graceful demeanour of an ordinary Bengali woman interested her greatly, and she describes in detail the sari of muslin that passed several times round the figure, as a remarkably graceful dress. She made a lively sketch of the Bengali lady with all the cosmetics and ornaments that adorned her body, and this is rated as one of the artist's best sketches.

William Simpson (1823-1899)

WILLIAM SIMPSON was one of the most talented travelling artists of the Victorian era. He was commissioned by the leading London firm of lithographers and publishers, Day and Sons, to visit India and record the sites and places affected by the events of the Mutiny. He was also to make a series of drawings of Indian views for a grand project of 250 lithographs modeled on the highly successful and popular work of David Roberts titled *The Holy Land.* A Scotsman raised in poverty, Simpson achieved recognition as an artist through sheer hard work and dedication. A prolific writer, a journalist, a keen observer and endowed with the creative imagination of the artist, Simpson looked for new themes and subjects for his work.

Simpson arrived in Calcutta in October 1859 and spent three years traveling across India. He visited Lahore, Peshawar, Simla, the upper reaches of the Sutluj as far as Chini in the Himalayas, Delhi, Agra and Lucknow. He also traveled to Central India and Rajasthan before the introduction of railways. He gives a graphic account of his palanquin travel and how he enjoyed sharing the food of the coolies who carried him. Sketching all the time, he was delighted to see the real village life of India in obscure distant places which few Europeans had ever seen before. Devoid of vanity and full of warmth and sympathetic curiosity for the people, his humanity made him objective and clear-sighted. He depicted his subjects with utmost fidelity and astonishing detail. Simpson took the second Himalayan tour in 1861 exploring the hills from Mussoorie up the valley of the Ganges to its source at Gangotri. He made a sketch of the small temple there and even followed the Hindu practice of purification by having a dip in the Ganges and drinking a little of the water. Later, he traveled to the Kashmir valley and was struck by its heavenly beauty with sparkling lakes and snow covered peaks. His last tour took him to Madras from where he went by a Government steamer to Bombay stopping enroute at Quilon, Cochin, Calicut and Mangalore on the Malabar Coast. He explored the neighbourhood of Bombay and then left for England in February 1862.

Simpson applied his talents to new and more challenging subjects not depicted before. His drawings presented a far more comprehensive and realistic picture of India. His sketches range from the picturesque landscape to the occupations and manners of the people of different classes, their festivities and rituals, public entertainers, ascetics and mendicants, thugs and dacoits. Like other British artists, Simpson was also curious about the way of life of the Indian women of aristocracy secluded in the zenana who did not sit for portraits by male artists. He was overjoyed when his host in Delhi, the editor of *Delhi Punch* who was married to an Anglo-Indian lady, arranged his visit to a zenana

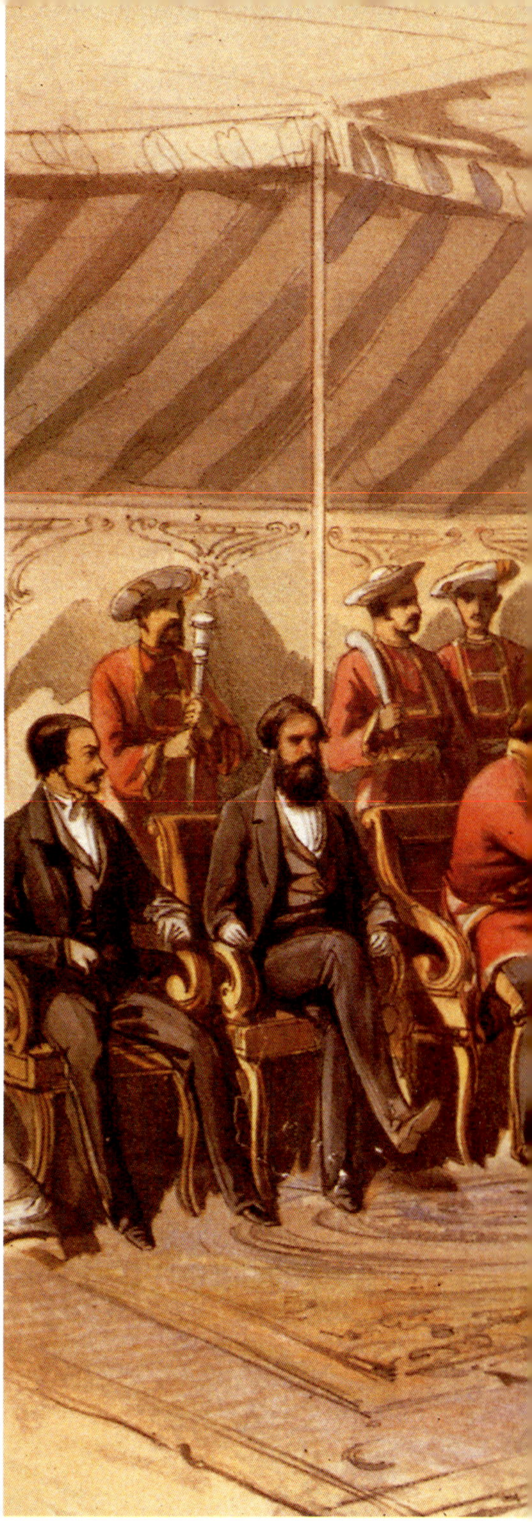

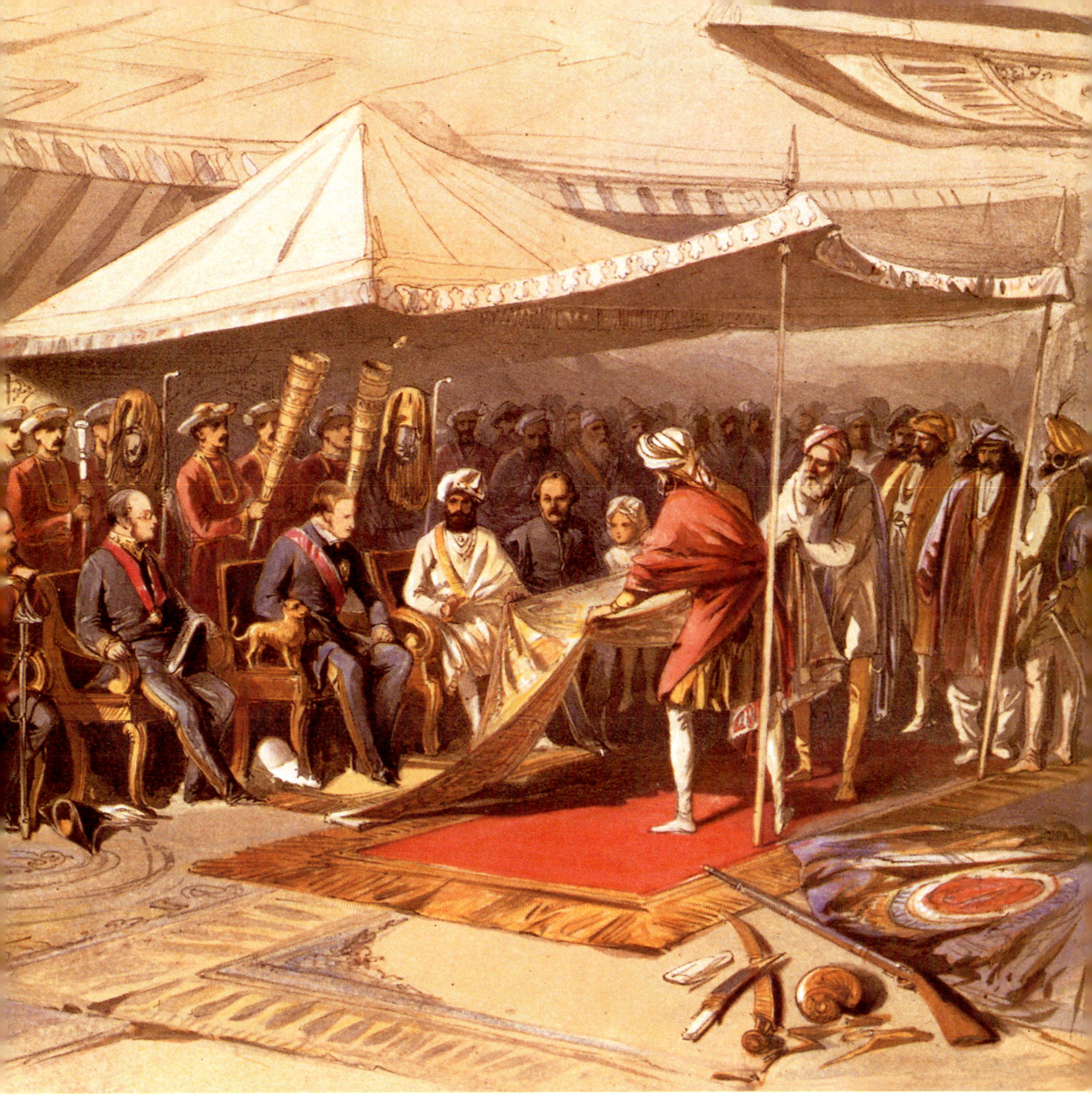

Return Visit of Viceroy to the Maharaja of Kashmir. Chromolithograph after a drawing by William Simpson, c.1860.

where he was allowed to make a portrait of the young beautiful Begum in her glittering attire and splendid jewellery.

After his return to England in 1862, Simpson spent four years transforming 250 sketches into finished watercolours to be reproduced in his magnum opus through chromolithographic process. But unfortunately disaster struck with the financial collapse of Day and Son, who then sold off the 250 water colours as bankrupt stock. Some fifty pictures had already been processed into lithographs and the creditors published a folio volume of these plates with a descriptive text by the historian John William Kaye titled *India Ancient and Modern* in 1867.

Glossary

Ayah An Indian nursemaid or a lady's maid
Baba A Young child.
Babu Bengali gentleman ; an English writing Indian clerk.
Bearer A personal servant
Begum A Muslim lady of rank ; a wife of a Muslim gentleman.
Bibi Wife ; unofficial native wives of British residents in India.
Brahman Hightest caste of Hindus.
Burra Sahib British civilian or military officer.
Bungalow Single-storeyed house with a lawn.
Budgerow A barge used by Europeans for journeys up and down the Ganges before the introduction of steamboats.
Cantonment Military Station of a British Indian army.
Charak Hook- swinging at a Hindu religious festival.
Chota Small or little.
Civil Lines Civilian area of a British Indian settlement.
Dak, Dawk Post by relay of men or horses.
Dak Bungalow A stopping place for the post (Dak) ; Place of stay for British officers on tour.
Durbar Public levee of Indian ruling princes, or British Governor-General ; Court of native rulers.
Durga Puja Hindu festival of worship of Goddess Durga.
Fakeer A religious mendicant or an ascetic ; a person without any material possessions.
Ghagra Long gathered skirt worn by Indian women.
Ghat, Ghaut Landing place for river craft and also bathing ghats.
Hookah Indian pipe for smoking tobacco through water, the fancy hubble – bubble.
Hooka burdar The servant who attends to his master's hooka.
Howdah A large chair or framed seat usually with a canopy on elephant's back.
Jamadar Chief servant in a household establishment.
Janpaun A sedan-Chair with poles used by the ladies in the hills.
Khansama Head table servant.
Mahout Driver and tender of an elephant.
Munshi A native teacher of languages.
Nabob Corruption of the Indian word Nawab used for an Englishman with wealth acquired in India.
Nautch Dance performed by Indian women.
Pukhah Proper, as in pukka sahib ; also a term for a building of bricks or stone.
Punkhah A large swinging cloth fan on a wooden frame suspended from the ceiling.
Purdah Curtain ; veil used by women to hide their faces.
Raj Rule, as in British Raj.
Rani A Hindu Queen.
Sadhu A sage or an ascetic.
Salaam A salutation.
Sepoy An Indian soldier in uniform in British service.
Suwar A rider.
Shikar A hunt.
Shooter Suwar A rider of swift camel.
Sunyasee A Hindu religious mendicant.
Suttee Old custom of self immolation of Hindu widows on their husband's funeral pyres.
Syce A groom for horses.
Tatty A mat screen made of fragrant khus-khus (grass).
Wallah A suffix added to any profession which denotes follower of that profession as in punkhah-wallah.
Wazir Minister.
Zenana A section of a house for women.

Bibliography

Acland, Rev. T.A. *Popular Account of the Manners and Customs of India.* London, 1847.

Archer, M. *British Drawings in the India Office Library,* 2 vols. London, 1969.

—*Company Drawings in the India Office Library.* London, 1972.

—*India and British Portraiture:* 1770–1825. London, 1979.

—*Early Views of India,* London, 1980.

Archer Mildred and W.G. *Indian Painting for the British 1770–1880.* Oxford, 1955.

Archer Mildred and Falk T. *The Passionate Quest—The Fraser Brothers in India.* London, 1989.

Bacon, Thomas. *First Impressions,* 2 vols. London, 1837.

Baden-Powell, R.S.S. *Pigsticking or Hosghunting.* London, 1889.

Ballhatchet, K. *Race, Sex, and class under the Raj.* New York, 1980.

Bayly, C.A. *An Illustrated History of Modern India,* London, 1990.

Bean, Susan S. *Yankee India.* Peabody Essex Museum: Salem, U.S.A., 2001.

Bellew, Capt. *Memoirs of a Griffin.* London, 1843.

Belnos, Mrs. S.C. *Twenty-four Plates Illustrative of Hindu and European Manners in Bengal.* London, 1832.

Braddon, E. *Thirty Years of Shikar.* Edinburgh, 1895.

Brown, H., ed. *The Sahibs, The Life and Ways of the British in India as Recorded by Themselves.* London, 1832.

Busteed, H.E. Echoes from old Calcutta. Calcutta, 1888.

Canby, Sheila, R. *Princes, Poets and Paladins:Islamic and Indian Paintings from the Collection of Prince and Princess Sadruddin Aga Khan.* London, 1998.

Carey, W.H. *The Good Old Days of Honourable John Company.* Calcutta, 1964.

Caunter Rev. *Oriental Annual* London 1834 1839.

Crill, R. *Arts of India 1550–1900.* V&A Museum: London, 1990.

Daniell Thomas & William.*Oriental Scenery.* London, 1795–1808.

Dodwell, H.H. *The Nabobs of Madras.* London, 1926.

Doyly, C. Tom Raw, *The Griffin.* London, 1882.

—*The Costumes and Customs of Modern India.* London, c 1824.

—*The European in India.* London, 1813.

Dubois, A.J.A. *Hindu Manners, Customs and Ceremonies.* Oxford, 1968 Reprint.

Dyson, K.K. *A Various Universe:A Study of the Journals and Memorirs of British Men and Woman in the India Subcontinent.* Oxford, 1978.

Eden, Emily, ed. H. Lawrence. *Up the Country.* London, 1901.

Edwards, M. *Glorious Sahibs.* London, 1968.

—*The Sahibs and the Lotus.* London, 1988.

—*British India (1772–1947).* London.

Edwin, A. *India Revisited.* London, 1886.

Forbes, J. *Oriental Memoirs,* 4 vols. London, 1813.

Foster, William ed. *Early Travels in India.* Reprinted, Delhi, 1968.

Graham, M. *Journal of a Residence in India.* Edinburgh, 1813.

Grose, J.H. *A Voyage to East Indies.* London, 1766.

Hall, Capt. Basil. *Travels in India,* London, 1931.

Hardgrave, Jr. Robert, L. *A Portrait of The Hindus: B. Solvyns and The European Images of India, 1760–1824* Ahmedabad, 2004.

Hart, W.H. *Everyday Life in Bengal and Other Indian Sketches.* London, 1906.

Heber, R. *Narrative of a Journey through the Upper Provinces of India from Calcutta to Bombay,* 2 vols. London, 1828.

Hervey, H. *The European in India.* London, 1913.

Hicks, F.C. *Forty Years among the Wild Animals of India.* Allahabad, 1910.

Hogdes, W. *Travels in India during the Years 1780-83.* London, 1793.

Hyam, R. *British Imperial Century.* London, 1976.

Johnson, Daniel. *Sketches of Indian Field Sports.* London, 1827.

Kaul, H.K. Travellers' *India: An Anthology.* New Delhi, 1979.

Kerr, S. *Selections from Calcutta Gazette.* 6 vols,

Calcutta, 1864.
Kincail, D. *British Social Life in India.* London, 1938.
Knighton, W. *Trophical Sketches,* 2 vols. London, 1855.
—*The Private Life of an Eastern King.* London, 1856.
Martyn, H. *Bengal Past and Present.* London, 1837.
Moorhouse, *G. India Britannica.* London, 1983.
Mundy, G.C. *Pen and Pencil Sketches,* 2 vols. London, 1832.
Nugent, Maria, *A Journal from the Year 1811 to the Year 1813.* London, 1984.
Pal, P. and Dehejia, V. *From Merchants to Emperors.* New York, 1986.
Parks, Fanny. *Wanderings of a Pilgrim in Search of the Picturesque,* 2 vols. London, 1850.
Princeep, V.C. *Imperial India.* London, 1879.
Rousselet, L. *India and its Native Princes.* London, 1875.
Savory, Isabel, *A Sportswoman in India.* London, 1900.
Sherwood, Mrs, M.M. *The Life and Times of Mrs. Sherwood (1775–1851)* ed. F.J. Harvey, Darton. London, 1910.
Skinner, Capt. T. *Excursions in India,* 2 vols. London.
Sleeman, W.H. *Rambles and Reflections of an Indian Official,* 2 vols. London, 1844.
—*A Journey through the Kingdom of Oudh,* 2 vols. London, 1858.
Solvyns, B. Les *Hindous,* 4 vols, Paris, 1808–1812.
Williamson, T. *The East India Vade Mecum,* 2 vols. London 1810.
—Oriental *Field Sports* 2 vols. London, 1819
Woodruff, P. *The Men Who Ruled India,* 2 vols. London, 1963.

Sources of Illustrations

Oriental Scenery (6 parts) ,Thomas and William Daniell London, 1795–1808. Pages 14, 16, 18, 19(bottom), 21(bottom), 22, 23, 29 (top), 30(bottom).

Oriental Drawings, Captain Charles Gold, London, 1806. Pages 45(bottom), 70, 73, 88, 98, 99, 129(top), 149.

The European in India, Charles Doyly, London, 1813. Pages 13, 38, 39, 40, 41, 42, 51, 68, 85, 89, 104, 105.

*Sketches Illustrating the Manners and Customs of the Indians and Anglo-Indians,*W. Tayler, London, 1842. Pages Cover, 6, 36.

Oriental Field Sports, Captain T Williamson, London, 1819. Pages 50, 52, 53, 54, 55.

Twenty Four Plates Illustrative of Hindoo and European Manners in Bengal, S. C. Belnos, London, 1832. Pages 37, 45(top), 67, 71, 78, 79(top), 84, 120.

India Ancient and Modern, J.W. Kaye, London, 1867. Pages 25, 27, 31, 61, 90, 102, 122, 153.

The Collection of Prince and Princess Sadruddin Aga Khan, Geneva. Pages 34, 82, 87

By permission of the British Library, Oriental and India Office Collections, London. Pages 43 (top), 56, 63, 76, 79, 101, 113, 117

The Trustees of the Victoria and Albert Museum, London. Pages 48, 62, 64, 66, 74, 80, 81, 94, 95, 111, 114, 116, 118, 119, 121, 130

The Royal Collection – Her Majesty Queen Elizabeth II. Page 83

National Gallery of Ireland, Dublin. Page 106

Yale Center of British Art, Paul Mellon Collection, New Haven, USA. Pages 12, 110.

National Gallery of Modern Art, New Delhi. Pages 96 (left), 138

Dr. Mildred Archer and Margaret Paish, London. Title page and page 86.

Dr Maurice Shellin, London. Page 137

Asiatic Society of Bengal, Kolkata. Page 10

Victoria Memorial Kolkata.Pages 14, 16, 18, 21(top), 65, 115, 132, 134

Courtesy Professor, Robert, L. Hardgrave, Jr. University of Texas at Austin, U.S.A. Pages 92, 128, 143.

Courtesy, Jagmohan Mahajan. Pages 8, 19(top), 28, 29(bottom), 32, 124.

INDEX